interchange

FIFTH EDITION

1

Student's Book

Jack C. Richards
with Jonathan Hull and Susan Proctor

WITH ONLINE
SELF-STUDY

CAMBRIDGE
UNIVERSITY PRESS

CAMBRIDGE
UNIVERSITY PRESS

University Printing House, Cambridge CB2 8BS, United Kingdom

One Liberty Plaza, 20th Floor, New York, NY 10006, USA

477 Williamstown Road, Port Melbourne, VIC 3207, Australia

4843/24, 2nd Floor, Ansari Road, Daryaganj, Delhi – 110002, India

79 Anson Road, #06–04/06, Singapore 079906

Torre de los Parques, Colonia Tlacoquemécatl del Valle, Mexico City CP 03200, Mexico

Cambridge University Press is part of the University of Cambridge.

It furthers the University's mission by disseminating knowledge in the pursuit of education, learning and research at the highest international levels of excellence.

www.cambridge.org
Information on this title: www.cambridge.org/9781316623909

First published 2005
Second edition 2013
20 19 18 17 16 15 14 13 12 11 10 9 8 7 6 5

Printed in Mexico by Editorial Impresora Apolo, S.A. de C.V.

A catalogue record for this publication is available from the British Library

ISBN	9781316620311	Student's Book with Online Self-Study 1
ISBN	9781316620359	Student's Book with Online Self-Study 1A
ISBN	9781316620427	Student's Book with Online Self-Study 1B
ISBN	9781316620441	Student's Book with Online Self-Study and Online Workbook 1
ISBN	9781316620458	Student's Book with Online Self-Study and Online Workbook 1A
ISBN	9781316620472	Student's Book with Online Self-Study and Online Workbook 1B
ISBN	9781316622476	Workbook 1
ISBN	9781316622544	Workbook 1A
ISBN	9781316622667	Workbook 1B
ISBN	9781316622681	Teacher's Edition with Complete Assessment Program 1
ISBN	9781316622261	Class Audio CDs 1
ISBN	9781316623909	Full Contact with Online Self-Study 1
ISBN	9781316623916	Full Contact with Online Self-Study 1A
ISBN	9781316623923	Full Contact with Online Self-Study 1B
ISBN	9781316622230	Presentation Plus Level 1

Additional resources for this publication at www.cambridge.org/interchange

Cambridge University Press has no responsibility for the persistence or accuracy of URLs for external or third-party internet websites referred to in this publication, and does not guarantee that any content on such websites is, or will remain, accurate or appropriate. Information regarding prices, travel timetables, and other factual information given in this work is correct at the time of first printing but Cambridge University Press does not guarantee the accuracy of such information thereafter.

Informed by teachers

Teachers from all over the world helped develop *Interchange Fifth Edition*. They looked at everything – from the color of the designs to the topics in the conversations – in order to make sure that this course will work in the classroom. We heard from 1,500 teachers in:

- Surveys
- Focus Groups
- In-Depth Reviews

We appreciate the help and input from everyone. In particular, we'd like to give the following people our special thanks:

Jader Franceschi, **Actúa Idiomas,** Bento Gonçalves, Rio Grande do Sul, Brazil

Juliana Dos Santos Voltan Costa, **Actus Idiomas,** São Paulo, Brazil

Ella Osorio, **Angelo State University,** San Angelo, TX, US

Mary Hunter, **Angelo State University,** San Angelo, TX, US

Mario César González, **Angloamericano de Monterrey, SC,** Monterrey, Mexico

Samantha Shipman, **Auburn High School,** Auburn, AL, US

Linda, **Bernick Language School,** Radford, VA, US

Dave Lowrance, **Bethesda University of California,** Yorba Linda, CA, US

Tajbakhsh Hosseini, **Bezmialem Vakif University,** Istanbul, Turkey

Dilek Gercek, **Bil English,** Izmir, Turkey

erkan kolat, **Biruni University, ELT,** Istanbul, Turkey

Nika Gutkowska, **Bluedata International,** New York, NY, US

Daniel Alcocer Gómez, **Cecati 92,** Guadalupe, Nuevo León, Mexico

Samantha Webb, **Central Middle School,** Milton-Freewater, OR, US

Verónica Salgado, **Centro Anglo Americano,** Cuernavaca, Mexico

Ana Rivadeneira Martínez and Georgia P. de Machuca, **Centro de Educación Continua – Universidad Politécnica del Ecuador,** Quito, Ecuador

Anderson Francisco Guimerães Maia, **Centro Cultural Brasil Estados Unidos,** Belém, Brazil

Rosana Mariano, **Centro Paula Souza,** São Paulo, Brazil

Carlos de la Paz Arroyo, Teresa Noemí Parra Alarcón, Gilberto

Bastida Gaytan, Manuel Esquivel Román, and Rosa Cepeda Tapia, **Centro Universitario Angloamericano,** Cuernavaca, Morelos, Mexico

Antonio Almeida, **CETEC,** Morelos, Mexico

Cinthia Ferreira, **Cinthia Ferreira Languages Services,** Toronto, ON, Canada

Phil Thomas and Sérgio Sanchez, **CLS Canadian Language School,** São Paulo, Brazil

Celia Concannon, **Cochise College,** Nogales, AZ, US

Maria do Carmo Rocha and CAOP English team, **Colégio Arquidiocesano Ouro Preto – Unidade Cônego Paulo Dilascio,** Ouro Preto, Brazil

Kim Rodriguez, **College of Charleston North,** Charleston, SC, US

Jesús Leza Alvarado, **Coparmex English Institute,** Monterrey, Mexico

John Partain, **Cortazar,** Guanajuato, Mexico

Alexander Palencia Navas, **Cursos de Lenguas, Universidad del Atlántico,** Barranquilla, Colombia

Kenneth Johan Gerardo Steenhuisen Cera, Melfi Osvaldo Guzman Triana, and Carlos Alberto Algarín Jiminez, **Cursos de Lenguas Extranjeras Universidad del Atlantico,** Barranquilla, Colombia

Jane P Kerford, **East Los Angeles College,** Pasadena, CA, US

Daniela, **East Village,** Campinas, São Paulo

Rosalva Camacho Orduño, **Easy English for Groups S.A. de C.V.,** Monterrey, Nuevo León, Mexico

Adonis Gimenez Fusetti, **Easy Way Idiomas,** Ibiúna, Brazil

Eileen Thompson, **Edison Community College,** Piqua, OH, US

Ahminne Handeri O.L Froede, **Englishouse escola de idiomas,** Teófilo Otoni, Brazil

Ana Luz Delgado-Izazola, **Escuela Nacional Preparatoria 5, UNAM,** Mexico City, Mexico

Nancy Alarcón Mendoza, **Facultad de Estudios Superiores Zaragoza, UNAM,** Mexico City, Mexico

Marcilio N. Barros, **Fast English USA,** Campinas, São Paulo, Brazil

Greta Douthat, **FCI Ashland,** Ashland, KY, US

Carlos Lizárraga González, **Grupo Educativo Anglo Americano, S.C.,** Mexico City, Mexico

Hugo Fernando Alcántar Valle, **Instituto Politécnico Nacional, Escuela Superior de Comercio y Administración-Unidad Santotomás, Celex Esca Santo Tomás,** Mexico City, Mexico

Sueli Nascimento, **Instituto Superior de Educação do Rio de Janeiro,** Rio de Janeiro, Brazil

Elsa F Monteverde, **International Academic Services,** Miami, FL, US

Laura Anand, **Irvine Adult School,** Irvine, CA, US

Prof. Marli T. Fernandes (principal) and Prof. Dr. Jefferson J. Fernandes (pedagogue), **Jefferson Idiomas,** São Paulo, Brazil

Herman Bartelen, **Kanda Gaigo Gakuin,** Tokyo, Japan

Cassia Silva, **Key Languages,** Key Biscayne, FL, US

Sister Mary Hope, **Kyoto Notre Dame Joshi Gakuin,** Kyoto, Japan

Nate Freedman, **LAL Language Centres,** Boston, MA, US

Richard Janzen, **Langley Secondary School,** Abbotsford, BC, Canada

Christina Abel Gabardo, **Language House,** Campo Largo, Brazil

Ivonne Castro, **Learn English International,** Cali, Colombia

Julio Cesar Maciel Rodrigues, **Liberty Centro de Línguas,** São Paulo, Brazil

Ann Gibson, **Maynard High School,** Maynard, MA, US

Martin Darling, **Meiji Gakuin Daigaku,** Tokyo, Japan

Dax Thomas, **Meiji Gakuin Daigaku,** Yokohama, Kanagawa, Japan

Derya Budak, **Mevlana University,** Konya, Turkey

B Sullivan, **Miami Valley Career Technical Center International Program,** Dayton, OH, US

Julio Velazquez, **Milo Language Center,** Weston, FL, US

Daiane Siqueira da Silva, Luiz Carlos Buontempo, Marlete Avelina de Oliveira Cunha, Marcos Paulo Segatti, Morgana Eveline de Oliveira, Nadia Lia Gino Alo, and Paul Hyde Budgen, **New Interchange-Escola de Idiomas,** São Paulo, Brazil

Patrícia França Furtado da Costa, Juiz de Fora, Brazil

Patricia Servín

Chris Pollard, **North West Regional College SK,** North Battleford, SK, Canada

Olga Amy, **Notre Dame High School,** Red Deer, Canada

Amy Garrett, **Ouachita Baptist University,** Arkadelphia, AR, US

Mervin Curry, **Palm Beach State College,** Boca Raton, FL, US

Julie Barros, **Quality English Studio,** Guarulhos, São Paulo, Brazil

Teodoro González Saldaña and Jesús Monserrrta Mata Franco, **Race Idiomas,** Mexico City, Mexico

Autumn Westphal and Noga La`or, **Rennert International,** New York, NY, US

Antonio Gallo and Javy Palau, **Rigby Idiomas,** Monterrey, Mexico Tatiane Gabriela Sperb do Nascimento, **Right Way,** Igrejinha, Brazil

Mustafa Akgül, **Selahaddin Eyyubi Universitesi,** Diyarbakır, Turkey

James Drury M. Fonseca, **Senac Idiomas Fortaleza,** Fortaleza, Ceara, Brazil

Manoel Fialho S Neto, **Senac – PE,** Recife, Brazil

Jane Imber, **Small World,** Lawrence, KS, US

Tony Torres, **South Texas College,** McAllen, TX, US

Janet Rose, **Tennessee Foreign Language Institute,** College Grove, TN, US

Todd Enslen, **Tohoku University,** Sendai, Miyagi, Japan

Daniel Murray, **Torrance Adult School,** Torrance, CA, US

Juan Manuel Pulido Mendoza, **Universidad del Atlántico,** Barranquilla, Colombia

Juan Carlos Vargas Millán, **Universidad Libre Seccional Cali,** Cali (Valle del Cauca), Colombia

Carmen Cecilia Llanos Ospina, **Universidad Libre Seccional Cali,** Cali, Colombia

Jorge Noriega Zenteno, **Universidad Politécnica del Valle de México,** Estado de México, Mexico

Aimee Natasha Holguin S., **Universidad Politécnica del Valle de México UPVM,** Tultitlàn Estado de México, Mexico

Christian Selene Bernal Barraza, **UPVM Universidad Politécnica del Valle de México,** Ecatepec, Mexico

Lizeth Ramos Acosta, **Universidad Santiago de Cali,** Cali, Colombia

Silvana Dushku, **University of Illinois Champaign,** IL, US

Deirdre McMurtry, **University of Nebraska – Omaha,** Omaha, NE, US

Jason E Mower, **University of Utah,** Salt Lake City, UT, US

Paul Chugg, **Vanguard Taylor Language Institute,** Edmonton, Alberta, Canada

Henry Mulak, **Varsity Tutors,** Los Angeles, CA, US

Shirlei Strucker Calgaro and Hugo Guilherme Karrer, **VIP Centro de Idiomas,** Panambi, Rio Grande do Sul, Brazil

Eleanor Kelly, **Waseda Daigaku Extension Centre,** Tokyo, Japan

Sherry Ashworth, **Wichita State University,** Wichita, KS, US

Laine Bourdene, **William Carey University,** Hattiesburg, MS, US

Serap Aydın, Istanbul, Turkey

Liliana Covino, Guarulhos, Brazil

Yannuarys Jiménez, Barranquilla, Colombia

Juliana Morais Pazzini, Toronto, ON, Canada

Marlon Sanches, Montreal, Canada

Additional content contributed by Kenna Bourke, Inara Couto, Nic Harris, Greg Manin, Ashleigh Martinez, Laura McKenzie, Paul McIntyre, Clara Prado, Lynne Robertson, Mari Vargo, Theo Walker, and Maria Lucia Zaorob.

Plan of Book 1

Titles/Topics	Speaking	Grammar

Pronunciation/Listening	Writing/Reading	Interchange Activity
Linked sounds Listening for names, countries, and school subjects	Writing questions requesting personal information "Is Your Name Trendy?": Reading about popular names	"Getting to know you": Collecting personal information about classmates PAGE 114
Syllable stress Listening to descriptions of jobs and daily routines	Writing a biography of a classmate "My Parents Don't Understand My Job!": Reading about four jobs	"What we have in common": Finding similarities in classmates' daily schedules PAGE 115
Sentence stress Listening to people shopping; listening for items, colors, and prices	Writing about favorite clothes "Online Shopping: The Crazy Things People Buy": Reading about unusual online items	"Flea market": Buying and selling things PAGES 116–117
Intonation in questions Listening for likes and dislikes	Writing text messages "The World's Most Powerful Female Musician": Reading about a famous musician	"Are you free this weekend?": Making plans; inviting and giving excuses PAGE 118
Intonation in statements Listening for family relationships	Writing an email about family "Do Families Spend a Lot of Time Together?": Reading about four families	"Is that true?": Finding out information about classmates' families PAGE 119
Intonation with direct address Listening to people talking about free-time activities; listening to descriptions of sports participation	Writing about weekly activities "Fit and Healthy? Take the Quiz!": Reading about health and taking a quiz	"What's your talent?": Finding out about classmates' abilities PAGE 120
Reduction of did you Listening to descriptions and opinions of past events and vacations	Writing a blog post "Awesome Vacations": Reading about different kinds of vacations	"Memories": Playing a board game PAGE 121
Reduction of there is/there are Listening for locations and descriptions of places	Writing about neighborhoods "Hip Neighborhoods of the World": Reading about popular neighborhoods	"Where are we?": describing and guessing locations PAGE 122

Titles/Topics	Speaking	Grammar

Pronunciation/Listening	Writing/Reading	Interchange Activity
Contrastive stress Listening to descriptions of people; identifying people	Writing an email describing a person "The Age of Selfies": Reading about the history of selfies	"Find the differences": Comparing two pictures of a party PAGES 123–124
Linked sounds Listening to descriptions of events	Writing an email to an old friend "Unique Experiences": Reading about four peoples' unusual experiences	"Fun survey": Finding out about a classmate's lifestyle PAGE 125
Can't and *shouldn't* Listening to descriptions of cities, towns, and countries	Writing about hometowns "A Big 'Hello!' From . . . ": Reading about interesting cities	"Welcome to our city!": Creating a guide to fun places in a city PAGE 126
Reduction of *to* Listening to health problems and advice	Writing a blog post "Toothache? Visit the Rain Forest!": Reading about a plant used as medicine	"What should I do?": Give suggestions for situations PAGE 127
Stress in responses Listening to restaurant orders	Writing a restaurant review "To Tip or Not to Tip?": Reading about tipping customs	"Planning a food festival": Creating a menu PAGE 128
Questions of choice Listening to a TV quiz show	Writing an article about a place "Earth's Cleanest Places": Reading about three very clean places	"How much do you know?": Taking a general knowledge quiz PAGE 129
Reduction of *could you* and *would you* Listening to telephone messages	Writing text message requests "Cell Phone Trouble!": Reading about cell phone problems	"Weekend plans": Finding out about classmates' weekend plans PAGE 130
Vowel sounds /oʊ/ and /ʌ/ Listening to descriptions of changes	Writing a plan for a class trip "A Goal Accomplished": Reading about a person's goals	"Our possible future": Planning a possible future PAGE 131

1 Where are you from?

▸ **Introduce oneself and others**
▸ **Talk about oneself and learn about others**

1 CONVERSATION Please call me Alexa.

▶ Listen and practice.

Arturo: Hello, I'm Arturo Valdez.

Alexa: Hi. My name is Alexandra Costa, but please call me Alexa.

Arturo: OK. Where are you from, Alexa?

Alexa: Brazil. How about you?

Arturo: I'm from Mexico.

Alexa: Oh, I love Mexico! It's really beautiful. Oh, good. Soo-jin is here.

Arturo: Who's Soo-jin?

Alexa: She's my classmate. We're in the same business class.

Arturo: Where's she from?

Alexa: South Korea. Let's go and say hello. Sorry, what's your last name again? Vargas?

Arturo: Actually, it's Valdez.

Alexa: How do you spell that?

Arturo: V-A-L-D-E-Z.

2 SPEAKING Checking information

A PAIR WORK Introduce yourself with your full name. Use the expressions in the box. Talk to the classmate sitting next to you and to three more classmates.

A: Hi! I'm Akemi Shimizu.

B: I'm sorry. What's your last name again?

A: Shimizu.

B: How do you spell that?

useful expressions
Hi! I'm . . .
I'm sorry. What's your first / last name again?
How do you spell that?
What do people call you?

B CLASS ACTIVITY Tell the class the name of the first classmate you talked to. Make a list of names.

"Her name is Akemi Shimizu. She spells her name . . ."

3 CONVERSATION This is Arturo Valdez.

A Listen and practice.

Alexa: Hi Soo-jin, this is Arturo Valdez. He's a biology student.

Soo-jin: Nice to meet you, Arturo. I'm Soo-jin Kim.

Arturo: Hi. So, you're from South Korea?

Soo-jin: That's right. I'm from Seoul.

Arturo: Cool! What's Seoul like?

Soo-jin: It's really nice. It's a very exciting city.

B Listen to the rest of the conversation. What city is Arturo from? What's it like?

4 PRONUNCIATION Linked sounds

Listen and practice. Notice how final consonant sounds are often linked to the vowels that follow them.

I'm a biology student.   My friend is over there.   My name is Alexandra Costa.

5 GRAMMAR FOCUS

Statements with *be*; possessive adjectives

Statements with *be*	Contractions of *be*	Possessive adjectives
I'm from Mexico.	**I'm** = I am	my
You're from Brazil.	**you're** = you are	your
He's from Japan.	**he's** = he is	his
She's a business student.	**she's** = she is	her
It's an exciting city.	**it's** = it is	its
We're in the same class.	**we're** = we are	our
They're my classmates.	**they're** = they are	their

GRAMMAR PLUS *see page 132*

A Complete these sentences. Then tell a partner about yourself.

1. _____My_____ name is Aiko Yoshida. _____ from Japan. _____ family is in Nagoya. _____ brother is a college student. _____ name is Haruki.

2. _____ name is Matias. _____ from Santiago. _____ a really nice city. _____ sister is a student here. _____ parents are in Chile right now.

3. _____ Angelica, but everyone calls me Angie. _____ last name is Newton. _____ a student at City College. _____ parents are on vacation this week. _____ in Las Vegas.

Where's your friend?	He's in class.
Who's Soo-jin?	She's my classmate.
What's Seoul **like**?	It's a very exciting city.
Where are you and Vanessa from?	We're from Brazil.
How are your classes?	They're pretty interesting.
What are your classmates **like**?	They're really nice.

GRAMMAR PLUS *see page 132*

For a list of countries and nationalities, see the appendix at the back of the book.

B Complete these questions. Then practice with a partner.

1. **A:** _____Who's_____ that?
   B: Oh, that's Mrs. Adams.

2. **A:** _____ she from?
   B: She's from San Diego.

3. **A:** _____ her first name?
   B: It's Caroline.

4. **A:** _____ the two students over there?
   B: Their names are Mason and Ava.

5. **A:** _____ they from?
   B: They're from Vancouver.

6. **A:** _____ they _____?
   B: They're shy, but very friendly.

C **GROUP WORK** Write five questions about your classmates. Then ask and answer the questions.

What's your last name?

Where's Jay from?

6 SNAPSHOT

SCHOOL SUBJECTS

1. _____math_____
2. _____
3. _____
4. _____
5. _____
6. _____
7. _____
8. _____

Write the names of the school subjects under the pictures.
What is (or was) your favorite school subject?
What subjects don't (or didn't) you like?

math	literature
history	chemistry
physics	geography
biology	physical education

CONVERSATION How's it going?

▶ Listen and practice.

Arturo	Hi, Soo-jin!
Soo-jin	Hey Arturo. How's it going?
Arturo	Great! How are you?
Soo-jin	I'm fine, thanks. So, are your classes interesting this semester?
Arturo	Yes, they are. I really love biology.
Soo-jin	Biology? Are you and Alexa in the same class?
Arturo	No, we aren't. My class is in the morning. Her class is in the afternoon.
Soo-jin	Oh, OK. Hey, do you have time for coffee?
Arturo	Sure. I'd love some coffee.

8 **GRAMMAR FOCUS**

▶ **Yes/No questions and short answers with *be***

Are you free?	Yes, I **am**.	No, I**'m not**.
Is Arturo from Mexico?	Yes, he **is**.	No, he**'s not**./No, he **isn't**.
Is Alexa's class in the morning?	Yes, it **is**.	No, it**'s not**./No, it **isn't**.
Are you and Alexa in the same class?	Yes, we **are**.	No, we**'re not**./No, we **aren't**.
Are your classes interesting?	Yes, they **are**.	No, they**'re not**./No, they **aren't**.

GRAMMAR PLUS *see page 132*

A Complete the conversations. Then practice with a partner.

1. **A:** ___Is___ Mr. Jones from the United States?
   B: Yes, he _____. _____ from Baltimore.

2. **A:** _____ English class at 2:00?
   B: No, it _____. _____ at 3:00.

3. **A:** _____ you and Giovanna from Italy?
   B: Yes, we _____. _____ from Milan.

4. **A:** _____ Mr. and Mrs. Flores Brazilian?
   B: No, they _____. _____ Peruvian.

B Answer these questions. If you answer "no," give the correct information.
Then ask your partner the questions.

1. Are you from the United States? _____
2. Is your teacher from Canada? _____
3. Is your English class in the morning? _____
4. Are you free after class? _____

C **GROUP WORK** Write five questions about your classmates. Then ask and answer the questions.

Are Kate and Phil from Chicago?

9 WORD POWER Hello and good-bye

A Do you know these expressions? Which ones are "hellos" and which ones are "good-byes"? Complete the chart. Add expressions of your own.

✓ Bye.
✓ Good morning.
   Good night.
   Have a good day.
   Hey.
   Hi.

How are you?
How's it going?
See you later.
See you tomorrow.
Talk to you later.
What's up?

Hello	Good-bye
Good morning.	Bye.

B Match each expression with the best response.

1. Have a good day.
2. Hi. How are you?
3. What's up?
4. Good morning.

   a. Oh, not much.
   b. Thank you. You, too.
   c. Good morning.
   d. Pretty good, thanks.

C **CLASS ACTIVITY** Practice saying hello. Then practice saying good-bye.

A: Hi, Sakura. How's it going?
B: Pretty good, thanks. How are you?

10 LISTENING Everyone calls me Bill.

▶ Listen to the conversations. Complete the information about each person.

First name	Last name	Where from?	What do they study?
1. William			
2.	Ortiz		
3. Min-soo			

11 INTERCHANGE 1 Getting to know you

Find out about your classmates. Go to Interchange 1 on page 114.

A Look at the names in the article. Are any of the names popular in your country? What similar names can you think of?

IS YOUR NAME *Trendy?*

Some people have names that are very unusual and unique. Think about the actress Emily Blunt, for example. Her daughters' names are Hazel (an eye color) and Violet (a flower). Alicia Keys has a son named Egypt. How cool is that? Are these names trendy? The answer is . . . maybe.

Many names seem to be trendy for a while, just like clothes. In the United States, some grandmothers and great-grandmothers have names like Mildred and Dorothy. For grandfathers and great-grandfathers, it's old names like Eugene or Larry. These names usually come from Greek and Latin, but they're not very popular now.

Parents sometimes choose names because they like an actor or a famous person. That's how trends usually start. For example, David and Victoria Beckham have a son named Brooklyn and a daughter named Harper. Now, Brooklyn is a popular boy's name and Harper is a popular girl's name. In the United Kingdom, baby boys often get the name George because of Prince George, Prince William and Kate Middleton's first child.

There is also a trend for names that are things or places (like Egypt). Flower names are becoming more popular: Poppy, Daisy, and Lotus, for example. Space names are cool, too. More and more babies have names like Orion (a star), Luna (the moon), or Mars (a planet).

POPULAR NAMES FOR BOYS & GIRLS

Can you guess who helped make these names popular?

BOYS	GIRLS
Bruno	January
Leonardo	Angelina
Liam	Audrey

Bruno Mars, Leonardo di Caprio, Liam Hemsworth, January Jones, Angelina Jolie, Audrey Hepburn

B Read the article. Then check (✓) the sentences that are true.

- ☐ **1.** Baby names like Mildred and Larry aren't so trendy now.
- ☐ **2.** Many babies are named after clothes.
- ☐ **3.** Alicia Keys has a son named Hazel.
- ☐ **4.** There is a famous prince named George.
- ☐ **5.** Some girls' names are the same as flower names.
- ☐ **6.** Babies never have names that are the same as planets or stars.

C **GROUP WORK** What names do you like? Can you think of anyone with an unusual name? Do you know how they got that name? Tell your classmates.

2 What do you do?

▶ Ask and answer questions about jobs
▶ Describe routines and daily schedules

1 SNAPSHOT

Six Popular Part-time Jobs in the United States

babysitter

fitness instructor

office assistant

sales associate

social media assistant

tutor

Which jobs are easy? difficult? exciting? boring? Why?
Are these good jobs for students? What are some other part-time jobs?

2 WORD POWER Jobs

A Complete the word map with jobs from the list.

✓ accountant
✓ cashier
  chef
✓ dancer
✓ flight attendant
  musician
  pilot
  receptionist
  server
  singer
  tour guide
  web designer

OFFICE WORK
accountant
_____
_____
_____
_____

FOOD SERVICE
cashier
_____
_____
_____
_____

JOBS

TRAVEL INDUSTRY
flight attendant
_____
_____
_____

ENTERTAINMENT BUSINESS
dancer
_____
_____
_____

B Add two more jobs to each category. Then compare with a partner.

3 SPEAKING Work and workplaces

GROUP WORK Form teams. One team member sits with his or her back to the board. Choose a job from page 8 or from the box. Write the job on the board. Your team member asks yes/no questions and tries to guess the job.

More jobs

carpenter	nurse
cook	office manager
dentist	police officer
doctor	reporter
engineer	restaurant host
firefighter	salesperson
front desk clerk	security guard
graphic designer	taxi driver
lawyer	teacher
mechanic	vendor

A: Does the person work in a hospital?
B: No, he or she doesn't.

A: Does he or she work in a restaurant?
C: Yes, that's right!

4 CONVERSATION I'm on my feet all day.

A Listen and practice.

Amy What do you do, Derek?

Derek I work part-time as a server.

Amy Oh, really? What restaurant do you work at?

Derek I work at Stella's Café downtown.

Amy That's cool. How do you like it?

Derek It's OK. I'm on my feet all day, so I'm always tired. What do you do?

Amy I'm a dancer.

Derek A dancer! How exciting!

Amy Yeah, it's great! I work with incredible people.

Derek That sounds really nice. But is it difficult?

Amy A little. I'm on my feet all day, too, but I love it.

B Listen to the rest of the conversation. Who does Amy travel with? Who does she meet in other cities?

5 GRAMMAR FOCUS

Simple present Wh-questions and statements

What do you **do**?	I'**m** a student. I **have** a part-time job, too.	**I/You**	**He/She**
Where do you **work**?	I **work** at a restaurant.	work	works
Where do you **go** to school?	I **go** to the University of Texas.	take	takes
		study	studies
What does Amy **do**?	She'**s** a dancer.	teach	teaches
Where does she **work**?	She **works** at a dance company.	do	does
	She **travels**, too.	go	goes
How does she **like** it?	She **loves** it.	have	has

GRAMMAR PLUS *see page 133*

A Complete these conversations. Then practice with a partner.

1. **A:** What _____do_____ you _____do_____?
   B: I'm a full-time student. I study the piano.
   A: And _____ do you _____ to school?
   B: I _____ to the Brooklyn School of Music.
   A: Wow! _____ do you like your classes?
   B: I _____ them a lot.

2. **A:** What _____ Tanya do?
   B: She's a teacher. She _____ an art class at a school in Denver.
   A: And what about Ryan? Where _____ he work?
   B: He _____ for a big computer company in San Francisco.
   A: _____ does he do, exactly?
   B: He's a web designer. He _____ fantastic websites.

3. **A:** What _____ Bruce and Ivy do?
   B: They _____ at an Italian restaurant. It's really good.
   A: That's nice. _____ is Ivy's job?
   B: Well, she manages the finances and Bruce _____ in the kitchen.

4. **A:** Where _____ Ali work?
   B: He _____ at the university. He _____ a part-time job.
   A: Really? What _____ he do?
   B: He _____ office work.
   A: How _____ he like it?
   B: Not much, but he _____ some extra money to spend!

B **PAIR WORK** Ask your partner questions like these about work and school. Take notes to use in Exercise 6.

What do you do?
Do you go to school or do you have a job?
How do you like . . . ?
Do you study another language?
What's your favorite . . . ?
What does your best friend do?

C **CLASS WORK** Tell the class about your partner.

"Regina goes to Chicago University, and she has a part-time job, too. She likes . . ."

6 WRITING A biography

A Use your notes from Exercise 5 to write a biography of your partner. Don't use your partner's name. Use *he* or *she* instead.

> My partner is a chef. She works in a very nice restaurant near
> our school. She cooks Italian food and bakes desserts. She likes
> her English classes a lot. Her favorite activities are speaking and
> vocabulary practice. She studies another language, too . . .

B **CLASS ACTIVITY** Pass your biographies around the class. Guess who each biography is about.

7 CONVERSATION I work in the afternoon.

▶ **A** Listen and practice.

KRISTINA I need to go to National Bank downtown, please. I'm late for a meeting.

TAXI DRIVER No problem. What time is your meeting?

KRISTINA In 10 minutes! I don't usually work in the morning.

TAXI DRIVER Really? What time do you usually go to work?

KRISTINA I work in the afternoon. I start at one.

TAXI DRIVER That's pretty late. Do you like to work in the afternoon?

KRISTINA Yes, I do. I work better in the afternoon. I finish at seven or eight, then I go home and eat dinner at around 10:30.

TAXI DRIVER Wow, you have dinner late! I go to bed every night at 8:00.

KRISTINA Really? That seems so early!

▶ **B** Listen to the rest of the conversation. What time does the taxi driver start work? What time does he finish?

8 PRONUNCIATION Syllable stress

▶ **A** Listen and practice. Notice which syllable has the main stress.

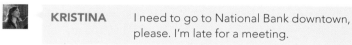

● ● ●
dancer

● ● ●
salesperson

● ● ●
accountant

_____ _____ _____

_____ _____ _____

▶ **B** Which stress pattern do these words have? Add them to the columns in part A. Then listen and check.

carpenter   musician   firefighter   reporter   server   tutor

9 GRAMMAR FOCUS

▶ Time expressions

				Expressing clock time
I get up	**at** 7:00	**in** the morning	**on** weekdays.	7:00
I leave work	**early**	**in** the afternoon	**on** Thursdays.	seven
I go to bed	**around** eleven	**in** the evening	**on** weeknights.	seven o'clock
I get home	**late**	**at** night	**on** weekends.	7:00 A.M. = 7:00 in the morning
I stay up	**until** midnight	**on** Fridays.		7:00 P.M. = 7:00 in the evening
I exercise	**before** noon	**on** Saturdays.		
I wake up	**after** noon	**on** Sundays.		

GRAMMAR PLUS see page 133

A Choose the correct word.

1. I get up **at** / **until** six **at** / **on** weekdays.
2. I have lunch **at** / **early** 11:30 **in** / **on** Mondays.
3. I have a snack **in** / **around** 10:00 **in** / **at** night.
4. **In** / **On** Fridays, I leave school **early** / **before**.
5. I stay up **before** / **until** 1:00 A.M. **in** / **on** weekends.
6. I sleep **around** / **until** noon **in** / **on** Sundays.

7. I have dinner **at** / **in** 7:00 **at** / **on** weeknights.
8. I read a book **after** / **before** I go to sleep.
9. **In** / **On** weekends, I go to bed **in** / **at** 1:00 A.M.
10. **In** / **On** Thursdays, I leave work **at** / **in** 9:00 P.M.
11. I work **late** / **until** on Wednesdays.
12. I study **around** / **until** 11:00 **after** / **early** dinner.

B Rewrite the sentences in part A so that they are true for you. Then compare with a partner.

C **PAIR WORK** Take turns asking and answering these questions.

1. Which days do you get up early? late?
2. What's something you do in the morning?
3. What's something you do before English class?
4. What's something you do on Saturday evenings?
5. Which days do you stay up late?
6. Which days do you go to bed early?
7. What do you do after dinner on weeknights?
8. What do you do after lunch on weekends?

10 LISTENING What hours do you work?

▶ **A** Listen to Aaron, Madison, and Kayla talk about their daily schedules. Complete the chart.

	Aaron	Madison	Kayla
Job	carpenter		
Gets up at . . .		7:00 a.m.	
Gets home at . . .			
Goes to bed at . . .			

B **CLASS ACTIVITY** Who do you think has the best daily schedule? Why?

11 INTERCHANGE 2 What we have in common

Find out about your classmates' schedules. Go to Interchange 2 on page 115.

A Read the title and skim the blog posts. What are these people's jobs? Why do you think their jobs are hard to understand?

MY PARENTS DON'T UNDERSTAND MY JOB!

DANNY BANGKOK, THAILAND

Do you know what a social media manager is? Right, of course you do, but my mom doesn't. Every week, I try to explain my job to her. I work for a company that makes cars. My job is to tell the world how great our cars are. How do I do that? I get up early and write posts for social media. On weekdays, I go online around 7:00 a.m. and sometimes I work until 9:00 at night. The problem is . . . my mom doesn't use social media.

CARLA BUENOS AIRES, ARGENTINA

It's so funny! I explain my job to my dad, but he just looks very confused. I'm a fashion designer. I always get up early on weekdays because I love my job. I have an office, and most days I draw pictures of cool new clothes, like dresses, jeans, and T-shirts. I also go to stores to look at fabrics to use for my clothes. My dad thinks I'm crazy! He just goes to a store and buys stuff to wear. He doesn't know someone has to design it first.

NICO ATHENS, GREECE

So, I'm a sociologist. I study people. Well, I study how people behave. I also study why we behave the way they do. My mom and dad don't understand why I do that. My mom says, "Nico, people are people! They just do normal things!" I don't agree. There are many reasons why people do the things they do, and I love to learn about that.

LISA LOS ANGELES, UNITED STATES

I'm a software engineer, but my dad doesn't know what that means. I tell him that software is the technology inside his computer, his phone, and his tablet. I make apps for smartphones. One app helps people exercise more. It's very cool because it tracks everything you do during the day. You put your phone in your pocket, and the app does the rest. The app tracks your walk to school, your bike ride on the weekend, and more.

B Read the article. Who does the following things? Check (✓) the correct boxes.

Who does something . . .	Danny	Carla	Nico	Lisa
1. . . . to help people get fit?	☐	☐	☐	☐
2. . . . to understand other people?	☐	☐	☐	☐
3. . . . to make things you can wear?	☐	☐	☐	☐
4. . . . to tell other people about their company?	☐	☐	☐	☐

C **PAIR WORK** Which of the four jobs do you think is the most interesting? the most useful? the hardest to explain? What other things are hard to explain? Think about different jobs, hobbies, or classes at school.

Units 1–2 Progress check

SELF-ASSESSMENT

How well can you do these things? Check (✓) the boxes.

I can . . .	Very well	OK	A little
Make an introduction and use basic greeting expressions (Ex. 1)	☐	☐	☐
Show I didn't understand and ask for repetition (Ex. 1)	☐	☐	☐
Ask and answer questions about myself and other people (Ex. 2)	☐	☐	☐
Ask and answer questions about work (Ex. 3, 4)	☐	☐	☐
Ask and answer questions about habits and routines (Ex. 5)	☐	☐	☐

1 ROLE PLAY Introductions

A PAIR WORK You are talking to someone at school. Have a conversation.
Then change roles and try the role play again.

A: Hi. How are you?
B: . . .
A: By the way, my name is . . .
B: I'm sorry. What's your name again?
A: . . .
B: I'm . . . . Are you a student here?
A: . . . And how about you?
B: . . .
A: Oh, really? And where are you from?

B GROUP WORK Join another pair.
Introduce your partner.

2 SPEAKING Interview

Write questions for these answers. Then use the questions to interview a classmate.

1. _What's_ _____?	My name is Midori Oki.
2. _____?	I'm from Kyoto, Japan.
3. _____?	Yes, my classes are very interesting.
4. _____?	My favorite class is English.
5. _____?	No, my teacher isn't American.
6. _____?	My classmates are very nice.
7. _____?	My best friend is Kiara.

3 SPEAKING What a great job!

A What do you know about these jobs? List three things each person does.

software engineer

caregiver

electrician

IT worker

works on a computer

_____

_____

_____

B GROUP WORK Compare your lists. Take turns asking about the jobs.

4 LISTENING At Dylan's party

A Listen to Austin and Haley talk about work and school. Complete the chart.

	Austin	Haley
What do you do?		
Where do you work/study?		
How do you like your job/classes?		
What do you do after work/school?		

B PAIR WORK Practice the questions in part A. Answer with your own information.

5 SPEAKING Survey: My perfect day

A Imagine your perfect day. Read the questions, then add one more. Then write your answers.

What time do you get up? _____

What do you do after you get up? _____

Where do you go? _____

What do you do in the evening? _____

When do you go to bed? _____

_____

B PAIR WORK Talk about your perfect day. Answer any questions.

WHAT'S NEXT?

Look at your Self-assessment again. Do you need to review anything?

3 How much are these?

▸ Ask about and describe prices
▸ Discuss preferences

1 SNAPSHOT

WHAT'S IN A COLOR?

white = hopeful
blue = truthful
brown = friendly
black = powerful

green = jealous
yellow = happy
orange = confident
red = exciting
pink = loving
purple = creative
gray = sad

Which words have a positive meaning? Which have a negative meaning?
What meanings do these colors have for you? What colors do you like to wear?

2 CONVERSATION I'll take it!

▶ **A** Listen and practice.

SALESCLERK Hi! Can I help you?

CUSTOMER Yes, please. I need a birthday present for my sister.

SALESCLERK That's so nice! What does she like?

CUSTOMER She loves anything blue. How much is this sweater?

SALESCLERK The light blue one? It's $150.

CUSTOMER That's pretty expensive. I love my sister, but I need to eat!

SALESCLERK Well, we have that one, too.

CUSTOMER Which one? The green one?

SALESCLERK Yes, and it's on sale for $28.99.

CUSTOMER Well, she also likes green. I'll take it!

▶ **B** Listen to the rest of the conversation. What else does the customer look at? Does he buy it?

16

3 GRAMMAR FOCUS

Demonstratives; one, ones

GRAMMAR PLUS see page 134

How much is	**this** T-shirt?	**that** T-shirt?	Which **one**?	
	this one?	**that one**?	The blue **one**.	**It's** $28.99.
How much are	**these** sneakers?	**those** sneakers	Which **ones**?	
	these?	**those**?	The gray **ones**.	**They're** $40.

saying prices

99¢ = ninety-nine cents
$28 = twenty-eight dollars
$28.99 = twenty-eight ninety-nine

A Complete these conversations. Then practice with a partner.

A: Excuse me. How much are
_____ *those* _____ jeans?
B: Which _____? Do you mean
_____?
A: No, the light blue _____.
B: Oh, _____ are $59.95.
A: Wow! That's expensive!

A: How much is _____ backpack?
B: Which _____?
A: The orange _____.
B: It's $36.99. But _____ green
_____ is only $22.25.
A: That's not bad. Can I see it, please?

B PAIR WORK Add prices to the items. Then ask and answer questions.

A: How much are these boots?
B: Which ones?
A: The brown ones.
B: They're $95.50.
A: That's expensive!

useful expressions

That's cheap.
That's reasonable.
That's OK/not bad.
That's expensive.

4 PRONUNCIATION Sentence stress

▶ **A** Listen and practice. Notice that the important words in a sentence have more stress.

Let's see . . .

Excuse me.
I'll take it.

That's expensive.
Can I help you?

Do you mean these?

B PAIR WORK Practice the conversations in Exercise 3, part B again. Pay attention to the sentence stress.

5 ROLE PLAY Can I help you?

A PAIR WORK Put items "for sale" on your desk, such as notebooks, watches, phones, or bags.

Student A: You are a salesclerk. Answer the customer's questions.

Student B: You are a customer. Ask the price of each item. Say if you want to buy it.

    A: Can I help you?
    B: Yes. I like this pen. How much is it?
    A: Which one?

B Change roles and try the role play again.

6 LISTENING Wow! It's expensive!

▶ **A** Listen to two friends shopping. Write the color and price for each item.

	1. tablet	2. headphones	3. sunglasses	4. T-shirt
color				
price				
Do they buy it?	☐ Yes ☐ No	☐ Yes ☐ No	☐ Yes ☐ No	☐ Yes ☐ No

▶ **B** Listen again. Do they buy the items? Check (✓) Yes or No.

7 INTERCHANGE 3 Flea market

See what kinds of deals you can make as a buyer and a seller.
Go to Interchange 3 on pages 116–117.

8 WORD POWER Materials

A What are these things made of? Label each one. Use the words from the list.

| cotton | gold | leather | plastic | rubber | silk | silver | wool |

1. a ___silk___ tie
2. a _____ bracelet
3. a _____ ring
4. a _____ shirt

5. a _____ belt
6. _____ earrings
7. _____ flip-flops
8. _____ socks

B **PAIR WORK** What other materials are the things in part A sometimes made of? Make a list.

C **CLASS ACTIVITY** Which materials can you find in your classroom?
"Min-hee has gold earrings, and Ray has a leather jacket."

9 CONVERSATION That's a good point.

A Listen and practice.

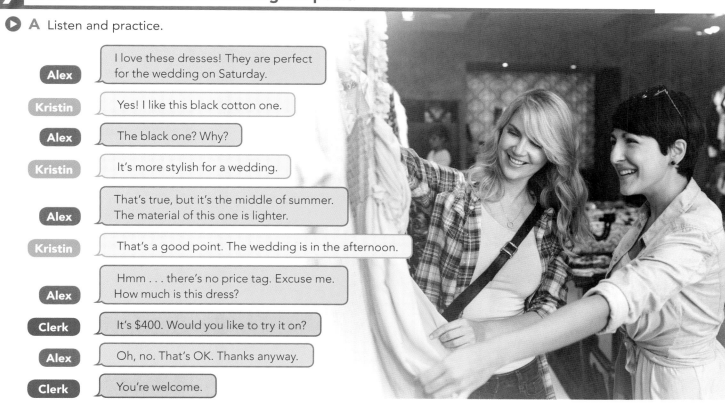

Alex: I love these dresses! They are perfect for the wedding on Saturday.

Kristin: Yes! I like this black cotton one.

Alex: The black one? Why?

Kristin: It's more stylish for a wedding.

Alex: That's true, but it's the middle of summer. The material of this one is lighter.

Kristin: That's a good point. The wedding is in the afternoon.

Alex: Hmm . . . there's no price tag. Excuse me. How much is this dress?

Clerk: It's $400. Would you like to try it on?

Alex: Oh, no. That's OK. Thanks anyway.

Clerk: You're welcome.

B Listen to the rest of the conversation. What does Alex buy? What does Kristin think of it?

10 GRAMMAR FOCUS

▶ Preferences; comparisons with adjectives

Which dress do you **prefer**?
   I **prefer** the blue one.
Which one do you **like more**?
   I **like** the blue one **more**.
Which one do you **like better**?
   I **like** the black one **better**.

It's **nicer than** the black one.

It's **lighter than** the black one.

It's **more stylish than** the blue one.

Spelling

cheap ⟶ cheap**er**
nice ⟶ nice**r**
big ⟶ bi**gger**
pretty ⟶ prett**ier**

GRAMMAR PLUS *see page 134*

A Complete these conversations. Then practice with a partner.

1. A: Which of these jackets
      do you like more?
   B: I prefer the leather
      one. The design is
      _____ (nice),
      and it looks
      _____ (expensive)
      the wool one.

2. A: These sweaters are nice.
      Which one do you prefer?
   B: I like the gray one
      better. The color is
      _____ (pretty). It's
      _____ (attractive)
      the brown and yellow
      one.

3. A: Which rings do you like
      better?
   B: I like the silver
      ones more. They're
      _____ (small) the
      gold ones. And they're
      _____ (cheap).

B **PAIR WORK** Compare the things in part A.
Give your own opinions.

A: Which jacket do you like more?
B: I like the wool one better. The color is prettier.

useful expressions

The color is prettier.
The design is nicer.
The style is more attractive.
The material is better.

11 WRITING My favorite clothes

A What do you like to wear? Write about your favorite clothes
and compare them to clothes you don't like as much.

> My favorite clothes are cotton T-shirts and jeans. T-shirts are
> more comfortable than shirts and ties, and I think jeans are nicer
> than pants. I know that suits are more stylish, but . . .

B **GROUP WORK** Take turns reading your descriptions.
Ask questions to get more information.

A Skim the article. Why do you think people shop online?

Home   Posts   Archives

ONLINE SHOPPING: The Crazy Things People Buy
In this week's blog, we look at some extraordinary things people can buy online.

1 A PIECE OF THE MOON: $27.50

It's true. You can own a piece of land on the moon. An acre, or about 4,000 square meters, of moon costs $27.50. That's a lot of space for your stuff. In fact, the price of each acre goes down when you buy more land. Imagine what you could do with all that space . . . if you could travel there! But don't worry, you get a certificate that says the land is yours.

2 SOMEONE TO STAND IN LINE FOR YOU: $25 AN HOUR

No one likes to stand in line, right? Now you don't have to! For $25 an hour, someone waits patiently in line to get the stuff you need. Imagine that! Some people pay for someone to stand in line for movie tickets or for a new video game that's on sale. Make a reservation online in just a few clicks.

3 SOME VERY EXPENSIVE SNEAKERS: $20,000 AND UP

Do you ever think your shoes are boring? Well, our sneakers are just what you need. Just go to our online store, look for a pair of sneakers you like, and place a bid. Maybe you'll win! Some of the sneakers are from famous basketball players.

4 NO TIME FOR A REAL PET: $12

Many people like dogs and cats, but they just don't have the time to take care of them. If that sounds like you, here's the answer to your problem: a digital pet rock. It's clean, it's quiet, and it doesn't need food. It comes in a box. We think it's just about the perfect pet. You plug it into your laptop, and it's always with you!

B Read the blog. Find the item and write its name. Then write the number of the paragraph where you find the answers.

Find something . . .
a. . . . that you can wear. _____
b. . . . that you use with your laptop. _____
c. . . . that saves you a lot of time. _____
d. . . . that is huge. _____

C **GROUP WORK** The person who invented the first pet rock, Gary Dahl, became a millionaire. Why do you think people bought pet rocks? Do you think Mr. Dahl was a smart man? Would you buy a pet rock? Would you buy any of the other things? How much would you spend? Tell your classmates.

4 Do you play the guitar?

▸ Discuss entertainment likes and dislikes
▸ Make, accept, and decline invitations

1 SNAPSHOT

MUSIC SALES
IN THE UNITED STATES

Country 11.2%
Electronic 3.4%
Latin 2.6%
Classical 1.4%
Jazz 1.4%
Rock 29%
Pop 14.9%
R&B and Hip-Hop 17.2%
Other 18.4%

What styles of music do you like? What styles do you dislike?
What styles of music are popular in your country?

2 WORD POWER That's entertainment!

A Complete the word map with words from the list. Some words can go in more than one category.

action	reality show
electronic	reggae
game show	salsa
horror	science fiction
musical	soap opera
rap	talk show

B Add two more words to each category. Then compare with a partner.

C GROUP WORK Number the items in each list from 1 (you like it the most) to 6 (you like it the least). Then compare your ideas.

ENTERTAINMENT

TV SHOWS

MOVIES

MUSIC

3 CONVERSATION What kind of music do you like?

A Listen and practice.

LEANNE I can't wait for the Taylor Swift concert this Friday!

SETH I think I know her. Does she play the violin?

LEANNE No. She's a pop star.

SETH Of course! I guess I don't listen to pop music a lot.

LEANNE Oh, really? What kind of music do you like?

SETH I really like hip-hop. Drake is my favorite musician.

LEANNE Doesn't Drake play the guitar?

SETH No, Leanne. He sings and raps.

LEANNE OK. Well, I think we need to teach each other about music!

B Listen to the rest of the conversation. Who is Seth's favorite band? Does Leanne like them?

4 GRAMMAR FOCUS

Simple present questions; short answers

		Object pronouns
Do you **like** country music? Yes, I **do**. I love it. No, I **don't**. I don't like it very much.	What kind of music **do** you **like**? I really like rap.	me
		you
Does she **play** the piano? Yes, she **does**. She plays very well. No, she **doesn't**. She doesn't play an instrument.	**What does** she **play**? She plays the guitar.	him
		her
		it
Do they **like** Imagine Dragons? Yes, they **do**. They like them a lot. No, they **don't**. They don't like them at all.	**Who do** they **like**? They like Maroon 5.	us
		them

GRAMMAR PLUS *see page 135*

Complete these conversations. Then practice with a partner.

1. **A:** I like Alabama Shakes a lot. _____ you know _____?
   B: Yes, I _____, and I love this song. Let's download _____.
2. **A:** _____ you like science fiction movies?
   B: Yes, I _____. I like _____ very much.
3. **A:** _____ Vinnie and Midori like soap operas?
   B: Vinnie _____, but Midori _____. She hates _____.
4. **A:** What kind of music _____ Maya like?
   B: Classical music. She loves Yo-Yo Ma.
   A: Yeah, he's amazing. I like _____ a lot.

Alabama Shakes

Do you play the guitar? **23**

5 PRONUNCIATION   Intonation in questions

▶ **A** Listen and practice. Yes/No questions usually have rising intonation.
Wh-questions usually have falling intonation.

Do you like pop music?   What kind of music do you like?

B **PAIR WORK** Practice these questions.

Do you like TV?   What shows do you like?
Do you like video games?   What games do you like?
Do you play a musical instrument?   What instrument do you play?

6 SPEAKING   Entertainment survey

A **GROUP WORK** Write five questions about entertainment and entertainers.
Then ask and answer your questions in groups.

What kinds of . . . do you like?
    (music, TV shows, video games)
Do you like . . . ?
    (reggae, game shows, action movies)
Who's your favorite . . . ?
    (singer, actor, athlete)

B **GROUP WORK** Complete this information about your group.
Ask any additional questions.

Our group
FAVORITES

What's your favorite kind of . . . ?

music _____

movie _____

TV show _____

What's your favorite . . . ?

song _____

movie _____

video game _____

Who's your favorite . . . ?

singer _____

actor _____

athlete _____

Adele

Steph Curry

Star Wars: The Force Awakens

Top Chef

C **CLASS ACTIVITY** Read your group's list to the class.
Find out the class favorites.

7 LISTENING The perfect date

A Listen to a host and four people on a TV game show. Three men want to invite Alexis on a date. What kinds of things do they like? Complete the chart.

Alexis

	Jacob	Tyler	Andrew	Alexis
Music				
Movies				
TV shows				

B **CLASS ACTIVITY** Who do you think is the best date for Alexis? Why?

8 CONVERSATION What time does it start?

A Listen and practice.

CONNOR I have tickets to my brother's concert on Friday night. Would you like to go?

CAMILA Thanks, I'd love to. What time does it start?

CONNOR At 8:00.

CAMILA Do you want to have dinner before? Maybe at 6:00?

CONNOR Well, I'd like to, but I have to work late. Let's just meet before the concert, around 7:30.

CAMILA No problem. We can have dinner another day. Let's meet at your office and go together.

CONNOR Sounds good! See you on Friday.

B Listen to Connor and Camila talking at the concert. Does Camila like the concert? Does Connor's brother play well?

9 GRAMMAR FOCUS

▶ *Would*; verb + *to* + verb

Would you **like to go** out on Friday?	**Would** you **like to go** to a concert?	**Contractions**
Yes, I **would**.	**I'd like to**, but I **have to work** late.	**I'd** = I would
Yes, **I'd love to**. Thanks.	**I'd like to**, but I **need to save** money.	
	I'd like to, but I **want to visit** my parents.	

GRAMMAR PLUS *see page 135*

A Respond to three invitations. Then write three invitations for the given responses.

1. A: I have tickets to the soccer game on Sunday. Would you like to go?

B: _____

2. A: Would you like to come over for dinner tomorrow night?

B: _____

3. A: Would you like to go to a hip-hop dance class with me this weekend?

B: _____

4. A: _____
_____

B: Yes, I'd love to. Thank you!

5. A: _____
_____

B: Well, I'd like to, but I have to study.

6. A: _____
_____

B: Yes, I would. I really like electronic music.

B **PAIR WORK** Ask and answer the questions in part A. Give your own responses.

C **PAIR WORK** Think of three things you would like to do. Then invite a partner to do them with you. Your partner responds and asks follow-up questions like these:

When is it?   Where is it?   What time does it start?   When does it end?

10 WRITING Text messages

A What do these text messages say?

text message abbreviations	
u = you	afaik = as far as I know
r = are	lol = laugh out loud
2 = to / too	idk = I don't know
pls = please	msg = message
thx = thanks	nm = never mind
imo = in my opinion	brb = be right back
tbh = to be honest	ttyl = talk to you later

B **GROUP WORK** Write a "text message" to each person in your group. Then exchange messages. Write a response to each message.

11 INTERCHANGE 4 Are you free this weekend?

Make weekend plans with your classmates. Go to Interchange 4 on page 118.

A Scan the article and look at the pictures. In what year did each event take place?

The World's Most Powerful FEMALE MUSICIAN

Beyoncé Knowles-Carter is a singer, songwriter, performer, actress, clothing designer, and Grammy Award–winning superstar. Many people call her one of the most powerful female musicians in history. Beyoncé works really hard for her success. As she says, "I wanted to sell a million records, and I sold a million records. I wanted to go platinum; I went platinum. I've been working nonstop since I was 15. I don't even know how to chill out."

Many people talk about Beyoncé's energy on stage. She's an amazing entertainer. Millions of fans love her singing and dancing. Beyoncé uses many different styles of music, including funk, soul, and pop. In her career so far, Beyoncé has sold over 100 million records as a solo artist and another 60 million records with her group Destiny's Child.

Beyoncé marries Jay-Z.

BEYONCÉ FAST FACTS

1981	Beyoncé is born in Houston, Texas.
1996	Her girl group, Destiny's Child, gets its first recording contract.
2001	Beyoncé experiences her first time acting. She stars in *Carmen: A Hip Hopera* on MTV.
2003	She releases her first solo album, *Dangerously in Love*.
2004	She wins five Grammys at the Grammy Awards.
2005	Beyoncé starts an organization to help hurricane victims.
2008	She marries rapper Jay-Z.
2010	She wins six Grammys at the Grammy Awards for her album *I Am . . . Sasha Fierce*.
2012	Beyoncé has a daughter and names her Blue Ivy.
2013	Beyoncé performs at the U.S. president's inauguration.
2013	She releases a secret album online named *Beyoncé*.
2016	Beyoncé performs her song "Formation" at a huge sporting event.

Beyoncé performs at the U.S. president's inauguration.

B Read the article. Then number these sentences from 1 (first event) to 8 (last event).

_____ **a.** She performs at a president's inauguration.

_____ **b.** She is born in Texas.

_____ **c.** She acts in a movie.

_____ **d.** She wins five Grammys.

_____ **e.** She releases her first solo album.

_____ **f.** She has a baby.

_____ **g.** Her group gets its first recording contract.

_____ **h.** She helps hurricane victims.

C **PAIR WORK** Who is your favorite musician? What do you know about his or her life?

Units 3–4 Progress check

SELF-ASSESSMENT

How well can you do these things? Check (✓) the boxes.

I can . . .	Very well	OK	A little
Give and understand information about prices (Ex. 1)	☐	☐	☐
Say what I like and dislike (Ex. 1, 2, 3)	☐	☐	☐
Explain why I like or dislike something (Ex. 2)	☐	☐	☐
Describe and compare objects and possessions (Ex. 2)	☐	☐	☐
Make and respond to invitiations (Ex. 4)	☐	☐	☐

1 LISTENING Price Cut City

▶ **A** Listen to a commercial for Price Cut City. Choose the correct prices.

B PAIR WORK What do you think of the items in part A? At what stores or websites can you find items like these at low prices? Give your own ideas and opinions.

2 ROLE PLAY Shopping trip

Student A: Choose things from Exercise 1 for your family. Ask for Student B's opinion.
Student B: Help Student A choose presents for his or her family.

> **A:** I want to buy a laptop for my parents. Which one do you like better?
> **B:** Well, I like . . . better. It's nicer, and . . .

Change roles and try the role play again.

3 SPEAKING Survey: Likes and dislikes

A Add one more question to the chart. Write your answers to these questions.

	Me	My classmate
When do you usually watch TV?		
What kinds of TV shows do you like?		
Do you like game shows?		
Do you read the news online?		
Who is your favorite singer?		
What do you think of hip-hop?		
What is your favorite movie?		
Do you like musicals?		
What kinds of movies do you dislike?		

B **CLASS ACTIVITY** Go around the class. Find someone who has the same answers as you. Write a classmate's name only once!

4 SPEAKING What an excuse!

A Make up three invitations to interesting activities. Write them on cards.

My friends and I are going to the amusement park on Sunday at 2 p.m. Would you like to come?

B Write three response cards. One is an acceptance card, and two are refusals. Think of silly or unusual excuses.

That sounds great! What time do you want to meet?

I'd like to, but I have to wash my cat tomorrow.

I'd love to, but I want to take my bird to a singing contest.

C **GROUP WORK** Shuffle the invitation cards together and the response cards together. Take three cards from each pile. Then invite people to do the things on your invitation cards. Use the response cards to accept or refuse.

WHAT'S NEXT?

Look at your Self-assessment again. Do you need to review anything?

5 What an interesting family!

▸ **Describe families**
▸ **Talk about habitual and current activities**

1 WORD POWER Family

A Look at Joseph's family tree. How are these people related to him? Add the words to the family tree.

cousin   niece
daughter sister-in-law
father   uncle
grandmother wife

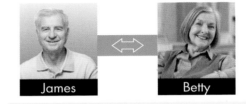

James   Betty

grandfather and _____

Robert   Patricia   Deborah   Arturo

_____ and mother   aunt and _____

Joseph   Keiko   Joshua   Nicole   Veronica

Joseph (husband) and his _____ brother and _____ _____

Andrew   Emily   Alyssa   Ethan

son and _____   _____ and nephew

B Draw your family tree (or a friend's family tree). Then take turns talking about your families. Ask follow-up questions to get more information.

A: There are six people in my family. I have one brother and two sisters.
B: How old is your brother?

2 LISTENING Famous relatives

▶ Listen to four conversations about famous people. How is the second person related to the first person?

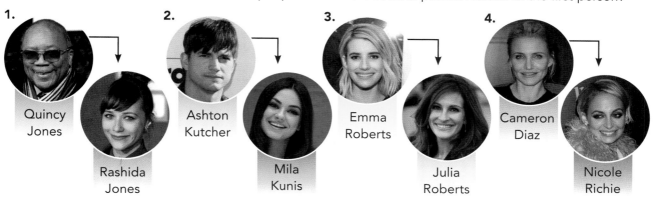

1. Quincy Jones → Rashida Jones

2. Ashton Kutcher → Mila Kunis

3. Emma Roberts → Julia Roberts

4. Cameron Diaz → Nicole Richie

3 CONVERSATION He's traveling in Thailand.

▶ **A** Listen and practice.

	MAX	Do you have brothers and sisters, Tina?
	TINA	Yes, I have a brother and a sister.
	MAX	Oh, what does your sister do?
	TINA	She's a surgeon. She works for a medical aid organization.
	MAX	Wow! And what about your brother?
	TINA	He's a writer. He travels and writes about his experiences for a magazine.
	MAX	What an interesting family! Can I meet them?
	TINA	Sure, but my sister's not here right now. She's treating patients in Cameroon.
	MAX	And your brother?
	TINA	He's traveling in Thailand, and then he wants to visit my sister. I miss them!

▶ **B** Listen to the rest of the conversation. Where do Max's parents live? What do his parents do?

4 PRONUNCIATION Intonation in statements

▶ **A** Listen and practice. Notice that statements usually have falling intonation.

She's working in Cameroon.   He's traveling in Thailand.

B PAIR WORK Practice the conversation in Exercise 3 again.

5 GRAMMAR FOCUS

Present continuous

Are you **living** at home now?	Yes, I **am**.	No, I**'m not**.
Is your sister **working** in another city?	Yes, she **is**.	No, she**'s not**./No, she **isn't**.
Are your parents **studying** English this year?	Yes, they **are**.	No, they**'re not**./No, they **aren't**.

Where **are** you **working** now?	I**'m not working**. I need a job.
What **is** your brother **doing**?	He**'s traveling** in Thailand.
What **are** your friends **doing** these days?	They**'re studying** for their exams.

GRAMMAR PLUS *see page 136*

A Complete these phone conversations using the present continuous.

A: Hi, Brittany. What _____ you _____ (do)?

B: Hey, Zach. I _____ (eat) a sandwich at O'Connor's.

A: Mmm! Is it good?

B: Yeah. It's delicious. Wait, they _____ (bring) my dessert now. It's chocolate cake with ice cream. Call you later! Bye!

A: So, Madison, how _____ you and your sister _____ (do) in college?

B: We _____ (have) a lot of fun, Mom!

A: Fun? OK, but _____ your sister _____ (go) to class every morning?

B: Yeah, Mom. She _____ (work) hard and I am, too. I'm serious!

B **PAIR WORK** Write a short dialogue using the present continuous, then practice it.

C **CLASS WORK** Read your dialogue to the class.

6 DISCUSSION What are you doing these days?

GROUP WORK Ask and answer questions about what you are doing. Use the topics in the box and your own ideas. Ask follow-up questions to get more information.

A: So, what are you doing these days?
B: I'm playing basketball in college.
A: That's nice. And are you enjoying it?

topics to talk about	
traveling	going to high school or college
playing a sport	learning a musical instrument
living alone	working or studying

7 INTERCHANGE 5 Family facts

Find out about your classmates' families. Go to Interchange 5 on page 119.

8 SNAPSHOT

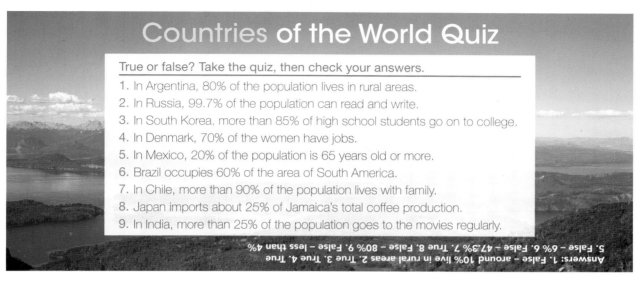

Countries of the World Quiz

True or false? Take the quiz, then check your answers.

1. In Argentina, 80% of the population lives in rural areas.
2. In Russia, 99.7% of the population can read and write.
3. In South Korea, more than 85% of high school students go on to college.
4. In Denmark, 70% of the women have jobs.
5. In Mexico, 20% of the population is 65 years old or more.
6. Brazil occupies 60% of the area of South America.
7. In Chile, more than 90% of the population lives with family.
8. Japan imports about 25% of Jamaica's total coffee production.
9. In India, more than 25% of the population goes to the movies regularly.

Answers: 1. **False** – around 10% live in rural areas 2. **True** 3. **True** 4. **True** 5. **False** – 6% 6. **False** – 47.3% 7. **True** 8. **False** – 80% 9. **False** – less than 4%

Which facts surprise you? Why?
What interesting facts do you know about your country?

9 CONVERSATION I didn't know that.

▶ **A** Listen and practice.

 LUIS What a great picture! Are those your parents?

VICKY Thanks! Yes, it's my favorite picture of us.

 LUIS It's really nice. So, do you have any brothers or sisters?

VICKY No, I'm an only child. Actually, a lot of families in China have only one child.

 LUIS Oh, really? I didn't know that.

VICKY What about you, Luis?

 LUIS I come from a big family. I have two brothers and four sisters.

VICKY Wow! Is that typical in Peru?

 LUIS I'm not sure. Many families are smaller these days. But big families are great because you get a lot of birthday presents!

▶ **B** Listen to the rest of the conversation. What does Vicky like about being an only child?

What an interesting family! **33**

10 GRAMMAR FOCUS

▶ Quantifiers

100%	**All**	
	Nearly all	families have only one child.
	Most	
	Many	
	A lot of	families are smaller these days.
	Some	
	Not many	couples have more than one child.
	Few	
0%	**No one**	gets married before the age of 18.

GRAMMAR PLUS *see page 136*

A Rewrite these sentences using quantifiers. Then compare with a partner.

1. In the U.S., 69% of high school students go to college.

_____

2. Seven percent of the people in Brazil are age 65 or older.

_____

3. In India, 0% of the people vote before the age of 18.

_____

4. Forty percent of the people in Sweden live alone.

_____

5. In Canada, 22% of the people speak French at home.

_____

B **PAIR WORK** Rewrite the sentences in part A so that they are true about your country.

> In the U.S., most high school students go to college.

11 WRITING An email to an online friend

A You have an online friend in another country. Write an email to your friend about your family.

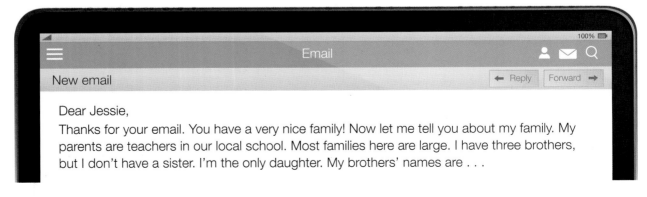

Dear Jessie,

Thanks for your email. You have a very nice family! Now let me tell you about my family. My parents are teachers in our local school. Most families here are large. I have three brothers, but I don't have a sister. I'm the only daughter. My brothers' names are . . .

B **GROUP WORK** Take turns reading your emails. Ask questions to get more information.

12 READING

A A journalist interviewed four people. Read the title of the article.
What do you think the answer will be? Check (✓) the answer.

☐ Yes, most families do.   ☐ No, most families don't.   ☐ Some families do, some families don't.

DO FAMILIES SPEND A LOT OF TIME TOGETHER?

We spend a lot of time together on the weekends. My husband and I always take our son, Oliver, and daughter, Samantha, out to do something fun. Some weeks we go for a long bike ride and get a lot of fresh air! We go to the beach in the summer, of course. In the evenings, we have a barbecue together. During the week, it's more difficult to spend time together because of work and school.
– Jane Chambers

It's a little sad, but most of the time we spend as a family is watching TV. We don't talk much. My mom and dad both work, and they're often tired when they get home. My sister just plays games on her tablet all evening. It's kind of boring. Maybe we spend about an hour a day together. It's never more than that.
– Billy Foster

I'm a stay-at-home dad, and I'm having a great time with my family! When the kids are in school, I do housework. When they come home, I help them with their homework. After that, we all have fun together. We play a lot of sports and read books. I love all the time I get with my two boys.
– Nick Ramos

We're always really busy, but we make an effort to spend time together. My grandparents come over to our house twice a week for dinner. I think family is very important. I often help my mom or dad cook the meals. Sometimes we all go to the movies. I like that a lot.
– Carla Costantini

B Read the interviews. Then check the correct names.

Who . . . ?	Jane	Billy	Nick	Carla
1. watches a lot of TV	☐	☐	☐	☐
2. sees their grandparents twice a week	☐	☐	☐	☐
3. spends time outdoors	☐	☐	☐	☐
4. stays at home with the kids	☐	☐	☐	☐
5. doesn't spend much time with family	☐	☐	☐	☐
6. does housework during the day	☐	☐	☐	☐

C **GROUP WORK** What do families look like in your country? Do dads stay at home with their children? Do you think that's a good thing or a bad thing? Is it important to you to spend time with your family?

How often do you run?

▶ Discuss sports and exercise habits
▶ Ask and answer questions about frequency of free-time activities

1 SNAPSHOT

Top Sports and Fitness Activities in the United States

Sports	Fitness Activities
☐ football	☐ treadmill
☐ baseball	☐ running/jogging
☐ soccer	☐ walking
☐ ice hockey	☐ bowling
☐ basketball	☐ weight training

Do people in your country enjoy any of these sports or activities?
Check (✓) the sports or fitness activities you enjoy.
Make a list of other activities you do. Then compare with the class.

2 WORD POWER Sports and fitness

A Which of these activities are popular with the following age groups in your country? Check (✓) the activities. Then compare with a partner.

	Children	Teens	Young adults	Middle-aged people	Older people
bike riding	☐	☐	☐	☐	☐
golf	☐	☐	☐	☐	☐
jogging	☐	☐	☐	☐	☐
martial arts	☐	☐	☐	☐	☐
Pilates	☐	☐	☐	☐	☐
soccer	☐	☐	☐	☐	☐
swimming	☐	☐	☐	☐	☐
volleyball	☐	☐	☐	☐	☐
yoga	☐	☐	☐	☐	☐

B **PAIR WORK** Which activities in part A are used with *do*, *go*, or *play*?

do martial arts	go bike riding	play golf
_____	_____	_____
_____	_____	_____

3 CONVERSATION I run every day.

▶ **A** Listen and practice.

Aaron: You have a lot of energy, Riley. Do you exercise a lot?

Riley: Well, I get up early and run on the treadmill for an hour every day.

Aaron: Seriously?

Riley: Sure. And I do weight lifting.

Aaron: Wow! How often do you lift weights?

Riley: I usually do it about three times a week. What about you?

Aaron: Oh, I hardly ever exercise. I usually just watch TV or listen to music in my free time. I guess I'm a real couch potato!

▶ **B** Listen to the rest of the conversation. What else does Riley do in her free time?

4 GRAMMAR FOCUS

▶ **Adverbs of frequency**

How often do you exercise?	Do you **ever** watch TV in the evening?
I run on the treadmill **every day**.	Yes, I **often** watch TV after dinner.
I go jogging **once a week**.	I **sometimes** watch TV before bed.
I play soccer **twice a month**.	**Sometimes** I watch TV before bed.*
I swim about **three times a year**.	I **hardly ever** watch TV.
I don't exercise very **often/much**.	No, I **never** watch TV.
Usually I exercise before class.*	

*__Usually__ and **sometimes** can begin a sentence.*

100%	always
	almost always
	usually
	often
	sometimes
	hardly ever
	almost never
0%	never

GRAMMAR PLUS *see page 137*

A Put the adverbs in the correct place. Sometimes there is more than one correct answer. Then practice with a partner.

1. **A:** Do you play sports? (ever)
   B: Sure. I play soccer. (twice a week)
2. **A:** What do you do on Saturday mornings? (usually)
   B: Nothing much. I sleep until noon. (almost always)
3. **A:** Do you lift weights at the gym? (often)
   B: No, I lift weights. (hardly ever)
4. **A:** Do you exercise on Sundays? (always)
   B: No, I exercise on Sundays. (never)
5. **A:** What do you do after class? (usually)
   B: I go out with my classmates. (about three times a week)
6. **A:** Do you go to the movies? (often)
   B: Yes, I go to the movies. (once a week)
7. **A:** Do you go bike riding? (ever)
   B: No, I ride a bike. (hardly ever)
8. **A:** Do you walk to school? (sometimes)
   B: Sure. I walk to school. (five days a week)

B **PAIR WORK** Take turns asking the questions in part A. Give your own information when answering.

5 PRONUNCIATION Intonation with direct address

A Listen and practice. Notice these statements with direct address.
There is usually falling intonation and a pause before the name.

You have a lot of energy, Riley.   You look tired, Aaron.   I feel great, Dr. Yun.

B **PAIR WORK** Write four statements using direct address. Then practice them.

6 SPEAKING Fitness programs

A **GROUP WORK** Take a poll in your group. Take turns asking each person these questions.
Each person gets two points for each *Yes* answer and one point for each *No* answer.

1 Do you have a regular fitness program?	2 Do you ever go to a gym?	3 Do you play any sports?	4 Do you ever take long walks?	5 Do you do anything else to keep fit?
YES ☐ NO ☐	YES ☐ NO ☐	YES ☐ NO ☐	YES ☐ NO ☐	YES ☐ NO ☐
How often do you exercise?	How often do you go? What do you do there?	Which ones? How often do you play them?	How often? Where do you go?	What do you do?

B **GROUP WORK** Add up your points and study the results of the poll.
Who in your group got at least six points?

C **CLASS WORK** Tell the class about one of the people in your group.

"Cynthia does Pilates twice a week, and sometimes she goes jogging. She doesn't . . ."

7 LISTENING I swim twice a week.

A Listen to three people discuss what they like to do in the evening.
Complete the chart.

	Activity	**How often?**
Joseph		
Victoria		
Carlos		

B Listen again. Who is most similar to you – Joseph, Victoria, or Carlos?

8 DISCUSSION Olympic sports and athletes

GROUP WORK Take turns asking and answering these questions.

Can you remember the names of five Olympic sports?
   What are they?
Do you ever watch Olympic sports on TV? Which ones?
Would you like to see Olympic sports live? Why? Why not?
Do you prefer the summer or winter Olympics? Why?
What's your favorite Olympic sport? Why?
What's an Olympic sport that you really don't like? Why not?
Who's a famous male athlete in your country? What sport
   does he play?
Who's a famous female athlete? What sport does she play?

9 WRITING Your weekly activities

A Write about your weekly activities. Include your favorite activity, but don't say which one is your favorite.

> I usually exercise four or five times a week. I always do yoga on Mondays and Wednesdays. I often go
> jogging in the morning on Tuesdays and Thursdays. I sometimes go to the beach and play volleyball
> with my friends on weekends. I . . .

B GROUP WORK Take turns reading your descriptions. Can you guess your partners' favorite activities?
"Your favorite activity is volleyball, right?"

10 CONVERSATION You're in great shape.

A Listen and practice.

STEPH You're in great shape, Mick.

MICK Thanks. I guess I'm a real fitness freak.

STEPH How often do you work out?

MICK Well, I go swimming and lift weights every day. And I play tennis three times a week.

STEPH Tennis? That sounds like a lot of fun.

MICK Oh, do you want to play sometime?

STEPH Uh . . . how well do you play?

MICK Pretty well, I guess.

STEPH Well, all right. But I'm not very good.

MICK No problem. I'll give you a few tips.

B Listen to Mick and Steph after their tennis match. Who's the winner?

11 GRAMMAR FOCUS

GRAMMAR PLUS see page 137

► Questions with *how*; short answers

How often do you work out?

   Every day.

   Twice a week.

   Not very often.

How long do you spend at the gym?

   Thirty minutes a day.

   Two hours a week.

   About an hour on weekends.

How well do you play tennis?

   Pretty well.

   About average.

   Not very well.

How good are you at sports?

   Pretty good.

   OK.

   Not so good.

A Complete these questions. Then practice with a partner.

1. **A:** _____ at sports?
   B: I guess I'm pretty good. I play a lot of different sports.
2. **A:** _____ spend online?
   B: About an hour after dinner. I like to chat with my friends.
3. **A:** _____ go to the beach?
   B: Once or twice a month. It's a good way to relax.
4. **A:** _____ swim?
   B: Not very well. I need to take swimming lessons.

B **GROUP WORK** Take turns asking the questions in part A. Give your own information when answering. Then ask more questions with *how often*, *how long*, *how well*, and *how good*.

12 LISTENING You're in great shape!

► Listen to Rachel, Nicholas, Zack, and Jennifer discuss sports and exercise. Who is a couch potato? a fitness freak? a sports nut? a gym rat?

a couch potato

a fitness freak

a sports nut

a gym rat

1. _____　　2. _____　　3. _____　　4. _____

13 INTERCHANGE ACTIVITY What's your talent?

Find out how well your classmates do different activities. Go to Interchange 6 on page 120.

A How healthy and fit do you think you are? Skim the questions. Then guess your health and fitness score from 0 (very unhealthy) to 50 (very healthy).

FIT AND HEALTHY?

Take the quiz!

1. **How many servings of fruits or vegetables do you eat each day?**

Five or more.	5
Between one and four.	3
I don't eat fruits or vegetables.	0

2. **How much sugar do you use in food and drinks?**

I hardly ever use sugar in my food and drink.	5
A little, but I'm careful.	3
A lot. I love sugar!	0

3. **How often do you eat junk food?**

Never.	5
Maybe once a week.	3
As often as possible.	0

4. **How many glasses of water do you drink each day?**

Eight or more.	5
Between one and three.	3
I almost always drink soda.	0

5. **Do you eat oily fish (for example, sardines, salmon)?**

Yes, I love fish!	5
Yes, about twice a month.	3
No, I really don't like fish.	0

6. **How often do you exercise?**

I usually exercise every day.	5
Two or three times a week.	3
What's exercise?	0

7. **Do you walk or bike to work or school?**

Yes, whenever I can.	5
I do when I have time.	3
No, never.	0

8. **Is fitness important to you?**

Yes, it's extremely important.	5
I think it's pretty important.	3
No, it's not important at all.	0

9. **What do you do on weekends?**

I play as many kinds of sports as I can!	5
I sometimes go for walks or bike rides.	3
I watch TV all day long.	0

10. **When you're at work or school, how active are you?**

Very active. I walk around a lot.	5
A little active. I go for a walk at lunchtime.	3
I sit at my desk and order lunch.	0

RATE YOURSELF!

42 to 50: Good job! You're doing all the right things for a healthy life.

28 to 41: You're on the right track. With a little more work, you'll be great.

15 to 27: Keep trying! You can be very fit and healthy, so don't give up!

14 or below: It's time to improve your health and fitness. You can do it!

B Take the quiz and add up your score. Is your score similar to your original guess? Do you agree with your score? Why or why not?

C **GROUP WORK** Compare your scores. Who is healthy and fit? What can your classmates do to improve their health and fitness?

SELF-ASSESSMENT

How well can you do these things? Check (✓) the boxes.

I can . . .	Very well	OK	A little
Ask about and describe present activities (Ex. 1, 2, 3)	☐	☐	☐
Describe family life (Ex. 3)	☐	☐	☐
Ask for and give personal information (Ex. 3)	☐	☐	☐
Give information about quantities (Ex. 3)	☐	☐	☐
Ask and answer questions about free time (Ex. 4)	☐	☐	☐
Ask and answer questions about routines and abilities (Ex. 4)	☐	☐	☐

1 LISTENING What are they doing?

▶ **A** Listen to people do different things.
What are they doing? Complete the chart.

B PAIR WORK Compare your answers.

A: In number one, someone is watching TV.
B: I don't think so. I think someone is . . .

What are they doing?
1. _____
2. _____
3. _____
4. _____

2 SPEAKING Memory game

GROUP WORK Choose a person in the room, but don't say who! Other students ask yes/no questions to guess the person.

A: I'm thinking of someone in the classroom.
B: Is it a man?
A: Yes, it is.
C: Is he sitting in the front of the room?
A: No, he isn't.
D: Is he sitting in the back?
A: Yes, he is.
E: Is he wearing a black T-shirt?
A: No, he isn't.
B: Is it . . . ?

The student with the correct guess has the next turn.

3 SPEAKING Family life survey

A GROUP WORK Add two more yes/no questions about family life to the chart. Then ask and answer the questions in groups. Write down the number of "yes" and "no" answers. (Remember to include yourself.)

	Number of "yes" answers	Number of "no" answers
1. Are you living with your family?		
2. Do your parents both work?		
3. Do you eat dinner with your family?		
4. Are you exercising these days?		
5. Are you studying something these days?		
6. Do you have brothers or sisters?		
7. _____		
8. _____		

B GROUP WORK Write up the results of the survey. Then tell the class.

> 1. In our group, most people are living with their families.
> 2. Nearly all of our mothers and fathers work.

Quantifiers	
All	100%
Nearly all	
Most	
Many	
A lot of	
Some	
Not many	
Few	
No one	0%

4 DISCUSSION Routines and abilities

GROUP WORK Choose three questions. Then ask your questions in groups. When someone answers "yes," think of more questions to ask.

Do you ever . . . ?

☐ cook for friends ☐ listen to English songs ☐ sing in the shower
☐ do yoga ☐ play video games ☐ tell jokes
☐ go jogging ☐ play volleyball ☐ write emails in English

A: Do you ever cook for friends?
B: Yes, I often do.
C: What do you cook?
B: I usually cook fish or pasta.
A: When do you cook?
B: On weekends.
C: How often do you cook?
B: Once a month.
A: How well do you cook?
B: About average. But they always ask for more!

WHAT'S NEXT?

Look at your Self-assessment again. Do you need to review anything?

7 We went dancing!

▶ Describe past daily and free-time activities
▶ Describe past vacations

1 SNAPSHOT

Free-time Activities

- ☐ check social media
- ☐ go dancing
- ☐ listen to music
- ☐ play video games
- ☐ read
- ☐ relax
- ☐ spend time with friends and family
- ☐ watch TV

Check (✓) the activities you do in your free time. List three other activities you do in your free time.
What are your favorite free-time activities? Are there activities you don't like? Which ones?

2 CONVERSATION What did you do last weekend?

▶ **A** Listen and practice.

NEIL So, what did you do last weekend, Cara?

CARA Oh, I had a great time. My friends and I had pizza on Saturday and then we all went dancing.

NEIL How fun! Did you go to The Treadmill?

CARA No, we didn't. We went to that new place downtown. How about you? Did you go anywhere?

NEIL No, I didn't go anywhere all weekend. I just stayed home and studied for today's Spanish test.

CARA Our test is today? I forgot about that!

NEIL Don't worry. You always get an A.

▶ **B** Listen to the rest of the conversation. What does Cara do on Sunday afternoons?

3 GRAMMAR FOCUS

Simple past

Did you **work** on Saturday?

    Yes, I **did**. I **worked** all day.

    No, I **didn't**. I **didn't work** at all.

Did you **go** anywhere last weekend?

    Yes, I **did**. I **went** to the movies.

    No, I **didn't**. I **didn't go** anywhere.

What **did** Neil **do** on Saturday?

    He **stayed** home and **studied** for a test.

How **did** Cara **spend** her weekend?

    She **went** to a club and **danced** with some friends.

GRAMMAR PLUS *see page 138*

A Complete these conversations. Then practice with a partner.

1. A: _____ you _____ (stay) home on Sunday?

   B: No, I _____ (call) my friend Anna. We _____ (drive) to a nice little restaurant for lunch.

2. A: How _____ you _____ (spend) your last birthday?

   B: I _____ (have) a party. Everyone _____ (enjoy) it, but the neighbors next door _____ (not, like) the noise.

3. A: What _____ you _____ (do) last night?

   B: I _____ (see) a sci-fi movie at the Cineplex. I _____ (love) it! Amazing special effects!

4. A: _____ you _____ (do) anything special over the weekend?

   B: Yes, I _____. I _____ (go) shopping. Unfortunately, I _____ (spend) all my money. Now I'm broke!

5. A: _____ you _____ (go) out on Friday night?

   B: No, I _____. I _____ (invite) friends over, and I _____ (cook) spaghetti for them.

regular verbs

work ⟶ work**ed**

invite ⟶ invit**ed**

study ⟶ stud**ied**

stop ⟶ stop**ped**

irregular verbs

buy ⟶ **bought**

do ⟶ **did**

drive ⟶ **drove**

have ⟶ **had**

go ⟶ **went**

sing ⟶ **sang**

see ⟶ **saw**

spend ⟶ **spent**

B PAIR WORK Take turns asking the questions in part A. Give your own information when answering.

A: Did you stay home on Sunday?

B: No, I didn't. I went dancing with some friends.

4 PRONUNCIATION Reduction of *did you*

A Listen and practice. Notice how **did you** is reduced in the following questions.

[dɪdʒə]

Did you have a good time?

[wədɪdʒə]

What did you do last night?

[haʊdɪdʒə]

How did you like the movie?

B PAIR WORK Practice the questions in Exercise 3, part A again. Pay attention to the pronunciation of **did you**.

5 WORD POWER Chores and activities

A PAIR WORK Find two other words or phrases from the list that usually go with each verb. Then add one more word or phrase to each verb.

a lot of fun	dancing	a good time	shopping	a bike ride
the bed	chores	the laundry	a trip	a video

do	my homework			
go	online			
have	a party			
make	a phone call			
take	a day off			

B GROUP WORK Choose the things you did last weekend. Then compare with your partners.

A: I went shopping with my friends. We had a good time. What about you?
B: I didn't have a very good time. I did chores.
C: I did chores, too. But I went dancing in the evening, and . . .

6 DISCUSSION Ask some questions!

GROUP WORK Take turns. One student makes a statement about the weekend. Other students ask questions. Each student answers at least three questions.

A: I went shopping on Saturday afternoon.
B: Where did you go?
A: To the Mayfair Center.
C: Who did you go with?
A: I went with my friends and my sister.
D: What time did you go?
A: We went around 3:00.

7 LISTENING Did you have a good holiday?

▶ **A** Listen to Andrew tell Elizabeth what he did yesterday. Check (✓) the things Andrew did.

Activities	Reasons
☐ went to the gym	_____
☐ played soccer	_____
☐ saw a movie	_____
☐ watched TV	_____
☐ went to a baseball game	_____
☐ spent time with family	_____

▶ **B** Listen again. Look at the activities Andrew didn't do. Why didn't he do them? Write the reason.

Play a board game. Go to Interchange 7 on page 121.

9 CONVERSATION Lucky you!

▶ **A** Listen and practice.

Leah: Hi, Cody. How was your vacation?

Cody: It was excellent! I went to California with my cousin. We had a great time.

Leah: Lucky you! How long were you there?

Cody: About a week.

Leah: Cool! Was the weather OK?

Cody: Not really. It was pretty cloudy. But we went surfing every day. The waves were amazing.

Leah: So, what was the best thing about the trip?

Cody: Well, something incredible happened. . . .

▶ **B** Listen to the rest of the conversation. What happened?

10 GRAMMAR FOCUS

▶ | **Past of *be*** | | |
|---|---|---|
| **Were** you in California? | Yes, I **was**. | **Contractions** |
| **Was** the weather OK? | No, it **wasn't**. | was**n't** = was **not** |
| **Were** you and your cousin on vacation? | Yes, we **were**. | were**n't** = were **not** |
| **Were** your parents there? | No, they **weren't**. | |
| How long **were** you away? | I **was** away for a week. | |
| How **was** your vacation? | It **was** excellent! | |

GRAMMAR PLUS *see page 138*

Complete these conversations. Then practice with a partner.

1. A: _____ you in New York last weekend?

   B: No, I _____. I _____ in Chicago.

   A: How _____ it?

   B: It _____ great! But it _____ cold and windy as usual.

2. A: How long _____ your parents in Chile?

   B: They _____ there for two weeks.

   A: _____ they in Santiago the whole time?

   B: No, they _____. They also went to Valparaiso.

3. A: _____ you away last week?

   B: Yes, I _____ in Madrid.

   A: Really? How long _____ you there?

   B: For almost a week. I _____ there on business.

We went dancing! **47**

11 DISCUSSION Past and future vacations

A **GROUP WORK** Ask your classmates about their last vacations.
Ask these questions or use your own ideas.

Where did you spend your last vacation?
How long was your vacation?
Who were you with?

What did you do?
How was the weather?
What would you like to do on
  your next vacation?

B **CLASS ACTIVITY** Who had an interesting vacation?
Tell the class who and why.

12 WRITING A blog post

A Read the blog post.

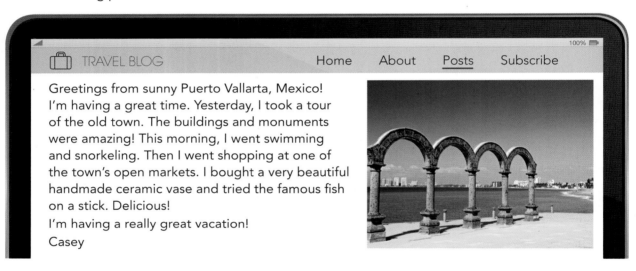

TRAVEL BLOG   Home   About   Posts   Subscribe

Greetings from sunny Puerto Vallarta, Mexico!
I'm having a great time. Yesterday, I took a tour
of the old town. The buildings and monuments
were amazing! This morning, I went swimming
and snorkeling. Then I went shopping at one of
the town's open markets. I bought a very beautiful
handmade ceramic vase and tried the famous fish
on a stick. Delicious!
I'm having a really great vacation!
Casey

B **PAIR WORK** Write a blog post to your partner about your last vacation. Then exchange posts.
Do you have any questions about your partner's vacation?

13 LISTENING I was on vacation.

A Listen to Daniel and Amanda talk about their vacations.
Did they have a good time? Check (✓) Yes or No.

	Yes	**No**
Daniel	☐	☐
Amanda	☐	☐

B Listen again. Complete the chart with information about their vacations.

Daniel's vacation		Amanda's vacation	
Place		Place	
Who with		Who with	
Activities		Activities	

A Look at the pictures. What do you think each person did on his or her vacation?

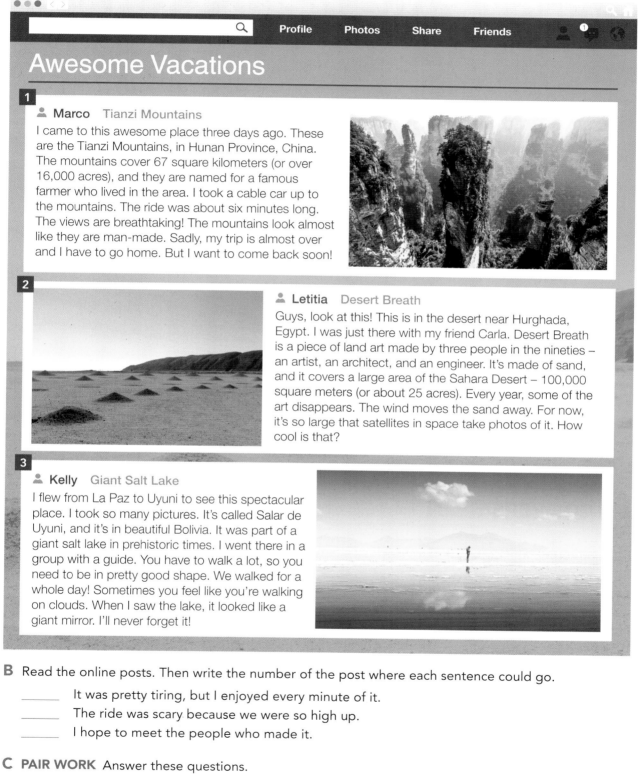

Awesome Vacations

1

👤 **Marco** Tianzi Mountains

I came to this awesome place three days ago. These are the Tianzi Mountains, in Hunan Province, China. The mountains cover 67 square kilometers (or over 16,000 acres), and they are named for a famous farmer who lived in the area. I took a cable car up to the mountains. The ride was about six minutes long. The views are breathtaking! The mountains look almost like they are man-made. Sadly, my trip is almost over and I have to go home. But I want to come back soon!

2

👤 **Letitia** Desert Breath

Guys, look at this! This is in the desert near Hurghada, Egypt. I was just there with my friend Carla. Desert Breath is a piece of land art made by three people in the nineties – an artist, an architect, and an engineer. It's made of sand, and it covers a large area of the Sahara Desert – 100,000 square meters (or about 25 acres). Every year, some of the art disappears. The wind moves the sand away. For now, it's so large that satellites in space take photos of it. How cool is that?

3

👤 **Kelly** Giant Salt Lake

I flew from La Paz to Uyuni to see this spectacular place. I took so many pictures. It's called Salar de Uyuni, and it's in beautiful Bolivia. It was part of a giant salt lake in prehistoric times. I went there in a group with a guide. You have to walk a lot, so you need to be in pretty good shape. We walked for a whole day! Sometimes you feel like you're walking on clouds. When I saw the lake, it looked like a giant mirror. I'll never forget it!

B Read the online posts. Then write the number of the post where each sentence could go.

_____ It was pretty tiring, but I enjoyed every minute of it.

_____ The ride was scary because we were so high up.

_____ I hope to meet the people who made it.

C **PAIR WORK** Answer these questions.

1. Which person used an unusual form of transportation?
2. Who saw a piece of art?
3. Who had a very active vacation?
4. Which place do you think is the most interesting? Why?

8 How's the neighborhood?

▶ Ask about and describe places
▶ Describe a neighborhood

1 WORD POWER Places and activities

A Match the places and the definitions. Then ask and answer the questions with a partner.

What's a . . . ?
1. clothing store _____
2. grocery store _____
3. hair salon _____
4. laundromat _____
5. newsstand _____
6. stadium _____
7. Wi-Fi hot spot _____

It's a place where you . . .
a. get food and small items for the home
b. can connect to the Internet
c. get a haircut
d. buy newspapers and magazines
e. see a game or a concert
f. find new fashions
g. wash and dry your clothes

B PAIR WORK Write definitions for these places.

| coffee shop | drugstore | gas station | library | post office |

It's a place where you drink coffee and tea and eat small meals. (coffee shop)

C GROUP WORK Read your definitions. Can your classmates guess the places?

2 CONVERSATION I just moved in.

▶ Listen and practice.

Greg: Excuse me! Hi, I'm your new neighbor, Greg. I just moved in.

Mrs. Cook: Oh. Yes?

Greg: I'm looking for a grocery store. Are there any around here?

Mrs. Cook: Yes, there are some on Pine Street.

Greg: Oh, good. And is there a laundromat near here?

Mrs. Cook: Well, I think there's one across from the shopping center.

Greg: Thank you.

Mrs. Cook: By the way, there's a hair salon in the shopping center.

Greg: A hair salon?

3 GRAMMAR FOCUS

There is, there are; one, any, some

Is there a laundromat near here?

    Yes, **there is**. There's **one** across from the shopping center.

    No, **there isn't**, but there's **one** next to the library.

Are there any grocery stores around here?

    Yes, **there are**. There are **some** nice stores on Pine Street.

    No, **there aren't**, but there are **some** on Third Avenue.

    No, **there aren't any** around here.

Prepositions
in
on
next to
near/close to
across from/opposite
in front of
in back of/behind
between
on the corner of

GRAMMAR PLUS *see page 139*

A Look at the map below. Write questions about these places.

an ATM	coffee shops	a department store	an electronics store	Wi-Fi hot spots
gas stations	grocery stores	a gym	hotels	a post office

Is there a gym around here?

Are there any restaurants on Main Street?

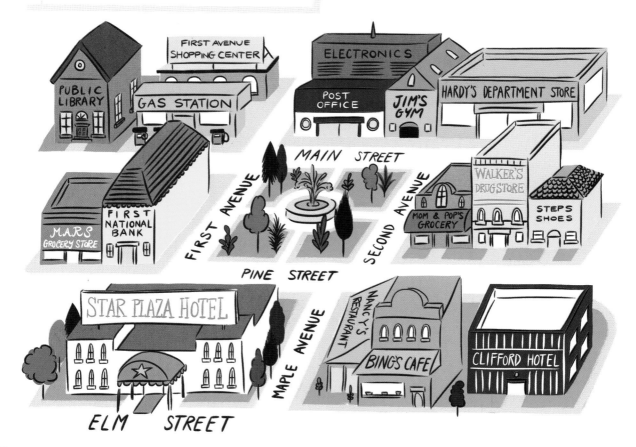

B PAIR WORK Ask and answer the questions you wrote in part A.

A: Is there a gym around here?

B: Yes, there is. There's one on Main Street next to the post office.

4 PRONUNCIATION Reduction of *there is/there are*

▶ **A** Listen and practice. Notice how *there is* and *there are* are reduced in conversation, except for short answers.

Is there a bank near here?

    Yes, **there is**. **There's** one on First Avenue.

Are there any coffee shops around here?

    Yes, **there are**. **There are** some on Pine Street.

B Practice the questions and answers in Exercise 3, part B again.

5 SPEAKING A nice neighborhood

A **PAIR WORK** Choose a neighborhood in your city or town. Fill in the chart with information about the neighborhood. Write three examples for each category. Go to Exercises 1 and 3 for ideas and use your own ideas, too.

There is a/an . . . (where?)	There are some . . . (where?)

There isn't a/an . . . (where?)	There aren't any . . . (where?)

B **GROUP WORK** Take turns asking and answering questions with another pair about the neighborhoods. If you don't know about a place your new partners ask about, answer, "Sorry, I don't know." Who gets more "Yes" answers?

A: Is there a gym in your neighborhood?
B: Yes, there's one across from the park.
C: Are there any coffee shops?
D: No, there aren't any in our neighborhood.
B: Is there a bookstore in your neighborhood?
A: Sorry, I don't know.

6 LISTENING We need some directions.

▶ **A** Listen to hotel guests ask about places to visit. Complete the chart.

Place	Location	Interesting? Yes	No
Flavors of Hollywood		☐	☐
Museum of Modern Art		☐	☐
City Zoo		☐	☐

B **PAIR WORK** Which place sounds the most interesting to you? Why?

7 SNAPSHOT

NEIGHBORHOODS

- downtown/main street
- the suburbs
- a shopping district
- a college campus
- a business district
- a theater district
- an industrial district
- a small town

What types of businesses are or aren't found in these neighborhoods?
Which areas do you visit often? Which areas do you hardly ever visit? Why?

8 CONVERSATION It's very convenient.

▶ Listen and practice.

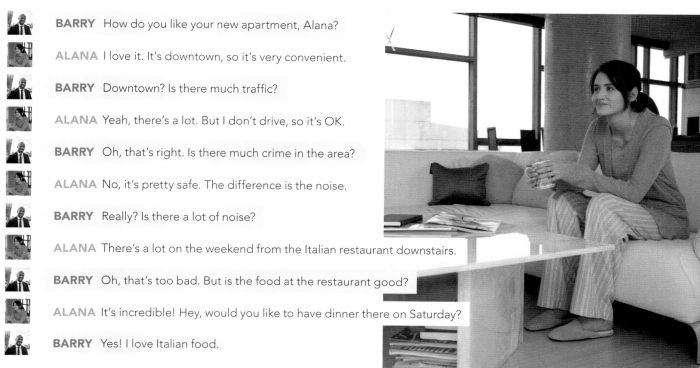

BARRY How do you like your new apartment, Alana?

ALANA I love it. It's downtown, so it's very convenient.

BARRY Downtown? Is there much traffic?

ALANA Yeah, there's a lot. But I don't drive, so it's OK.

BARRY Oh, that's right. Is there much crime in the area?

ALANA No, it's pretty safe. The difference is the noise.

BARRY Really? Is there a lot of noise?

ALANA There's a lot on the weekend from the Italian restaurant downstairs.

BARRY Oh, that's too bad. But is the food at the restaurant good?

ALANA It's incredible! Hey, would you like to have dinner there on Saturday?

BARRY Yes! I love Italian food.

9 GRAMMAR FOCUS

> **Quantifiers; *how many* and *how much***

Count nouns	Noncount nouns
Are there **many restaurants**?	Is there **much crime**?
Yes, there are **a lot**.	Yes, there's **a lot**.
There are **a few**.	There's **a little**.
No, there are**n't many**.	No, there is**n't much**.
No, there are**n't any**.	No, there is**n't any**.
No, there are **none**.	No, there's **none**.
How many restaurants are there?	**How much** crime is there?
There are 10 or 12.	There's a lot of crime.

GRAMMAR PLUS see page 139

A Write answers to these questions about your neighborhood. Then practice with a partner.

1. Is there much parking?
2. Are there many apartment buildings?
3. How much traffic is there?
4. How many drugstores are there?
5. Is there much noise?
6. Are there many shopping malls?
7. Is there much pollution?
8. How many fast-food restaurants are there?

B **GROUP WORK** Write questions like those in part A about these topics. Then ask and answer the questions.

cafés   crime   parks   trash   public transportation   schools   traffic lights

10 INTERCHANGE 8 Where are we?

Play a guessing game. Go to Interchange 8 on page 122.

11 WRITING My neighborhood

A Read this paragraph Kate wrote about her neighborhood.

B Now write a paragraph about your neighborhood. Describe what type of neighborhood it is and what places are or aren't in your area.

C **PAIR WORK** Read your partner's paragraph. Ask follow-up questions to get more information.

60%

Menu   Log out

I live in a very nice neighborhood near my office, so I walk or ride my bike to work every morning. It's a very green area with many trees and a small but beautiful park. It's also very convenient. There is a shopping mall behind my building. In the mall, there are two drugstores, a bank, and a grocery store. And there is a café with great food and good prices. I get coffee there every morning. But there isn't a library, and most books at the bookstore are expensive. Oh well, nothing is perfect!

12 READING

A Scan the article. Check (✓) the neighborhood that is famous for nightlife.

☐ Roma Norte ☐ Shimokitazawa ☐ Pigneto

Locations   Reservations   Shop   Sign in   Register   🔍

HIP NEIGHBORHOODS OF THE WORLD

Ⓐ Shimokitazawa, Tokyo

This is the place to be for fans of indie music! Head over to this creative neighborhood and discover record stores, concert halls, and theaters in the narrow streets. Shimokitazawa (or Shimokita, for short) is a relaxed place full of young people who visit the cafés and live music venues. Every year, there is a theater festival here. It's a very popular place for students.

Ⓑ Pigneto, Rome

La Sapienza, a famous college in Rome, is near this neighborhood. It's an extremely cool place to hang out. Pigneto has a huge choice of restaurants, cafés, and ice cream stores. Pigneto is famous for its nightlife. As you walk around, you hear electronic music coming from different clubs. People also come here for the Nuovo Cinema Aquila, the best place to see indie movies from around the world.

Ⓒ Roma Norte, Mexico City

This place is popular with artists, students, tourists, and musicians. Feeling hungry? Go to a huge food market, Mercado Roma, to taste delicious ceviche, squid torta, and other Mexican specialties. Next, check out the trendy restaurants for dinner, or shop for beautiful fashion items in the boutiques. There are hip T-shirts and sneakers for sale everywhere. There's locally made jewelry you can buy, too!

B Read the article. Then write the letter of the paragraph where these things are mentioned.

1. _____ local jewelry
2. _____ festivals
3. _____ indie movies
4. _____ record stores
5. _____ food specialties
6. _____ a college
7. _____ theaters
8. _____ ice cream

C **PAIR WORK** What's your favorite neighborhood in your city or country? What is interesting about it? What do you like to do there?

Units 7–8 Progress check

SELF-ASSESSMENT

How well can you do these things? Check (✓) the boxes.

I can . . .	Very well	OK	A little
Understand descriptions of past events (Ex. 1)	☐	☐	☐
Describe events in the past (Ex. 1)	☐	☐	☐
Ask and answer questions about past activities (Ex. 2)	☐	☐	☐
Give and understand simple directions (Ex. 3)	☐	☐	☐
Talk about my neighborhood (Ex. 4)	☐	☐	☐

1 LISTENING Jimmy's weekend

▶ **A** A thief robbed a house on Saturday. A detective is questioning Jimmy.
The pictures show what Jimmy really did on Saturday. Listen to
their conversation. Are Jimmy's answers true (**T**) or false (**F**)?

1:00 P.M. T F   3:00 P.M. T F   5:00 P.M. T F   6:00 P.M. T F   8:00 P.M. T F   10:30 P.M. T F

B **PAIR WORK** What did Jimmy really do? Use the pictures to retell the story.

2 DISCUSSION How good is your memory?

A Do you remember what you did yesterday? Check (✓) the
things you did. Then add two other things you did.

☐ got up early   ☐ went to class   ☐ did the laundry   ☐ went to bed late
☐ exercised   ☐ ate at a restaurant   ☐ did the dishes   ☐ _____
☐ texted a friend   ☐ went shopping   ☐ went online   ☐ _____

B **GROUP WORK** Ask questions about each thing in part A.

A: Did you get up early yesterday?
B: No, I didn't. I got up at 10:00. I was very tired.

3 SPEAKING What's your neighborhood like?

A Create a neighborhood. Add five places to "My map." Choose from this list.
Add plural words two or more times.

| a bank | a bookstore | cafés | drugstores | gas stations | a gym | a theater |

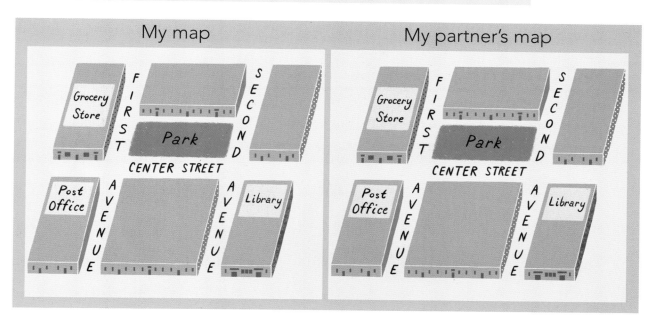

B **PAIR WORK** Ask questions about your partner's map. (But don't look!)
Draw the places on "My partner's map." Then compare your maps.

A: Are there any gas stations in the neighborhood?
B: Yes, there are two. There's one on the corner of Center Street and
First Avenue and one on Center Street across from the park.

4 ROLE PLAY Tell me about your neighborhood.

Student A: Imagine you are a visitor in Student B's neighborhood.
Ask questions about it.
Student B: Imagine a visitor wants to find out about your
neighborhood. Answer the visitor's questions.

> **A:** Is there much crime?
> **B:** There isn't much. It's a very safe neighborhood.
> **A:** Is there much noise?
> **B:** Well, yes, it's a shopping district, so . . .

Change roles and try the role play again.

topics to ask about
buildings
crime
noise
parking
parks
places to shop
pollution
public transportation
schools
traffic

WHAT'S NEXT?

Look at your Self-assessment again. Do you need to review anything?

9 What does she look like?

▶ Describe people's physical appearance
▶ Identify people by describing how they look and what they're doing

1 WORD POWER Physical appearance

A Look at these expressions. What are three more words or expressions to describe people? Write them in the box below.

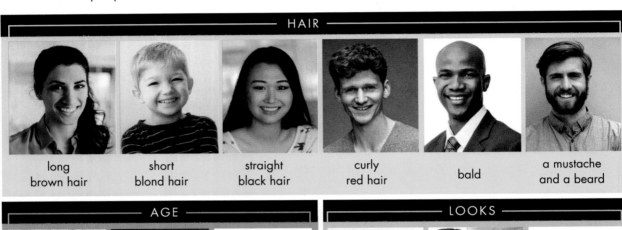

HAIR

long brown hair short blond hair straight black hair curly red hair bald a mustache and a beard

AGE

young middle-aged elderly

LOOKS

handsome good-looking pretty

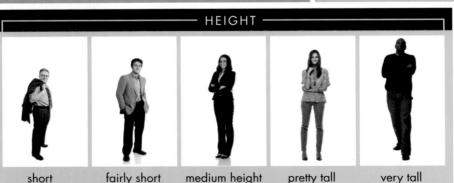

HEIGHT

short fairly short medium height pretty tall very tall

Other words or expressions

_____
_____
_____

B **PAIR WORK** Choose at least four expressions to describe yourself and your partner. Then compare. Do you agree?

A: You have long blond hair. You're pretty tall.
B: I don't think so. My hair isn't very long.

Me	My partner

2 CONVERSATION She's so pretty!

▶ **A** Listen and practice.

Lauren: I hear you have a new girlfriend, Justin.
Justin: Yes. Her name's Tiffany. She's really smart, and she's so pretty!
Lauren: Really? What does she look like?
Justin: Well, she's very tall.
Lauren: How tall?
Justin: About 5 foot 10, I suppose.
Lauren: Yeah, that *is* pretty tall. What color is her hair?
Justin: She has beautiful brown hair.
Lauren: And how old is she?
Justin: I don't know. I think it's a little rude to ask.

▶ **B** Listen to the rest of the conversation. What else do you learn about Tiffany?

3 GRAMMAR FOCUS

▶ **Describing people**

General appearance	Height	Hair	Age
What does she look like?	How tall is she?	How long is her hair?	How old is she?
She's tall, with brown hair.	She's 1 meter 78.	It's pretty short.	She's about 32.
She's pretty.	She's 5 foot 10.		She's in her thirties.
Does he wear glasses?	How tall is he?	What color is his hair?	How old is he?
No, he wears contacts.	He's medium height.	It's dark/light brown.	He's in his twenties.

Saying heights

	U.S.	Metric
	five (foot) ten.	one meter seventy-eight tall.
Tiffany is	five foot ten inches (tall).	1 meter 78.
	5'10".	178 cm.

GRAMMAR PLUS *see page 140*

A Write questions to match these statements. Then compare with a partner.

1. _____ ? My father is 52.
2. _____ ? I'm 167 cm (5 foot 6).
3. _____ ? My cousin has red hair.
4. _____ ? No, he wears contact lenses.
5. _____ ? He's tall and very good-looking.
6. _____ ? My sister's hair is medium length.
7. _____ ? I have dark brown eyes.

B **PAIR WORK** Choose a person in your class. Don't tell your partner who it is. Your partner will ask questions to guess the person's name.

A: Is it a man or a woman?   **A:** What color is his hair?
B: It's a man.   **B:** . . .

4 LISTENING Which one is Justin?

▶ **A** Listen to descriptions of six people. Number them from 1 to 6.

▶ **B** Listen again. How old is each person?

5 INTERCHANGE 9 Find the differences

Compare two pictures of a party. Student A go to Interchange 9A on page 123.
Student B go to Interchange 9B on page 124.

6 WRITING Describing physical appearance

A You are helping to organize a special event at your school with sports, arts, and a surprise celebrity guest. Write an email to a friend inviting him or her to the event, and describe the celebrity. Don't give the celebrity's name.

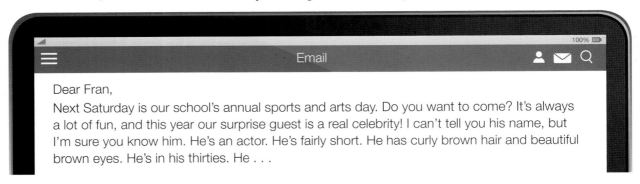

Email

Dear Fran,
Next Saturday is our school's annual sports and arts day. Do you want to come? It's always a lot of fun, and this year our surprise guest is a real celebrity! I can't tell you his name, but I'm sure you know him. He's an actor. He's fairly short. He has curly brown hair and beautiful brown eyes. He's in his thirties. He . . .

B GROUP WORK Read your email to the group. Can they guess the celebrity you are describing?

7 SNAPSHOT

New York Street Fashion

Boho (Bohemian)

The boho girl wears comfortable clothes – long skirts and flowy dresses in colorful floral prints.

Classic Prep

The preppy guy wears shirts and sweaters in pastel colors, khaki pants, and leather belts.

Hipster

The hipster wears hip hats, jewelry, and large glasses. Black is a popular color. The men often have unique hairstyles and long beards.

Streetwear

The streetwear fan wears casual and trendy clothes: jeans, basketball jerseys, baseball caps, T-shirts with logos, and cool sneakers.

Do you see your style(s)? Which one(s)?
Which style(s) do you like? Which do you dislike? Why?
Do you see any of these styles on the streets in your town or city? Which one(s)?

8 CONVERSATION Which one is she?

A Listen and practice.

Brooke: Hi, Diego! Good to see you! Is Cora here, too?

Diego: Oh, she couldn't make it. She went to a concert with Alanna.

Brooke: Oh! Let's go talk to my friend Paula. She doesn't know anyone here.

Diego: Paula? Which one is she? Is she the woman wearing a long skirt over there?

Brooke: No, she's the tall one in jeans and a scarf. She's standing near the window.

Diego: OK. I'd like to meet her.

B Listen to the rest of the conversation. Label Liam, Hina, Sierra, and Matt in the picture.

9 GRAMMAR FOCUS

> **Modifiers with present participles and prepositions**
>
> | | | **Participles** |
> | --- | --- | --- |
> | Who's Diego? | He's **the man** | **wearing** a blue shirt. |
> | Which one is Diego? | He's **the one** | **talking** to Brooke. |
> | | | **Prepositions** |
> | Who's Brooke? | She's **the woman** | **with** long black hair. |
> | Which one is Paula? | She's **the tall one** | **in** jeans. |
> | Who are the Harrisons? | They're **the people** | **next to** the window. |
> | Which ones are the Harrisons? | They're **the ones** | **on** the couch. |
>
> **GRAMMAR PLUS** *see page 140*

A Rewrite these statements using modifiers with participles or prepositions.

1. Kyle is the tall guy. He's wearing a yellow shirt and brown pants.
   <u>Kyle is the tall guy wearing a yellow shirt and brown pants.</u>

2. Mark and Eve are the middle-aged couple. They're talking to Michael.
   _____

3. Alexis is the young girl. She's in a white T-shirt and blue jeans.
   _____

4. Britney is the woman in the green dress. She's sitting to the left of Javier.
   _____

5. J.P. is the serious-looking boy. He's playing a video game.
   _____

B **PAIR WORK** Complete these questions using your classmates' names and information. Then take turns asking and answering the questions.

1. Who's the guy (man) sitting next to _____?
2. Who's the girl (woman) wearing _____?
3. Who is _____?
4. Which one is _____?
5. Who are the people _____?
6. Who are the ones _____?

10 PRONUNCIATION Contrastive stress in responses

A Listen and practice. Notice how the stress changes to emphasize a contrast.

A: Is Rob the one wearing the red shirt?

B: No, he's the one wearing the black shirt.

A: Is Rachel the woman on the couch?

B: No, Jen is the woman on the couch.

B Mark the stress changes in these conversations. Listen and check. Then practice the conversations.

A: Is Sophie the one sitting next to Judy?

B: No, she's the one standing next to Judy.

A: Is David the one on the couch?

B: No, he's the one behind the couch.

A Match the descriptions with the pictures. Write the letter.

This picture is out of this world! _____

My life in fashion. _____

An old idea meets the twenty-first century. _____

The real me or the "perfect" me? _____

THE AGE OF [○] SELFIES

THE BIRTH OF THE SELFIE

Most of us take selfies now and then. Presidents, rock stars, actors, and sports stars all take them. It's very easy to take selfies on a smartphone. But the selfie isn't really a new idea. Back in 1839, a man named Robert Cornelius took the very first selfie. Cornelius was a photographer from Philadelphia, in the U.S. He took the picture of himself by setting up his camera and then running to stand in front of it. On the back of the picture, Cornelius wrote: "The first light picture ever taken. 1839."

WORLD'S BEST SELFIE?

Astronaut Aki Hoshide is the third Japanese astronaut to walk in space. But that's not the only reason he's famous. Hoshide created an amazing image! The astronaut took this picture while he was at the International Space Station. The photo shows him, the sun, and deep space in the same shot. He named it "Orbiting Astronaut Self-Portrait."

THE PSYCHOLOGY OF SELFIES

Why do people want to take pictures of themselves? Psychologists say that it's a way of understanding who we are. It's also a way of controlling how other people see us. When we take selfies, we can choose the flattering ones – the ones that make us look really good – and share them with our friends on social media or over text. Some people take their selfies very seriously. There are even apps people can use to make their faces look "perfect."

THE DAILY SELFIE

Several years ago, Poppy Dinsey started a fashion blog. She had a simple but great idea. Every day for a year she posted a selfie of herself wearing a different outfit. So one day, she's wearing jeans. Another day, she's wearing skinny pants and a baggy sweater. The next day, she's wearing a hip dress. People loved Poppy's blog. Many people started their own fashion blogs because they liked her so much.

B Read the blog. Match each question with the correct answer.

1. What is Poppy Dinsey famous for? _____
2. Where did Aki Hoshide take a selfie? _____
3. Who says selfies are a way of understanding ourselves? _____
4. Who took the first selfie? _____
5. Where do many people post selfies? _____
6. What is Hoshide's job? _____

a. at the International Space Station
b. astronaut
c. on social media
d. psychologists
e. a fashion blog
f. a man from Philadelphia

C **PAIR WORK** What do you think of selfies? When and where do you take selfies? What's the main reason you take selfies?

10 Have you ever been there?

▶ Describe recent activities
▶ Describe experiences from the recent and distant past

1 SNAPSHOT

Fun for everyone around Orlando!

☐ go to a theme park ☐ go dancing ☐ visit a space center ☐ eat Cuban food ☐ see an alligator

Which activities have you done?
Check (✓) the activities you would like to try.
Where can you do these or similar activities in your country?

2 CONVERSATION My feet are killing me!

▶ **A** Listen and practice.

Erin: It's great to see you again, Carlos! Have you been in Orlando long?

Carlos: You too, Erin! I've been here for about a week.

Erin: I can't wait to show you the city. Have you been to the theme parks yet?

Carlos: Yeah, I've already been to three. The lines were so long!

Erin: OK. Well, how about shopping? I know a great store. . .

Carlos: Well, I've already been to so many stores. I can't buy any more clothes.

Erin: I know what! I bet you haven't visited the Kennedy Space Center. It's an hour away.

Carlos: Actually, I've already been to the Space Center and met an astronaut!

Erin: Wow! You've done a lot! Well, is there anything you want to do?

Carlos: You know, I really just want to take it easy today. My feet are killing me!

▶ **B** Listen to the rest of the conversation. What do they plan to do tomorrow?

3 GRAMMAR FOCUS

Present perfect; *already, yet*

The present perfect is formed with the verb *have* + the past participle.

Have you **been** to a jazz club?

   Yes, I**'ve been** to several.   No, I **haven't been** to one.

Has Carlos **visited** the theme parks?

   Yes, he**'s visited** three or four.   No, he **hasn't visited** any parks.

Have they **eaten** dinner yet?

   Yes, they**'ve** already **eaten**.   No, they **haven't eaten** yet.

Contractions		
I**'ve**	=	I have
you**'ve**	=	you have
he**'s**	=	he has
she**'s**	=	she has
it**'s**	=	it has
we**'ve**	=	we have
they**'ve**	=	they have
has**n't**	=	has not
have**n't**	=	have not

GRAMMAR PLUS *see page 141*

A How many times have you done these things in the past week? Write your answers. Then compare with a partner.

1. cook dinner
2. wash the dishes
3. listen to music
4. do the laundry
5. go to a restaurant
6. clean the house

> I've cooked dinner twice this week.
>
> OR
>
> I haven't cooked dinner this week.

regular past participles

visit	⟶	visited
like	⟶	liked
stop	⟶	stopped
try	⟶	tried

irregular past participles

be	⟶	been
do	⟶	did
eat	⟶	eaten
go	⟶	gone
have	⟶	had
hear	⟶	heard
make	⟶	made
ride	⟶	ridden
see	⟶	seen

B Complete these conversations using the present perfect. Then practice with a partner.

1. **A:** _____Have_____ you _____done_____ much exercise this week? (do)

   B: Yes, I _____ already _____ to Pilates class four times. (be)

2. **A:** _____ you _____ any sports this month? (play)

   B: No, I _____ the time. (not have)

3. **A:** How many movies _____ you _____ to this month? (be)

   B: Actually, I _____ any yet. (not see)

4. **A:** _____ you _____ to any interesting parties recently? (be)

   B: No, I _____ to any parties for quite a while. (not go)

5. **A:** _____ you _____ any food this week? (cook)

   B: Yes, I _____ already _____ dinner twice. (make)

6. **A:** How many times _____ you _____ out to eat this week? (go)

   B: I _____ at fast-food restaurants a couple of times. (eat)

C **PAIR WORK** Take turns asking the questions in part B. Give your own information when answering.

4 CONVERSATION Have you ever had a Cuban sandwich?

A Listen and practice.

Erin: I'm sorry I'm late. Have you been here long?

Carlos: No, only for a few minutes. So, have you chosen a restaurant yet?

Erin: I can't decide. We can go to a big restaurant or a have a sandwich at a café. Have you ever had a Cuban sandwich?

Carlos: No, I haven't. Are they good?

Erin: They're delicious. I've had them many times.

Carlos: You really like Cuban food! Have you ever been to Cuba?

Erin: No, but I went to college in Miami. I ate empanadas and rice and beans all the time!

B Listen to the rest of the conversation. Where do they decide to go after lunch?

5 GRAMMAR FOCUS

Present perfect vs. simple past

	Use the present perfect for an indefinite time in the past.	Use the simple past for a specific event in the past.
Have you ever **eaten** Cuban food?	Yes, I **have**. I've **had** it many times. No, I **haven't**. I **haven't tried** it yet.	I **ate** a lot of Cuban food when I **lived** in Miami. No, I never **tried** it when I **lived** in Miami.
Have you ever **seen** an alligator?	Yes, I **have**. I've **seen** a few alligators in my life. No, I **haven't**. I've never **seen** one.	I **saw** a big alligator at the new park last week. I **didn't go** to the alligator park last week, so I **didn't see** any.

GRAMMAR PLUS see page 141

A Complete these conversations. Use the present perfect and simple past of the verbs given and short answers.

1. **A:** _____ you ever _____ in public? (sing)
   B: Yes, I _____. I _____ at a friend's birthday party.

2. **A:** _____ you ever _____ something valuable? (lose)
   B: No, I _____. But my brother _____ his cell phone on a trip once.

3. **A:** _____ you ever _____ a traffic ticket? (get)
   B: Yes, I _____. Once I _____ a ticket and had to pay $50.

4. **A:** _____ you ever _____ a live concert? (see)
   B: Yes, I _____. I _____ Adele at the stadium last year.

5. **A:** _____ you ever _____ late for an important event? (be)
   B: No, I _____. But my sister _____ two hours late for her wedding!

B **PAIR WORK** Take turns asking the questions in part A. Give your own information when answering.

> ### *For* and *since*

How long **did** you **live** in Miami?	I **lived** there **for** four years. It was a great experience.
How long **have** you **lived** in Orlando?	I**'ve lived** here **for** three years. I'm very happy here.
	I**'ve worked** at the hotel **since** last year. I love it there.

GRAMMAR PLUS *see page 141*

C Complete these sentences with *for* or *since*. Then compare with a partner.

1. Maura was in Central America _____ a month last year.
2. I've been a college student _____ almost four years.
3. Hiroshi has been at work _____ 6:00 A.M.
4. I haven't gone to a party _____ a long time.
5. Sean lived in Bolivia _____ two years as a kid.
6. My parents have been on vacation _____ Monday.
7. Jennifer was engaged to Theo _____ six months.
8. Alex and Brianna have been best friends _____ high school.

expressions with *for*
two weeks
a few months
several years
a long time

expressions with *since*
6:45
last weekend
2009
elementary school

D **PAIR WORK** Ask and answer these questions.

How long have you had your current hairstyle?
How long have you studied at this school?
How long have you known your best friend?
How long have you been awake today?

6 PRONUNCIATION Linked sounds

A Listen and practice. Notice how final /t/ and /d/ sounds in verbs are linked to the vowels that follow them.

A: Have you cooked lunch yet?
                /t/
B: Yes, I've already cooked it.

A: Have you ever tried Key Lime Pie?
                /d/
B: Yes, I tried it once in Miami.

B **PAIR WORK** Ask and answer these questions. Use *it* in your responses. Pay attention to the linked sounds.

Have you ever cut your own hair?
Have you ever tasted blue cheese?
Have you ever tried Vietnamese food?
Have you ever lost your ID?
Have you looked at Unit 11 yet?

7 LISTENING Great to see you!

Listen to Nicole tell Tyler about some interesting things she's done recently. Complete the chart.

Places Nicole went	What she did there	Has Tyler been there before?	
1.		☐ Yes	☐ No
2.		☐ Yes	☐ No

Have you ever been there? **67**

8 WORD POWER Life experiences

A Find two phrases to go with each verb. Write them in the chart.

a bike	your English books	a costume	a truck	your phone	a motorcycle
sushi	chocolate soda	iced coffee	octopus	a sports car	a uniform

eat	_____	_____	_____
drink	_____	_____	_____
drive	_____	_____	_____
lose	_____	_____	_____
ride	_____	_____	_____
wear	_____	_____	_____

B Add another phrase for each verb in part A.

9 SPEAKING Have you ever . . . ?

A GROUP WORK Ask your classmates questions about the activities in Exercise 8 or your own ideas.

A: Have you ever worn a costume?
B: Yes, I have.
C: Really? Where were you?

B CLASS ACTIVITY Tell the class one interesting thing you learned about a classmate.

10 WRITING An email to an old friend

A Write an email to someone you haven't seen for a long time. Include three things you've done since you last saw that person.

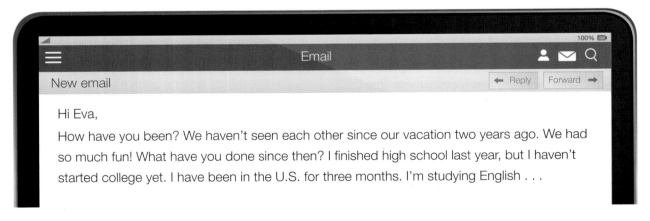

Hi Eva,

How have you been? We haven't seen each other since our vacation two years ago. We had so much fun! What have you done since then? I finished high school last year, but I haven't started college yet. I have been in the U.S. for three months. I'm studying English . . .

B PAIR WORK Exchange emails with a partner. Write a response about the three things your partner has done.

11 INTERCHANGE 10 Fun survey

How much fun do you have? Go to Interchange 10 on page 125.

12 READING

A Look at the photos. Skim the blog posts. What did Jennifer Aniston do in her sleep? How did Mervyn Kincaid cross the Irish Sea?

UNIQUE EXPERIENCES

How much is that pizza?!

Do you like pizza? Do you *really* like pizza? Do you like pizza enough to spend over $100 on one? Some people do! And here's the reason why. Truffles are similar to mushrooms, but they grow underground. They're extremely expensive. They can cost hundreds of dollars each. Pizza usually only costs a few dollars, but some people have paid as much as $178 to eat pizza with fresh white truffles on it. Celebrity TV chef Gordon Ramsay has won a place in the Guinness Book of Records for inventing this expensive dish.

Do you sleepwalk?

Did you know that some people walk in their sleep? Well, you probably do because it's a surprisingly common problem. In fact, almost a third of the U.S. population has sleepwalked at some point in their lives. The actress Jennifer Aniston is one of them. Jennifer has set off the burglar alarm in her own house by walking around while she was asleep.

Set sail in a bathtub!

Have you ever dreamed of going on a really big adventure? One man has crossed the Irish Sea . . . in a bathtub! Yes, you heard that right. Mervyn Kincaid has sailed from Ireland to Scotland in a bathtub with a small engine attached. Even better, Mervyn has raised a lot of money for charity. His friends and family have all made donations.

Oh no! I hit "send"!

Have you ever pushed "send" on a text message and then realized you've just sent a text to the wrong person? Hopefully not! But Burt Brown has. This 30-year-old software engineer has just sent 30 cute pictures of his baby to his boss instead of his mom! Luckily, his boss is a good guy and understood the mistake.

B Read the news reports. Check (✓) True or False.

	True	False
1. Pizza is very expensive in the U.S.	☐	☐
2. Truffles grow underground.	☐	☐
3. Mervyn Kincaid didn't use a boat for his journey.	☐	☐
4. Mervyn Kincaid crossed the Irish Sea to pay for his bathtub.	☐	☐
5. Sleepwalking is extremely rare.	☐	☐
6. There was a lot of noise when Jennifer Aniston walked in her sleep.	☐	☐
7. Burt Brown sent photos to his boss.	☐	☐
8. Burt's boss was very angry about the baby pictures.	☐	☐

C **GROUP WORK** What unique experiences have you had in your life? Were they fun? Were they embarrassing? Tell your classmates.

SELF-ASSESSMENT

How well can you do these things? Check (✓) the boxes.

I can . . .	Very well	OK	A little
Ask about and describe people's appearance (Ex. 1)	☐	☐	☐
Identify people by describing what they're doing, what they're wearing, and where they are (Ex. 2)	☐	☐	☐
Find out whether or not things have been done (Ex. 3)	☐	☐	☐
Understand descriptions of experiences (Ex. 4)	☐	☐	☐
Ask and answer questions about experiences (Ex. 4)	☐	☐	☐
Find out how long people have done things (Ex. 5)	☐	☐	☐

1 ROLE PLAY Missing person

Student A: One of your classmates is lost. You are talking to a police officer. Answer the officer's questions and describe your classmate.

Student B: You are a police officer. Someone is describing a lost classmate. Ask questions to complete the form. Can you identify the classmate?

Change roles and try the role play again.

> ## MISSING PERSON REPORT
>
> NAME _____
>
> HEIGHT: _____ WEIGHT: _____ AGE: _____
>
> EYE COLOR:
> ☐ BLUE   ☐ BROWN
> ☐ GREEN   ☐ HAZEL
>
> HAIR COLOR:
> ☐ BLOND   ☐ BROWN
> ☐ RED   ☐ BLACK
> ☐ GRAY   ☐ BALD
>
> CLOTHING: _____
> _____
>
> GLASSES, ETC: _____

2 SPEAKING Which one is . . . ?

A Look at this picture. How many sentences can you write to identify the people?

> Mia and Derek are the people
>   in sunglasses.
> They're the ones looking at the tablet.

B PAIR WORK Try to memorize the people in the picture. Then close your books. Take turns asking about the people.

A: Which one is Allen?
B: I think Allen is the guy eating . . .

3 SPEAKING "To do" lists

A Imagine you are preparing for these situations. Make a list of four things you need to do for each situation.

You are going to go to the beach this weekend.
Your first day of school is in a week.
You are going to move to a new apartment.

> *"To do" list: trip to the beach*
> 1. *buy a swimsuit*

B **PAIR WORK** Exchange lists. Take turns asking about what has been done. When answering, decide what you have or haven't done.

A: Have you bought a swimsuit yet?
B: Yes, I've already gotten one.

4 LISTENING I won a contest!

▶ **A** Alyssa has just met a friend in San Diego. Listen to her talk about things she has done. Check (✓) the correct things.

Alyssa has . . .

☐ won a contest.	☐ gone windsurfing.
☐ flown in a plane.	☐ lost her wallet.
☐ stayed in an expensive hotel.	☐ gotten sunburned.
☐ met a famous person.	☐ posted on a blog.

B **GROUP WORK** Have you ever done the things in part A? Take turns asking about each thing.

5 SURVEY How long have you . . . ?

A Add one more question to the chart. Write answers to these questions using *for* and *since*.

How long have you . . . ?	My answers	Classmate's name
owned this book		
studied English		
known your teacher		
lived in this town or city		
been a student		

B **CLASS ACTIVITY** Go around the class. Find someone who has the same answers. Write a classmate's name only once.

WHAT'S NEXT?

Look at your Self-assessment again. Do you need to review anything?

11 It's a really nice city.

▶ Describe hometowns, cities, and countries
▶ Make recommendations about places to visit

1 WORD POWER Adjectives to describe places

A PAIR WORK Match each word in column A with its opposite in column B. Then add two more pairs of adjectives to the list.

A	B
1. beautiful	**a.** boring
2. cheap	**b.** crowded
3. clean	**c.** dangerous
4. interesting	**d.** expensive
5. quiet	**e.** noisy
6. relaxing	**f.** polluted
7. safe	**g.** stressful
8. spacious	**h.** ugly
9. _____	**i.** _____
10. _____	**j.** _____

beautiful

ugly

B PAIR WORK Choose two places you know. Describe them to your partner using the words in part A.

2 CONVERSATION It looks so relaxing.

▶ **A** Listen and practice.

Ron That photo is really cool! Where is that?

Camila That's a beach near my house in Punta Cana, in the Dominican Republic.

Ron It looks so relaxing. I've heard the area is really beautiful.

Camila Yeah, it is. The weather is great, and there are some fantastic beaches. The water is really clear, too.

Ron Is it expensive there?

Camila Well, it's not cheap. But prices for tourists can be pretty reasonable.

Ron Hmm . . . and how far is it from Santo Domingo?

Camila It's not *too* far from the capital. About 200 kilometers . . . a little over 120 miles.

Ron It sounds very interesting. I should plan a trip there sometime.

▶ **B** Listen to the rest of the conversation. What does Camila say about entertainment in Punta Cana?

Punta Cana, Dominican Republic

Adverbs before adjectives

		adverbs
Punta Cana is **really** nice.	It's a **really** nice place.	too
It's **fairly** expensive.	It's a **fairly** expensive destination.	extremely
It's not **very** big.	It's not a **very** big city.	very/really
New York is **too** noisy, and it's **too** crowded for me.		pretty
		fairly/somewhat

A Match the questions with the answers. Then practice the conversations with a partner.

1. What's Seoul like? Is it an interesting place? _____
2. Do you like your hometown? Why or why not? _____
3. What's Sydney like? I've never been there. _____
4. Have you ever been to São Paulo? _____
5. What's the weather like in Chicago? _____

a. Oh, really? It's beautiful and very clean. It has a great harbor and beautiful beaches.
b. Yes, I have. It's an extremely large and crowded place, but I love it. It has excellent restaurants.
c. It's really nice in the summer, but it's too cold for me in the winter.
d. Not really. It's too small, and it's really boring. That's why I moved away.
e. Yes. It has amazing shopping, and the people are pretty friendly.

Conjunctions

Los Angeles is a big city, **and** the weather is nice.	It's a big city. It's not too big, **though**.
Boston is a big city, **but** it's not too big.	It's a big city. It's not too big, **however**.

GRAMMAR PLUS *see page 142*

B Choose the correct conjunctions and rewrite the sentences.

1. Kyoto is very nice. Everyone is extremely friendly. (and / but)

   _____

2. The streets are crowded during the day. They're very quiet at night. (and / though)

   _____

3. The weather is nice. Summers get pretty hot. (and / however)

   _____

4. You can rent a bicycle. It's expensive. (and / but)

   _____

5. It's an amazing city. I love to go there. (and / however)

   _____

C **GROUP WORK** Describe three cities or towns in your country. State two positive features and one negative feature for each.

A: Singapore is very exciting and there are a lot of things to do, but it's too expensive.
B: The weather in Bogotá is . . .

Kyoto, Japan

4 LISTENING Descriptive hometowns

A Listen to Abby and Christopher talk about their hometowns.
What do they say about them? Choose the correct words.

Abby's hometown	Christopher's hometown
a fairly / not very large town	a really / fairly stressful place
somewhat / extremely beautiful	pretty / too crowded
pretty / very cheap	not very / extremely clean
_____ quiet	_____ expensive

B Listen again. Write another adverb you hear them use to describe their hometowns.

5 WRITING A great place to live

A Write about interesting places for tourists to visit in your hometown.

> Otavalo is a very interesting town in Ecuador. It's to the north of Quito.
> It has a fantastic market, and a lot of tourists go there to buy handmade
> art and crafts. The scenery around Otavalo is very pretty and . . .

B **PAIR WORK** Exchange papers and read each other's articles.
What did you learn about your partner's hometown?

6 SNAPSHOT

SIX WORLD-FAMOUS LANDMARKS

1. The Grand Canyon Arizona, U.S. ☐
2. The Louvre Paris, France ☐
3. The pyramids Giza, Egypt ☐
4. The Colosseum Rome, Italy ☐
5. Sugarloaf Mountain Rio de Janeiro, Brazil ☐
6. Taj Mahal Agra, India ☐

Which places would you like to visit? Why?
Put the places you would like to visit in order from most interesting (1) to least interesting (6).
Which interesting places around your country or the world have you already visited?
What three other places around the world would you like to visit? Why?

7 CONVERSATION What should I do there?

▶ **A** Listen and practice.

JASON Can you tell me a little about Mexico City?

CLAUDIA Sure. What would you like to know?

JASON Well, I'm going to be there for a few days next month. What should I do there?

CLAUDIA Oh! You should definitely visit the National Museum of Anthropology. It's amazing.

JASON OK. It's on my list now! Anything else?

CLAUDIA You shouldn't miss the Diego Rivera murals. They're incredible. Oh, and you can walk around the historic center.

JASON That sounds perfect. And what about the food? What should I eat?

CLAUDIA You can't miss the street food. The tacos, barbecue, fruit . . . it's all delicious.

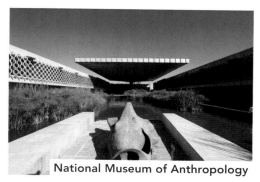
National Museum of Anthropology

Diego Rivera murals

▶ **B** Listen to the rest of the conversation. Where is Jason from? What should you do there?

8 GRAMMAR FOCUS

▶ **Modal verbs *can* and *should***

What **can** I do in Mexico City?

    You **can** walk around the historic center.

    You **can't** miss the street food.

What **should** I see there?

    You **should** visit the National Museum of Anthropology.

    You **shouldn't** miss the Diego Rivera murals.

GRAMMAR PLUS *see page 142*

A Complete these conversations using *can, can't, should,* or *shouldn't.* Then practice with a partner.

1. **A:** I _____ decide where to go on my vacation.
   B: You _____ go to Morocco. It's my favorite place to visit.
2. **A:** I'm planning to go to Puerto Rico next year. When do you think I _____ go?
   B: You _____ go anytime. The weather is nice almost all year.
3. **A:** _____ I rent a car when I arrive in New York? What do you recommend?
   B: No, you _____ definitely use the subway. It's fast and not too expensive.
4. **A:** Where _____ I get some nice jewelry in Istanbul?
   B: You _____ miss the Grand Bazaar. It's the best place for bargains.
5. **A:** What _____ I see from the Eiffel Tower?
   B: You _____ see all of Paris, but in bad weather, you _____ see anything.

B Write answers to these questions about your country. Then compare with a partner.

What time of year should you go there?

What are three things you can do there?

What can you do for free?

What shouldn't a visitor miss?

9 PRONUNCIATION *Can't* and *shouldn't*

▶ **A** Listen and practice these statements. Notice how the *t* in **can't** and **shouldn't** is not strongly pronounced.

You can get a taxi easily.
You can't get a taxi easily.
You should visit in the summer.
You shouldn't visit in the summer.

Las Vegas, United States

▶ **B** Listen to four sentences. Choose the modal verb you hear.

1. can / can't
2. should / shouldn't
3. can / can't
4. should / shouldn't

10 LISTENING Where should you go?

▶ **A** Listen to speakers talk about three countries. Complete the chart.

Country	Largest city	What visitors should see or do
1. ___Japan___	_____	_____
2. _____	_____	_____
3. _____	_____	_____

▶ **B** Listen again. What else do the speakers say about the countries?

11 SPEAKING What can visitors do there?

GROUP WORK Has anyone visited an interesting place in your country or in another country? Find out more about it. Start like this and ask questions like the ones below.

A: I visited Jeju Island once.
B: Really? What's the best time of year to visit?
A: Springtime is very nice. I went in May.
C: What's the weather like then?

What's the best time of year to visit?
What's the weather like then?
What should tourists see and do there?
What special foods can you eat?
What's the shopping like?
What things should people buy?
What else can visitors do there?

Jeju Island, South Korea

12 INTERCHANGE 11 Welcome to our city!

Make a guide to fun places in your city. Go to Interchange 11 on page 126.

A Skim the emails. What city is famous for small plates of food? Where is
a good place to ride your bike at night?

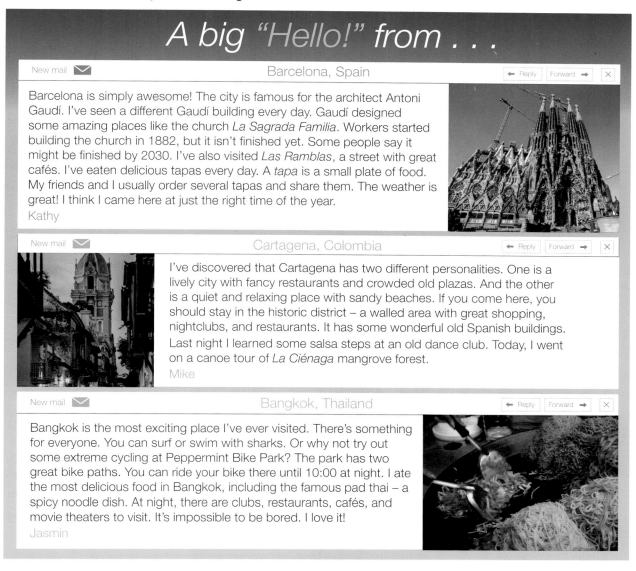

A big "Hello!" from . . .

New mail ✉   Barcelona, Spain   ← Reply Forward → ✕

Barcelona is simply awesome! The city is famous for the architect Antoni
Gaudí. I've seen a different Gaudí building every day. Gaudí designed
some amazing places like the church *La Sagrada Familia*. Workers started
building the church in 1882, but it isn't finished yet. Some people say it
might be finished by 2030. I've also visited *Las Ramblas*, a street with great
cafés. I've eaten delicious tapas every day. A *tapa* is a small plate of food.
My friends and I usually order several tapas and share them. The weather is
great! I think I came here at just the right time of the year.
Kathy

New mail ✉   Cartagena, Colombia   ← Reply Forward → ✕

I've discovered that Cartagena has two different personalities. One is a
lively city with fancy restaurants and crowded old plazas. And the other
is a quiet and relaxing place with sandy beaches. If you come here, you
should stay in the historic district – a walled area with great shopping,
nightclubs, and restaurants. It has some wonderful old Spanish buildings.
Last night I learned some salsa steps at an old dance club. Today, I went
on a canoe tour of *La Ciénaga* mangrove forest.
Mike

New mail ✉   Bangkok, Thailand   ← Reply Forward → ✕

Bangkok is the most exciting place I've ever visited. There's something
for everyone. You can surf or swim with sharks. Or why not try out
some extreme cycling at Peppermint Bike Park? The park has two
great bike paths. You can ride your bike there until 10:00 at night. I ate
the most delicious food in Bangkok, including the famous pad thai – a
spicy noodle dish. At night, there are clubs, restaurants, cafés, and
movie theaters to visit. It's impossible to be bored. I love it!
Jasmin

B Read the emails. Check (✓) the cities where you can do these things.
Then complete the chart with examples from the emails.

Activity	Barcelona	Cartagena	Bangkok	Examples
1. swim with sharks	☐	☐	☐	
2. see a famous church	☐	☐	☐	
3. eat spicy food	☐	☐	☐	
4. go dancing	☐	☐	☐	
5. take a boat tour	☐	☐	☐	
6. eat small plates of local food	☐	☐	☐	

C **PAIR WORK** Which city is the most interesting to you? Why? Which other
city or cities in the world would you like to visit? Why?

12 It's important to get rest.

▸ **State health problems and give advice**
▸ **Ask for advice and give suggestions about health products**

1 SNAPSHOT

Common Health Problems

☐ a headache ☐ a cough ☐ a cold ☐ the flu

☐ a stomachache ☐ a backache ☐ sore muscles ☐ insomnia

How many times have you been sick in the past year?
Check (✓) the health problems you have had recently.
What do you do for the health problems you checked?

2 CONVERSATION It really works!

▶ **A** Listen and practice.

Mila: Are you all right, Keith?
Keith: Not really. I don't feel so well. I have a terrible cold.
Mila: Oh, that's too bad. You shouldn't be at the gym, then.
Keith: Yeah, I know. But I need to run for an hour every day.
Mila: Not today, Keith! It's really important to get some rest.
Keith: Yeah, you're right. I should be in bed.
Mila: Well, yeah! And have you taken anything for your cold?
Keith: No, I haven't. What should I take?
Mila: Well, you know, pain medicine, lots of water. Sometimes it's helpful to drink garlic tea. Just chop up some garlic and boil it for a few minutes, then add lemon and honey. Try it! It really works!
Keith: Yuck! That sounds awful!

▶ **B** Listen to advice from Keith's next-door neighbors. What do they suggest?

3 GRAMMAR FOCUS

> ## Adjective + infinitive; noun + infinitive
>
> | What should you do for a cold? | It's **important** | **to get** some rest. |
> | | It's sometimes **helpful** | **to drink** garlic tea. |
> | | It's **a good idea** | **to take** some vitamin C. |
>
> GRAMMAR PLUS *see page 143*

A Look at these health problems. Choose several pieces of good advice for each problem.

a sore throat

Problems

1. a backache _____
2. a bad headache _____
3. a burn _____
4. a cough _____
5. a fever _____
6. the flu _____
7. a sore throat _____
8. a toothache _____

Advice

a. drink lots of liquids
b. get some medicine
c. go to bed and rest
d. put it under cold water
e. put a heating pad on it
f. put some cream on it
g. see a dentist
h. see a doctor
i. take some pain medicine
j. take some vitamin C

a fever

B **GROUP WORK** Talk about the problems in part A and give advice. What other advice do you have?

A: What should you do for a backache?
B: It's a good idea to put a heating pad on it.
C: It's also important to see a doctor and . . .

C Write advice for these problems. (You will use this advice in Exercise 4.)

| an earache | a cold | a sunburn | sore muscles |

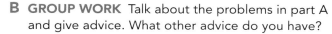

For an earache, it's a good idea to . . .

a toothache

a burn

4 PRONUNCIATION Reduction of *to*

A Listen and practice. In conversation, **to** is often reduced to /tə/.

A: What should you do for a toothache?
B: It's sometimes helpful **to** take some pain medicine. And it's important **to** see a dentist.

B **PAIR WORK** Look back at Exercise 3, part C. Ask for and give advice about each health problem. Pay attention to the pronunciation of **to**.

5 INTERCHANGE 12 What should I do?

Play a board game. Go to Interchange 12 on page 127.

6 DISCUSSION Good advice

A GROUP WORK Imagine these situations are true for you. Get three suggestions for each one from your partners.

I sometimes feel really stressed.
I need to study, but I can't concentrate.
I feel sick before every exam.
I forget about half the new words I learn.
I get nervous when I speak English to foreigners.
I get really hungry before I go to bed.

A: I sometimes feel really stressed. What should I do?
B: It's a good idea to take a hot bath.
C: It's sometimes helpful to go for a walk.

B CLASS ACTIVITY Have any of the above situations happened to you recently? Share what you did with the class.

7 WORD POWER Containers

A Use the words in the list to complete these expressions. Then compare with a partner. Sometimes more than one answer is correct.

bag   jar
bottle   pack
box   stick
can   tube

1. a _____ of pain medicine
2. a _____ of bandages
3. a _____ of cough drops
4. a _____ of deodorant
5. a _____ of face cream
6. a _____ of shaving cream
7. a _____ of tissues
8. a _____ of toothpaste

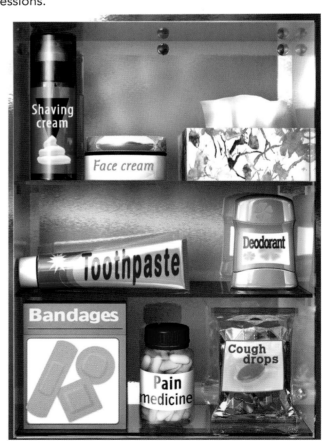

B PAIR WORK What is one more thing you can buy in each of the containers above?

"You can buy a bag of breath mints."

C PAIR WORK What are the five most useful items in your medicine cabinet?

8 CONVERSATION Can you suggest anything?

▶ **A** Listen and practice.

Pharmacist: Hi. May I help you?

Mr. Peters: Yes, please. Could I have something for a backache? My muscles are really sore.

Pharmacist: Well, it's a good idea to use a heating pad. And why don't you try this cream? It works really well.

Mr. Peters: OK, I'll take one tube. Also, my wife has a bad cough. Can you suggest anything?

Pharmacist: She should try these cough drops.

Mr. Peters: Thanks! May I have a large bag? And what do you suggest for insomnia?

Pharmacist: Well, you could get a box of chamomile tea. Is it for you?

Mr. Peters: Yes, I can't sleep.

Pharmacist: A sore back and your wife's bad cough? I think I know why you can't sleep!

▶ **B** Listen to the pharmacist talk to the next customer. What does the customer want?

9 GRAMMAR FOCUS

▶ **Modal verbs *can*, *could*, and *may* for requests; suggestions**

Can/May I help you?	What do you suggest/have for a backache?
Can I have a bag of cough drops?	You could try this new cream.
Could I have something for a cough?	You should get a heating pad.
May I have a bottle of pain medicine?	Why don't you try these pills?

GRAMMAR PLUS *see page 143*

Choose the correct words. Then compare and practice with a partner.

1. **A: Can / Could** I help you?
   B: What do you **suggest / try** for dry skin?
   A: Why don't you **suggest / try** this lotion? It's excellent.
   B: OK. I'll take it.
2. **A: May / Do** I have something for itchy eyes?
   B: Sure. You **could / may** try a bottle of eyedrops.
3. **A:** Could I **suggest / have** a box of bandages, please?
   B: Here you are.
   A: And what do you **suggest / try** for insomnia?
   B: You **should / may** try this herbal tea. It's very relaxing.
   A: OK. Thanks.

10 LISTENING What's wrong?

▶ Listen to four people talking about problems and giving advice. Write the problem and the advice.

	Problem	Advice
1. John		
2. Ashley		
3. Brandon		
4. Rachel		

11 ROLE PLAY Can I help you?

Student A: You are a customer in a drugstore. You need:

something for a backache
something for dry skin
something for the flu
something for low energy
something for sore feet
something for an upset stomach

Ask for some suggestions.

Student B: You are a pharmacist in a drugstore.
A customer needs some things.
Make some suggestions.

Change roles and try the role play again.

12 WRITING Reacting to a blog post

A Read this health and fitness blog post on how to avoid stress.

Home	About	Healthy living		🔍

Suggestions for a Relaxing Life
Tuesday, March 29   healthyandhappy

Can we avoid stress in our lives? What should we do to have a relaxing life?
Everyone wants the answers to these questions. Well, we have a few suggestions:
- We should not work long hours or work on our days off.
- We should try to exercise three or four times a week.
- It's a good idea to buy only the things we really need.
- It's really important to have fun. Fun is the perfect remedy for stress!

B Now imagine you have your own blog. Write a post with your ideas on how to reduce stress and have a relaxing life. Think of an interesting name for your blog.

C **GROUP WORK** Exchange blog posts. Read your partners' blogs and write a suggestion at the bottom of each post. Then share the most interesting blog and suggestions with the class.

A Skim the article. Then check the best description of the article.

- [ ] The article gives the author's opinion about the subject.
- [ ] The article gives information and facts.
- [ ] The article tells a story about a scientist.

Toothache?
Visit the rain forest!

acmella oleracea

A Nobody likes having a toothache, and not many people enjoy visiting the dentist's office. Exciting new research suggests that there is a different way to treat a toothache – one that doesn't need an appointment with a dentist.

B Scientists say that a very rare red and yellow plant from the Amazon rain forest could stop a toothache. It's more powerful than taking pain medicine, and it's more effective than most treatments you get in the dentist's chair. The plant, named *acmella oleracea,* has been used as a remedy for toothaches by the Keshwa Lamas, a Peruvian community, for many years.

C Dr. Françoise Barbira Freedman is an anthropologist – a scientist who studies humans. She learned about the plant 30 years ago on a trip to Peru. One day, she got a terrible toothache. The people in the village where she was living gave her the remedy and her pain disappeared.

D Now this amazing plant has been made into a gel. Many tests show that it really helps with the pain of toothaches and even helps babies who are getting their first teeth. To thank the Keshwa Lamas for this remedy, there is a plan to give some of the money from the gel back to the community. So it's good news for everyone.

B Read the article. Then answer these questions. Write the letter of the paragraph where you find the answers.

1. _____ When did Dr. Freedman learn about the plant?

2. _____ What has the plant been made into?

3. _____ What is the plant's scientific name?

4. _____ Who gave Dr. Freedman the remedy?

5. _____ What will be given back to the Keshwa Lamas?

6. _____ Where can you find the plant?

C GROUP WORK What are some other reasons why rain forests are important?

Units 11–12 Progress check

SELF-ASSESSMENT

How well can you do these things? Check (✓) the boxes.

I can . . .	Very well	OK	A little
Understand descriptions of towns and cities (Ex. 1)	☐	☐	☐
Get useful information about towns and cities (Ex. 1, 2)	☐	☐	☐
Describe towns and cities (Ex. 2)	☐	☐	☐
Ask for and make suggestions (Ex. 2, 3, 4)	☐	☐	☐
Ask and answer questions about experiences (Ex. 3, 4)	☐	☐	☐
Ask for and give advice about problems (Ex. 4)	☐	☐	☐

1 LISTENING So, you're from Hawaii?

▶ **A** Listen to Megan talk about Honolulu. What does she say about these things? Complete the chart.

1. size of city _____	**3.** prices of things _____
2. weather _____	**4.** Waikiki Beach _____

B Write sentences comparing Honolulu with your hometown. Then discuss with a partner.

Honolulu isn't too big, but Seoul is really big.

2 ROLE PLAY My hometown

Student A: Imagine you are planning to visit Student B's hometown. Ask questions to learn more about the place. Use the questions in the box and your own ideas.

Student B: Answer Student A's questions about your hometown.

A: What's your hometown like?
B: It's very interesting, but it's crowded and polluted.

Change roles and try the role play again.

possible questions

What's your hometown like?
How big is it?
What's the weather like?
Is it expensive?
What should you see there?
What can you do there?

3 DISCUSSION Medicines and remedies

A GROUP WORK Write your suggestions for these common problems and then discuss your ideas in groups.

a stomachache

an insect bite

the hiccups

a nosebleed

For a stomachache, it's a good idea to . . .

A: What can you do for a stomachache?
B: I think it's helpful to drink herbal tea.
C: Yes. And it's a good idea to see a doctor.

B GROUP WORK What health problems do you visit a doctor for? go to a drugstore for? use a home remedy for? Ask for advice and remedies.

4 SPEAKING What's your advice?

A GROUP WORK Read these people's problems. Suggest advice for each problem. Then choose the best advice.

I'm visiting the United States. I'm staying with a family while I'm here. What small gifts can I get for them?

My co-worker always talks loudly to his friends during work hours. I can't concentrate! What can I do?

Our school wants to buy some new gym equipment. Can you suggest some good ways to raise money?

A: Why doesn't she give them some flowers? They're always nice.
B: That's a good idea. Or she could bring chocolates.
C: I think she should . . .

B CLASS ACTIVITY Share your group's advice for each problem with the class.

WHAT'S NEXT?

Look at your Self-assessment again. Do you need to review anything?

13 What would you like?

▶ Agree and disagree about food preferences
▶ Order food in a restaurant

1 SNAPSHOT

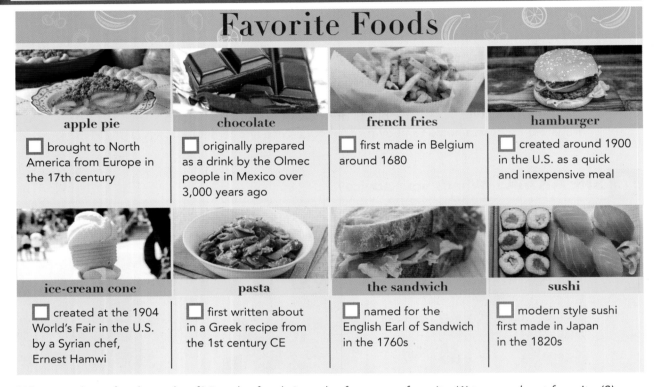

Favorite Foods

apple pie
☐ brought to North America from Europe in the 17th century

chocolate
☐ originally prepared as a drink by the Olmec people in Mexico over 3,000 years ago

french fries
☐ first made in Belgium around 1680

hamburger
☐ created around 1900 in the U.S. as a quick and inexpensive meal

ice-cream cone
☐ created at the 1904 World's Fair in the U.S. by a Syrian chef, Ernest Hamwi

pasta
☐ first written about in a Greek recipe from the 1st century CE

the sandwich
☐ named for the English Earl of Sandwich in the 1760s

sushi
☐ modern style sushi first made in Japan in the 1820s

What are these foods made of? Put the foods in order from your favorite (1) to your least favorite (8). What are three other foods you enjoy? Which have you eaten recently?

2 CONVERSATION I'm tired of shopping.

▶ **A** Listen and practice.

Simon: Hey, do you want to get something to eat?
Kristin: Sure. I'm tired of shopping.
Simon: So am I. What do you think of Thai food?
Kristin: I love it, but I'm not really in the mood for it today.
Simon: Yeah. I'm not either, I guess. It's a bit spicy.
Kristin: What about Japanese food?
Simon: Fine by me! I love Japanese food.
Kristin: So do I. There's a great restaurant on the first floor. It's called Kyoto Garden.
Simon: Perfect. Let's go try it.

▶ **B** Listen to the rest of the conversation. What do they decide to do after eating? Is there something they don't want to do?

▶ *So, too, neither, either*

	Agree	Disagree
I'm crazy about Italian food.	So am I./I am, too.	Oh, I'm not.
I can eat really spicy food.	So can I./I can, too.	Really? I can't.
I like Japanese food a lot.	So do I./I do, too.	Oh, I don't (like it very much).
I'm not in the mood for Indian food.	Neither am I./I'm not either.	Really? I am.
I can't stand fast food.	Neither can I./I can't either.	Oh, I love it!
I don't like salty food.	Neither do I./I don't either.	Oh, I like it a lot.

GRAMMAR PLUS *see page 144*

bland

delicious

greasy

healthy

rich

salty

spicy

A Write responses to show agreement with these statements.
Then compare with a partner.

1. I'm not crazy about Italian food. _____
2. I can eat any kind of food. _____
3. I think Indian food is delicious. _____
4. I can't stand greasy food. _____
5. I don't like salty food. _____
6. I'm in the mood for something spicy. _____
7. I'm tired of fast food. _____
8. I don't enjoy rich food very much. _____
9. I always eat healthy food. _____
10. I can't eat bland food. _____

B **PAIR WORK** Take turns responding to the statements in part A again.
Give your own opinion when responding.

C Write statements about these things. (You will use the statements in Exercise 4.)

1. two kinds of food you like
2. two kinds of food you can't stand
3. two kinds of food you would like to eat today

4 PRONUNCIATION Stress in responses

▶ **A** Listen and practice. Notice how the last word of each response is stressed.

●	●	●	●
I do, too.	So do I.	I don't either.	Neither do I.
I am, too.	So am I.	I'm not either.	Neither am I.
I can, too.	So can I.	I can't either.	Neither can I.

B **PAIR WORK** Read and respond to the statements your partner wrote for Exercise 3, part C. Pay attention to the stress in your responses.

5 WORD POWER Food categories

A Complete the chart. Then add one more word to each category.

bread   fish   mangoes   peas   shrimp
chicken   grapes   octopus   potatoes   strawberries
corn   lamb   pasta   rice   turkey

Fruit	Vegetables	Grains	Meat	Seafood

B **GROUP WORK** What's your favorite food in each category? Are there any you haven't tried?

6 CONVERSATION May I take your order?

▶ **A** Listen and practice.

Server May I take your order?

Customer Yes, please. I'd like the veggie burger.

Server All right. And would you like soup or salad with your burger?

Customer What's the soup of the day?

Server It's chicken soup. We also have cream of potato soup and onion soup.

Customer I'll have the onion soup, please.

Server And would you like anything to drink?

Customer Yes, I'd like a lemonade, please.

Today's Specials
soup of the day
chicken curry and mango salad
veggie burger with soup or salad
red bean chili and chips

▶ **B** Listen to the server talk to the next customer. What does he order?

7 GRAMMAR FOCUS

▶ **Modal verbs *would* and *will* for requests**

What **would** you **like**?	I**'d like** the veggie burger.	**Contractions**
	I**'ll have** a mango salad.	I**'ll** = I will
What kind of soup **would** you **like**?	I**'d like** onion soup, please.	I**'d** = I would
	I**'ll have** the soup of the day.	
What **would** you **like** to drink?	I**'d like** a lemonade.	
	I**'ll have** a large orange juice.	
Would you **like** anything else?	Yes, please. I**'d like** some coffee.	
	That's all, thanks.	

GRAMMAR PLUS *see page 144*

Complete this conversation. Then practice with a partner.

Server: What _____ you like to order?

Customer: I _____ have the spicy fish.

Server: _____ you like salad or potatoes?

Customer: I _____ like potatoes, please.

Server: OK. And _____ you like anything to drink?

Customer: I _____ just have a glass of water.

Server: Would you _____ anything else?

Customer: No, that's all for now, thanks.

Later

Server: Would you _____ dessert?

Customer: Yes, I _____ like ice cream.

Server: What flavor _____ you like?

Customer: Hmm. I _____ have mint chocolate chip, please.

8 ROLE PLAY At a coffee shop

Student A: You are a customer at a coffee shop. Order what you want for lunch.
Student B: You are the server. Take your customer's order.

TODAY'S LUNCH SPECIALS

Cheeseburger with onion rings	Lamb curry and potatoes
Spicy shrimp and rice	Sushi plate with miso soup
Chicken salad sandwich	Vegetarian pizza and salad

Drinks		Desserts	
Coffee	Fresh juice	Ice cream	Lemon pie
Tea	Sparkling water	Chocolate cake	Fresh fruit salad
Soda			

Change roles and try the role play again.

9 LISTENING Working late

▶ **A** Steven and Sarah are working late. Listen as their boss asks what they would like for dinner. What do they order? Fill in their choices.

Steven	Sarah
_____ pizza	_____ pizza
Salad with _____	Salad with _____ dressing
Drink: _____ with _____	Drink: _____ with _____
Dessert: a piece of _____	Dessert: a slice of _____

▶ **B** Listen to their conversation after the food arrives. Choose the two items that are missing from the order.

10 INTERCHANGE 13 Planning a food festival

Create a menu to offer at a food festival. Go to Interchange 13 on page 128.

11 WRITING A restaurant review

A Have you eaten out recently? Write a review of a restaurant, café, or food truck. Choose at least five questions from the list. Answer these questions and add ideas of your own.

What's the name of the place?
When did you go there?
What time did you go?
Who did you go with?
What did you have to eat?
What did you have to drink?
Did you order dessert?
What did you like about the place?
What didn't you like about it?
Would you recommend it? Why? Why not?

B **GROUP WORK** Take turns reading your reviews. Which place would you like to try?

USER REVIEW

Last Saturday, my sister and I tried Burger To Go, a new restaurant in our town. I had a classic cheeseburger and fries. The burger wasn't very big, but it was delicious. The fries were hot and crispy but a little too salty. For dessert, I had apple pie. It wasn't bad, but I've had better. I would recommend Burger To Go for their burgers and their very friendly service. I hope they improve with time!
– Emilia

A Scan the article. In which country do people usually leave a 15–20% tip on food? In which country is tipping unnecessary?

TO TIP OR NOT TO TIP?

WHAT'S A TIP?

The verb *to tip* means to give money, and the noun *tip* is the money that you give to someone. It's a slang word from Old English. Around the world, many people give tips to people who provide a service for them. It's a way of saying thank you. But did you know that tipping customs around the world *vary* a lot?

WHO AND WHERE TO TIP

In some countries, like the United States, it's common to give a tip in a lot of different places. Almost everybody gives tips to servers in restaurants and cafés. Servers *rely on* those tips to add to the low *wages* they get paid for their jobs. People also tip taxi drivers and hairstylists. If an airport worker or a hotel bellhop helps you with a heavy suitcase, you tip them as well. In Japan, though, it's a very different story. In Japan, tipping isn't part of the culture, so it rarely happens. In fact, a tip might be *confusing* to the server. And in France, a "service charge" is included on all restaurant checks, so in fact, you've already tipped your server.

HOW MUCH TO TIP?

The amount people tip in the United States varies between 15 and 20% on restaurant checks. So, for example, if a restaurant total is $40, people give the server around $6–8. That seems like a lot of money for some visitors who come from countries where tipping isn't *customary*. According to one news source, the average tip in a New York restaurant is 19.1% of the total, but in London it's 11.8%. That's a big difference.

WHO'S THE BEST TIPPER?

A millionaire named Benjamin Olewine probably wins the prize for giving the world's most *generous* tip. Mr. Olewine paid for his server's nursing school fees as a tip! The waitress, Melissa, was working in a restaurant to save money for school. One day, she served breakfast to Mr. Olewine. The check was $3.45. The tip was more than $20,000!

B Read the article. Find the words in italics, then check (✓) the correct meaning of each word.

1. *vary*
☐ change
☐ stay the same

2. *rely on*
☐ ask for
☐ need

3. *wages*
☐ regular pay for a job
☐ tips received for a job

4. *confusing*
☐ unnecessary
☐ difficult to understand

5. *customary*
☐ usual
☐ unusual

6. *generous*
☐ very rich
☐ giving more than enough

C Check (✓) the statements that describe correct tipping behavior. For the items you don't check, what is acceptable?

☐ **1.** You're eating at a restaurant in London. You leave a 25% tip.
☐ **2.** You give your New York server a 15% tip.
☐ **3.** You give a large tip after your meal in Tokyo.
☐ **4.** Your bellhop in Chicago helps you carry your suitcase. You give him a tip.
☐ **5.** You pay your check in Paris and don't leave a tip.

D GROUP WORK Is tipping customary in your country? If it is, who do you tip and how much? If it isn't, what do you think about tipping?

▸ **Describe and compare different places in the world**
▸ **Describe temperatures, distances, and measurements**

1 WORD POWER Places around the world

A Match the words from the list to the letters in the picture. Then compare with a partner.

1. beach _____
2. desert _____
3. forest _____
4. hill _____
5. island _____
6. lake _____
7. mountain _____
8. ocean _____
9. river _____
10. valley _____
11. volcano _____
12. waterfall _____

B **PAIR WORK** What other geography words can you think of? Do you see any of these places in the picture above?

C **GROUP WORK** Try to think of famous examples for each item in part A.

A: A famous beach is Shirahama Beach in Japan.

B: And the Sahara is a famous . . .

2 CONVERSATION I love quizzes!

▶ **A** Listen and practice.

Claire: This is one of the best airline magazines I've ever read. Oh, look! A quiz! "Our world – How much do you know?"

Steve: Oh, I love quizzes! Ask me the questions.

Claire: Sure. First question: Which country is larger, Mexico or Australia?

Steve: I know. Australia is larger than Mexico.

Claire: OK, next. What's the longest river in the world?

Steve: That's easy. It's the Nile!

Claire: All right. Here's a hard one. Which country is more crowded, Malta or England?

Steve: I'm not sure. I think Malta is more crowded.

Claire: Really? OK, one more. Which city is the most expensive: Hong Kong, London, or Paris?

Steve: Oh, that's easy. Paris is the most expensive.

▶ **B** Listen to the rest of the conversation. How many questions did Steve get right?

3 GRAMMAR FOCUS

▶ **Comparisons with adjectives**

Which country is **larger**, Australia or Mexico?		
Australia is **larger than** Mexico.		
Which country is **the largest** in the world?		
Russia is **the largest** country.		
Which is **more crowded**? Malta or England?		
Malta is **more crowded than** England.		
Malta is **the most crowded** country in Europe.		

Adjective	Comparative	Superlative
long	longer	the longest
large	larger	the largest
dry	drier	the driest
big	bigger	the biggest
beautiful	more beautiful	the most beautiful
crowded	more crowded	the most crowded
expensive	more expensive	the most expensive
good	better	the best
bad	worse	the worst

GRAMMAR PLUS *see page 145*

A Complete questions 1 to 4 with comparatives and questions 5 to 8 with superlatives. Then ask and answer the questions.

1. Which country is _____, Monaco or Vatican City? (small)
2. Which waterfall is _____, Niagara Falls or Victoria Falls? (high)
3. Which city is _____, Hong Kong or Cairo? (crowded)
4. Which lake is _____, Lake Michigan or Lake Baikal? (large)
5. Which is _____: Mount Aconcagua, Mount Everest, or Mount Fuji? (high)
6. What is _____ river in the Americas, the Mississippi, the Colorado, or the Amazon? (long)
7. Which city is _____: London, Tokyo, or Moscow? (expensive)
8. What is _____ ocean in the world, the Pacific, the Atlantic, or the Arctic? (deep)

B **CLASS ACTIVITY** Write four questions like those in part A about your country or other countries. Then ask your classmates the questions.

4 PRONUNCIATION Questions of choice

▶ **A** Listen and practice. Notice how the intonation in questions of choice drops, then rises, and then drops again.

Which city is more crowded, Hong Kong or Cairo?

Which city is the most expensive: London, Tokyo, or Moscow?

B PAIR WORK Take turns asking these questions. Pay attention to your intonation. Do you know the answers?

Which desert is bigger, the Gobi or the Atacama?
Which city is higher, Bogotá or La Paz?
Which ocean is the smallest: the Arctic, the Indian, or the Atlantic?
Which mountains are the highest: the Andes, the Rockies, or the Himalayas?

5 SPEAKING Travelers' tips

GROUP WORK Imagine these people are planning to visit your country. What would they enjoy doing? Agree on a recommendation for each person.

Jana

"I like all kinds of outdoor activities, especially hiking and bike riding. I can't stand crowded and polluted cities."

Neil

"I enjoy visiting museums, trying local food, and shopping at small stores. I don't like boring tourist places."

Sammie

"I love nightlife. My favorite activity is going dancing and meeting new people! I really don't like small towns."

6 LISTENING Quiz Show!

▶ Listen to three people on a TV quiz show. Check (✓) the correct answers.

1.	☐ the Eiffel Tower	☐ the Statue of Liberty	☐ the Panama Canal
2.	☐ Victoria Falls	☐ Niagara Falls	☐ Angel Falls
3.	☐ gold	☐ butter	☐ all
4.	☐ the Arctic Ocean	☐ the Southern Ocean	☐ the Indian Ocean
5.	☐ São Paulo	☐ Mexico City	☐ Seoul
6.	☐ Africa	☐ Antarctica	☐ Australia

7 INTERCHANGE 14 How much do you know?

You probably know more than you think! Take a quiz. Go to Interchange 14 on page 129.

8 SNAPSHOT

8 Surprising Facts

1 The hottest place in the world is Death Valley, California. The temperature there has reached 134°F (56.7°C).

2 Antarctica is the largest desert on Earth. It is 5.4 million square miles (14 million square kilometers). It's also the coldest, windiest continent.

3 *NCIS* is the world's most watched TV show. Over 55 million people across the world have watched it.

4 The largest cat in the world is the Siberian tiger. At 700 pounds (320 kilos), it is bigger than a lion.

5 France is the most popular country to visit. It gets over 80 million visitors a year.

6 The highest price for a car at an auction was just over $38 million for a 1962 Ferrari. The auction happened in 2014.

7 The best-selling music album of all time is Michael Jackson's *Thriller*. The 1982 album has sold around 65 million copies.

8 The planet in our Solar System with the most moons, 67 total, is Jupiter. The largest one, Ganymede, is the ninth largest object in the Solar System.

Which facts do you find surprising? Why?
What are some facts about your country? What's the tallest building?
  the busiest airport? the most popular city to visit?

9 CONVERSATION That's freezing!

▶ **A** Listen and practice.

Alberto: Hi, Lily. You're from Canada, right? I'm going to Toronto in January.

Lily: Actually, I'm from the U.S., but I went to school in Toronto. Winter there can be pretty cold.

Alberto: How cold is it on average?

Lily: Um, I think the average in January is around 20° or maybe 25°.

Alberto: Twenty-five degrees? But that's warm!

Lily: Twenty-five degrees Fahrenheit. That's about . . . minus 3 or 4 Celsius.

Alberto: Minus 3 or 4? That's freezing!

Lily: Oh, come on, that's not *so* cold, at least not where I'm from.

Alberto: Really? Where are you from?

Lily: Well, I live in Fairbanks, Alaska, around 3,000 miles from Toronto. That's . . . let me check on my phone . . . Yes, that's about 4,800 kilometers.

Alberto: Wow. . . . So, is it colder than Toronto?

Lily: It's much colder than Toronto. It's the coldest city in the United States!

▶ **B** Listen to the rest of the conversation. Is Fairbanks a small town? What else does Lily say about it?

10 GRAMMAR FOCUS

▶ Questions with *how*

How cold is Toronto in the winter?	It gets down to minus 25° Celsius.	(-13° Fahrenheit)
How hot is Fairbanks in the summer?	It gets up to about 20° Celsius.	(68° Fahrenheit)
How far is Toronto from Fairbanks?	It's about 4,800 kilometers.	(3,000 miles)
How big is Seoul?	It's 605 square kilometers.	(233.6 square miles)
How high is Mount Everest?	It's 8,848 meters **high**.	(29,028 feet)
How long is the Mississippi River?	It's about 3,700 kilometers **long**.	(2,300 miles)
How deep is the Grand Canyon?	It's about 1,828 meters **deep**.	(6,000 feet)

GRAMMAR PLUS see page 145

A Write the questions to these answers. Then practice with a partner.

1. **A:** _____ ?
   B: Niagara Falls is 52 meters (170 feet) high.

2. **A:** _____ ?
   B: California is about 423,970 square kilometers (163,670 square miles).

3. **A:** _____ ?
   B: The Nile is 6,670 kilometers (4,145 miles) long.

4. **A:** _____ ?
   B: Osaka is about 400 kilometers (250 miles) from Tokyo.

5. **A:** _____ ?
   B: Mexico City gets up to about 28° Celsius (82° Fahrenheit) in the summer.

B **GROUP WORK** Think of five questions with *how* about places in your country or other countries you know. Ask and answer your questions.

11 WRITING An article about a place

A Write an article about a place in your country or in another country that you think tourists would like to visit. Describe a place from the list.

a beach
a desert
an island
a lake
a mountain
a river
a volcano
a waterfall

B **PAIR WORK** Read your partner's article. Ask questions to get more information.

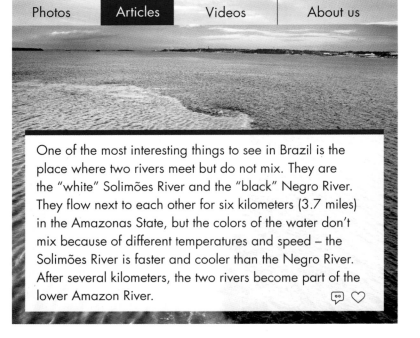

Photos	Articles	Videos	About us

One of the most interesting things to see in Brazil is the place where two rivers meet but do not mix. They are the "white" Solimões River and the "black" Negro River. They flow next to each other for six kilometers (3.7 miles) in the Amazonas State, but the colors of the water don't mix because of different temperatures and speed – the Solimões River is faster and cooler than the Negro River. After several kilometers, the two rivers become part of the lower Amazon River.

A Look at the title of the article and the pictures. Why do you think these places are so clean?

Earth's Cleanest Places

Lake Vostok, Antarctica

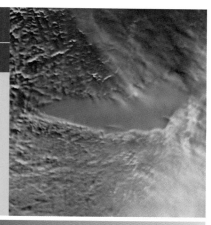

About four kilometers (2.5 miles) under a large area of ice in Antarctica, there's a lake named Lake Vostok. It covers 15,690 square kilometers (6,058 square miles) and is 800 meters (2,625 feet) deep in some places. Lake Vostok is prehistoric – millions of years old – but until 1956, no one even knew it existed. It's a fresh water lake, and it has been hidden from sunlight for 15 million years. What this means is that the water is some of the cleanest, purest water on Earth.

Cape Grim, Australia

We all know that air pollution is a problem all around the world, so where do you go if you want really clean air? Well, Cape Grim in Tasmania, Australia is probably the best idea. Cape Grim has some of the cleanest air on Earth. Cape Grim also has beautiful, clean water. Why is this? Wind! Special winds called "The Roaring Forties" cross the Southern Ocean, bringing with them wonderfully clean water and air. In fact, in Cape Grim, people are allowed to put rain water into bottles and sell it. That's how clean it is!

Singapore

The tiny island of Singapore has a population of about 5.7 million people. It also has very strict rules about the way its people behave. Singapore is one of the cleanest cities on the planet because of these rules. People are not allowed to chew gum unless it's from a doctor, and all used chewing gum has to go in a trash can. That means that you don't find gum on the sidewalks. In fact, no one drops trash in the street. There are big fines for people who don't respect the rules, but most people are happy to keep their city clean and healthy.

B Read the article. What is the main goal of the article? Check (✓) the correct answer.

☐ to entertain people ☐ to inform people ☐ to persuade people to do something

C Read the article and answer the questions.

1. When did people discover Lake Vostok? _____
2. How long has Lake Vostok been hidden? _____
3. What two things is Cape Grim famous for? _____
4. What's the main reason that Cape Grim is so clean? _____
5. About how many people live in Singapore? _____
6. What happens when people break the rules in Singapore? _____

D **GROUP WORK** What do you think is the cleanest place in your country? Why is it so clean? How would you describe it to a friend?

Units 13–14 Progress check

SELF-ASSESSMENT

How well can you do these things? Check (✓) the boxes.

I can . . .	Very well	OK	A little
Say what I like and dislike (Ex. 1)	☐	☐	☐
Agree and disagree with other people (Ex. 1)	☐	☐	☐
Understand a variety of questions in a restaurant (Ex. 2)	☐	☐	☐
Order a meal in a restaurant (Ex. 3)	☐	☐	☐
Describe and compare things, people, and places (Ex. 4, 5)	☐	☐	☐
Ask questions about distances and measurements (Ex. 5)	☐	☐	☐

1 SPEAKING Survey: food preferences

A Answer these questions. Write your responses under the column "My answers."
Then add one more question to the chart.

	My answers	Classmate's name
What food are you crazy about?		
What food can't you stand?		
Do you like vegetarian food?		
Can you eat very spicy food?		
How often do you go out to eat?		
What restaurant do you like a lot?		

B **CLASS ACTIVITY** Go around the class. Find someone who has the same opinions or habits.

A: I'm crazy about Japanese food.
B: I am, too./So am I. OR Oh, I'm not. I'm crazy about . . .

2 LISTENING In a restaurant

▶ Listen to six requests in a restaurant. Check (✓) the best response.

1. ☐ Yes. This way, please.
☐ Yes, please.

2. ☐ No, I don't.
☐ Yes, I'll have tea, please.

3. ☐ I'd like the fish, please.
☐ Yes, I would.

4. ☐ I'll have a green salad.
☐ Italian, please.

5. ☐ Broccoli, please.
☐ Yes, I would.

6. ☐ Yes, I'd like more water.
☐ No, I don't think so.

3 ROLE PLAY May I take your order?

Student A: Imagine you are a server and Student B is a customer. Take his or her order and write it on the check.

Student B: Imagine you are a hungry customer at any restaurant you choose. Student A is a server. Order a meal.

Change roles and try the role play again.

THANK YOU   TOTAL: ....

4 SPEAKING Your hometown quiz

A PAIR WORK Write down six facts about your town or city using comparatives or superlatives. Then write six Wh-questions based on your facts.

> 1. The longest street is Independence Street.
>   What's the longest street in our city?

B GROUP WORK Join another pair. Take turns asking the other pair your questions. How many can they answer correctly?

5 GAME What's the question?

A Think of three statements that can be answered with *how* questions or Wh-questions with comparatives and superlatives. Write each statement on a separate card.

B CLASS ACTIVITY Divide into Teams A and B. Shuffle the cards together. One student from Team A picks a card and reads it to a student from Team B. That student tries to make a question for it.

A: The Atacama is drier than the Sahara.
B: Which desert is drier, the Atacama or the Sahara?

Keep score. The team with the most correct questions wins.

> June and July are the coldest months in our city.

> The Atacama is drier than the Sahara.

> It's about two kilometers from my house to the school.

WHAT'S NEXT?

Look at your Self-assessment again. Do you need to review anything?

15 What are you doing later?

- ▸ Discuss future activities and plans
- ▸ Give messages

1 SNAPSHOT

HOW TO DECLINE AN INVITATION POLITELY

A friend has invited you to go out, but you can't make it. Follow our advice and learn how you can decline an invitation politely and keep your friend.

To thank your friend, you can say:
"Thanks so much for asking me. It sounds like a lot of fun."
"Thanks so much for the invite."

To apologize and explain why you can't accept, you can say:
"Sorry, but I already have plans."
"Sorry, but I have something else going on that day."
"I'm so sorry, but I can't make it. I'm really busy these days."

To offer another time to do something together, you can say:
"This week is crazy, but let's shoot for next week."
"Maybe another time? I'm free next week."
"Can I take a rain check?"

Do you feel comfortable declining friends' invitations? Why? Why not?
What polite excuses have you used? Which are effective? Which are not?
What is the best tip, in your opinion? Why?

2 CONVERSATION Are you doing anything tomorrow?

▶ **A** Listen and practice.

Alicia: Hey, Mike, what are you doing tonight? Do you want to go see the new photo exhibit?

Mike: Thanks so much for asking me, but I can't. I'm going to have dinner with my parents.

Alicia: Oh, well, maybe some other time.

Mike: Are you doing anything tomorrow? We could go then.

Alicia: Tomorrow sounds fine. I have class until four.

Mike: So let's go around five.

Alicia: OK. Afterward, maybe we can get some dinner.

Mike: Sounds great.

▶ **B** Listen to the rest of the conversation. Where are Alicia and Mike going to have dinner? Who are they going to meet for dinner?

3 GRAMMAR FOCUS

Future with present continuous and *be going to*

With present continuous	With *be going to* + verb	Time expressions
What **are** you **doing** tonight?	What **is** she **going to do** tomorrow?	tonight
I**'m going** to a party.	She**'s going to see** a play.	tomorrow
Are you **doing** anything tomorrow?	**Are** they **going to see** the photo exhibit?	on Friday
No, I**'m** not (**doing** anything).	Yes, they **are** (**going to see** it).	this weekend
		next week

GRAMMAR PLUS see page 146

A Complete the invitations in column A with the present continuous used as future. Complete the responses in column B with *be going to*.

A

1. What _____ you _____ (do) tonight? Would you like to go out?

2. _____ you _____ (do) anything on Friday night? Do you want to see a movie?

3. We _____ (have) friends over for a barbecue on Sunday. Would you and your parents like to come?

4. _____ you _____ (stay) in town next weekend? Do you want to go for a hike?

B

a. I _____ (be) here on Saturday, but not Sunday. Let's try to go on Saturday.

b. Well, my father _____ (visit) my brother at college. But my mother and I _____ (be) home. We'd love to come!

c. Sorry, I can't. I _____ (work) late tonight. How about tomorrow night?

d. Can we go to a late show? I _____ (stay) at the office till 7:00.

B Match the invitations in column A with the responses in column B. Then practice with a partner.

4 WORD POWER Free-time activities and events

A Complete the chart with words and phrases from the list. Then add one more example to each category.

a rock concert   a barbecue   a wedding   a hip-hop dance performance

a soccer game   a film festival   a musical   a video game tournament

a birthday party   a class reunion   a car race   a baseball game

Sports and games	Friends and family	Art and performances

B **PAIR WORK** Are you going to do any of the activities in part A? When are you doing them? Talk with a partner.

5 ROLE PLAY Accept or refuse?

Student A: Choose an activity from Exercise 4 and invite a partner to go with you. Be ready to say where and when the activity is.

> **A:** So, are you doing anything on . . . ? Would you like to . . . ?

Student B: Your partner invites you out. Either accept the invitation and ask for more information or say you can't go and give an excuse.

Accept

B: OK. That sounds fun. Where is it?

Refuse

B: Oh, I'm sorry, I can't. I'm . . .

Change roles and try the role play again.

6 INTERCHANGE Weekend plans

Find out what your classmates are going to do this weekend. Go to Interchange 15 on page 130.

7 CONVERSATION Can I take a message?

▶ **A** Listen and practice.

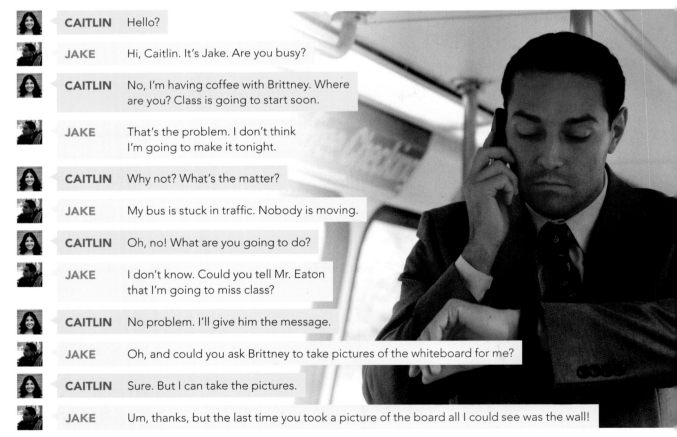

CAITLIN	Hello?
JAKE	Hi, Caitlin. It's Jake. Are you busy?
CAITLIN	No, I'm having coffee with Brittney. Where are you? Class is going to start soon.
JAKE	That's the problem. I don't think I'm going to make it tonight.
CAITLIN	Why not? What's the matter?
JAKE	My bus is stuck in traffic. Nobody is moving.
CAITLIN	Oh, no! What are you going to do?
JAKE	I don't know. Could you tell Mr. Eaton that I'm going to miss class?
CAITLIN	No problem. I'll give him the message.
JAKE	Oh, and could you ask Brittney to take pictures of the whiteboard for me?
CAITLIN	Sure. But I can take the pictures.
JAKE	Um, thanks, but the last time you took a picture of the board all I could see was the wall!

▶ **B** Listen to three other phone calls. Write the callers' names.

8 GRAMMAR FOCUS

▶ **Formal and informal messages with *tell* and *ask***

Statements

I'm going to miss class tonight.

Messages with a statement: *tell*

(Please) **Tell him (that)** I'm going to miss class.

Could you tell him (that) I'm going to miss class?

Would you tell him (that) I'm going to miss class?

informal
↓
formal

Requests

Could she take a picture of the board?

Messages with a request: *ask*

(Please) **Ask her** to take a picture of the board.

Could you ask her to take a picture of the board?

Would you ask her to take a picture of the board?

informal
↓
formal

GRAMMAR PLUS *see page 146*

A Unscramble these messages. Then compare with a partner.

1. tell / that / is / please / Haru / the barbecue / on Saturday

_____.

2. call me / at / 4:00 / you / Caitlin / could /ask / to

_____?

3. is / that / Mia / tonight / could / you / the dance performance / tell

_____?

4. tell / is / Casey / in the park / would / you / that / the picnic

_____?

5. meet me / to / you / would / Maika / ask / at the stadium

_____?

6. ask / to the rock concert / please / bring / Garrett / to / the tickets

_____.

B **PAIR WORK** Imagine that you are far from school and cannot come to class. "Call" your partner and ask him or her to give a message to your teacher and to one of the students in your group.

A: Could you tell Ms. Clark that . . . And could you ask Joel to . . .

9 WRITING Text message requests

A **PAIR WORK** "Text" your partner. Write messages to each other with requests for your classmates. Write as many messages as you can in three minutes.

> A: Hi, Sandra. Would you ask Marcella to have dinner with us after class?
>
> B: OK, Chris. And could you tell Jules that we have a test tomorrow?

B **CLASS ACTIVITY** Give the messages to your classmates.

A: Hi, Jules. I have a message from Sandra. We have a test tomorrow.

B: Hi, Marcella. I have a message from Chris. Would you like to have dinner with us after class?

10 PRONUNCIATION Reduction of *could you* and *would you*

▶ **A** Listen and practice. Notice how **could you** and **would you** are reduced in conversation.

[cʊdʒə]
Could you tell him I'm going to miss class?

[wʊdʒə]
Would you ask him to call me after class?

B PAIR WORK Practice these questions with reduced forms.

Could you tell them I'm in bed with a cold?

Would you ask her to be on time?

Could you ask her to return my dictionary?

Would you tell him there's a food festival tomorrow?

11 LISTENING I'm going to be late.

▶ Listen to four people leaving messages. Who is the message from?
Who is it for? What is the message? Complete the chart.

1
Message from: _____
Message for: _____
Message: _____
_____

2
Message from: _____
Message for: _____
Message: _____
_____

3
Message from: _____
Message for: _____
Message: _____

4
Message from: _____
Message for: _____
Message: _____
_____

12 ROLE PLAY Who's calling?

Student A: You have a computer repair store. A client, Sophie Green, has left her laptop at your store. Call her to tell her this:

The computer needs a new motherboard. It's going to cost $250.
She can buy a used motherboard for $90. Could she please call you before 5:00?

Student B: Someone calls for your mother, Sophie Green. She isn't at home. Take a message for her.

Change roles and try another role play.

Student A: You are a receptionist at Techniware Industries. Someone calls for your boss, Mr. Yun. He isn't in. Take a message for him.

Student B: Call Mr. Yun at Techniware Industries to tell him this:

You can't make your lunch meeting at 12:00 next Wednesday. You would like to meet at 12:30 at the same place instead. Could he please call you to arrange the new time?

useful expressions
Caller
May I speak to . . . ?
Can I leave a message?
Receiver
Sorry, but . . . isn't here.
Can I take a message?
I'll give him/her the message.

A Scan the article. Why did some people go to the wrong address?

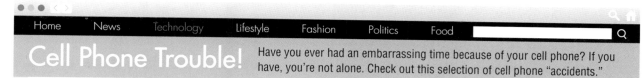

| Home | News | Technology | Lifestyle | Fashion | Politics | Food |

Cell Phone Trouble!

Have you ever had an embarrassing time because of your cell phone? If you have, you're not alone. Check out this selection of cell phone "accidents."

Security cameras in a fancy hotel captured a video of a well-dressed woman, about 30 years old, texting on her phone. There's nothing unusual about that, is there? Well, yes, this time there is. The woman was so busy on her phone that she walked right into a pool of water in the hotel lobby . . . fully dressed! Nobody knows who the woman is or where the watery adventure happened, but almost half a million people have watched the video on the Internet!

A New Yorker was riding the subway home from work one evening. He was very excited by the video game he was playing on his smartphone. When he won the game, he threw his arms in the air in excitement . . . At that moment, the subway doors opened to let people on and off the train. The problem is that the man threw his phone right out of the subway car and on to the tracks below. Oops! No more video games for a while!

A lot of people are so busy looking at their smartphones that they often walk into lampposts and hurt themselves. The problem is so big that Brick Lane in London is now a "safe text" zone. Every lamppost in the street is covered in soft padding just in case somebody walks into it.

Most of us use map apps on our phones to get to the places we want to go. But sometimes, these apps get a little confused. A demolition company (a company that tears down buildings) used a map app to find a house. So far so good, right? Well, no. The map led the workers to the wrong house, a house one block away from the correct house in a town in Texas. The workers tore the house down. Imagine the owner's reaction when she arrived back home later that day!

B Read the article. Which advice best summarizes the article?

1. London is a great place to visit if you like using cell phones.
2. Be careful when you use your cell phone.
3. Lampposts and water are extremely dangerous.

C Check the facts that are mentioned in the article.

☐ **1.** A woman on a subway fell into some water while she was using her phone.
☐ **2.** Many people have watched a video of a woman falling into water.
☐ **3.** A man on a subway lost his phone.
☐ **4.** The man on the subway didn't like the video game he was playing.
☐ **5.** London has an area where you can text more safely.
☐ **6.** Every lamppost in London is padded.
☐ **7.** A demolition company tore down someone's home.
☐ **8.** The torn down building was in Texas.

D **PAIR WORK** Have you ever had a cell phone "accident?" What happened? What advice about cell phone safety would you give to a child?

16 How have you changed?

- ▶ Describe life changes
- ▶ Describe plans for the future

1 SNAPSHOT

LIFE-CHANGING EXPERIENCES

Change schools

Move to a new house

Turn 18

Get a driver's license

Graduate from college

Get a job

Move to a new city

Travel abroad

Fall in love

Get married

Have children

Retire

Which of these events are the most important changes? Why?
What changes have you gone through in the last year? Which do you expect to happen soon?
What other things bring about change in our lives?

2 CONVERSATION I haven't seen you in ages.

▶ **A** Listen and practice.

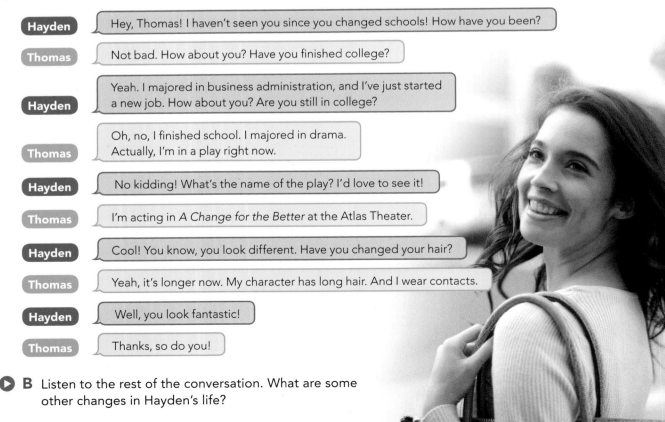

Hayden Hey, Thomas! I haven't seen you since you changed schools! How have you been?

Thomas Not bad. How about you? Have you finished college?

Hayden Yeah. I majored in business administration, and I've just started a new job. How about you? Are you still in college?

Thomas Oh, no, I finished school. I majored in drama. Actually, I'm in a play right now.

Hayden No kidding! What's the name of the play? I'd love to see it!

Thomas I'm acting in *A Change for the Better* at the Atlas Theater.

Hayden Cool! You know, you look different. Have you changed your hair?

Thomas Yeah, it's longer now. My character has long hair. And I wear contacts.

Hayden Well, you look fantastic!

Thomas Thanks, so do you!

▶ **B** Listen to the rest of the conversation. What are some other changes in Hayden's life?

3 GRAMMAR FOCUS

Describing changes

With the present tense

I'm **not** in school anymore.

I **wear** contacts now.

With the past tense

I **majored** in business administration.

I **got** engaged.

With the present perfect

I'**ve** just **started** a new job.

I'**ve bought** a new apartment.

With the comparative

It's **less noisy** than downtown.

My hair is **longer** now.

GRAMMAR PLUS *see page 147*

A How have you changed in the last five years? Check (✓) the statements that are true for you. If a statement isn't true, give the correct information.

- [ ] **1.** I dress differently now.
- [ ] **2.** I've changed my hairstyle.
- [ ] **3.** I've made some new friends.
- [ ] **4.** I got a pet.
- [ ] **5.** I've joined a gym.
- [ ] **6.** I moved into my own apartment.
- [ ] **7.** I'm more outgoing than before.
- [ ] **8.** I'm not in high school anymore.
- [ ] **9.** My life is easier now.
- [ ] **10.** I got married.

B **PAIR WORK** Compare your responses in part A. Have you changed in similar ways?

C **GROUP WORK** Write five sentences describing other changes in your life. Then compare in groups. Who in the group has changed the most?

4 LISTENING Online photo albums

Madison and Zachary are looking through online photo albums. Listen to their conversation. How have they changed? Write down three changes.

Changes
_____
_____
_____

5 WORD POWER Changes

A Complete the word map with phrases from the list. Then add two more examples to each category.

dye my hair
get a bank loan
get a credit card
get a pay raise
grow a beard
improve my English vocabulary
learn a new sport
learn how to dance
open a savings account
pierce my ears
start a new online course
wear contact lenses

APPEARANCE
_____
_____
_____
_____
_____

MONEY
_____
_____
_____
_____

CHANGES

SKILLS
_____
_____
_____
_____
_____
_____

B **PAIR WORK** Have you changed in any of these areas? Tell your partner about a change in each category.

A: I started an Italian cooking class last month. I've always loved Italian food.

B: I've improved my English vocabulary a lot. I always watch movies with English subtitles now.

6 CONVERSATION Planning your future

A Listen and practice.

Matt: So, what are you going to do this year? Any New Year's resolutions?

Robin: Well, I'd love to learn how to play the guitar, so I plan to take lessons.

Matt: That sounds great. I don't have any musical talents, but I'd like to learn how to dance. Maybe I can learn to salsa!

Robin: Why not? I hope to learn to play some Latin music, too.

Matt: I know! We can take a trip to Puerto Rico and spend a month learning guitar and dancing. How about that?

Robin: Uh . . . Matt? I don't have any money. Do you?

Matt: I don't either, but I hope to get a new job soon.

Robin: Have you started looking?

Matt: Not yet, but I plan to start right after the holidays.

B Listen to the rest of the conversation. What kind of job does Matt want? What other plans does Robin have for the new year?

7 GRAMMAR FOCUS

▶ Verb + infinitive

What **are** you **going to do** this year?

I**'m** (not) **going to take** a trip to the Caribbean.
I (don't) **plan to take** guitar lessons.
I (don't) **want to learn** to dance.

I **hope to get** a new job.
I**'d like to travel** around the United States.
I**'d love to play** the guitar.

GRAMMAR PLUS *see page 147*

A Complete these statements so that they are true for you. Use verb + infinitive as shown in the grammar box. Then add two more statements of your own.

1. I _____ travel abroad.
2. I _____ live with my parents.
3. I _____ get married.
4. I _____ have a lot of children.
5. I _____ make a lot of money!
6. I _____ become famous.
7. I _____ buy a sports car.
8. I _____ learn another language.
9. _____
10. _____

B PAIR WORK Compare your responses with a partner. How are you the same? How are you different?

C GROUP WORK What are your plans for the future? Take turns asking and answering these questions.

What are you going to do after this English class is over?
Do you plan to study English again next year?
What other languages would you like to learn?
What countries would you like to visit? Why?
Do you want to get a (new) job in a few years?
What other changes do you hope to make in your life? Why?

8 PRONUNCIATION Vowel sounds /oʊ/ and /ʌ/

▶ **A** Many words spelled with *o* are pronounced /oʊ/ or /ʌ/. Listen to the difference and practice.

/oʊ/ = don't	smoke	go	loan	own	hope
/ʌ/ = month	love	some	does	young	touch

▶ **B** Listen to these words. Check (✓) the correct pronunciation.

	both	cold	come	home	honey	money	mother	over
/oʊ/	☐	☐	☐	☐	☐	☐	☐	☐
/ʌ/	☐	☐	☐	☐	☐	☐	☐	☐

9 INTERCHANGE 16 Our possible future

Imagine you could do anything, go anywhere, and meet anybody.
Go to Interchange 16 on page 131.

10 SPEAKING An English course abroad

A GROUP WORK You want to take an English course abroad
in an English-speaking country. Groups get special
discounts, so your whole group has to agree on a trip.
Talk about these details and take notes on your
group's decisions.

> 1. Where you'd like to study (choose an English-
>   speaking country and city)
> 2. When you'd like to travel (choose month of the year)
> 3. How long you want to stay there
> 4. Where you'd like to stay (choose one): a family home,
>   a dorm, a hostel, an apartment, a hotel
> 5. Courses you plan to take (choose two):
>   grammar, writing, pronunciation, conversation,
>   business English
> 6. Tourist places you hope to see

A: Where would you like to study?
B: How about Australia?
C: Australia is great, but it's going to be too expensive.
I'd love to go to London. I've never been there.
D: When do you want to go? I think May and June are
the best months.

B CLASS ACTIVITY Present your ideas to the class. If the whole class agrees on one trip,
you can get a bigger discount.

11 WRITING Travel plans

A GROUP WORK Work with the same group from Exercise 10. As a group,
write to your teacher about your plans for the class trip abroad.

Dear . . .
Our group has decided to spend three weeks studying English in London. We are going in May
because the weather is nice and things are a little less expensive. We all want to take conversation
and pronunciation courses, so that was an easy decision. We plan to share an apartment there, but
we haven't found a good one yet. We really hope to visit the British Museum and see Big Ben and
Buckingham Palace. We'd love to . . .

B PAIR WORK Get together with a student from another group and read
each other's messages. Do you have similar plans?

A Read the article. What is it about? Check (✓) the correct answer.

☐ Students in the Netherlands ☐ An important invention ☐ Vacations near the ocean

A Goal Accomplished

Boyan Slat has one huge goal. It's a goal that could benefit people and animals all over the world. Amazingly, it looks like he's going to accomplish it.

When he was 16, Dutch engineering student Boyan Slat was on vacation in Greece, and he started to think about all the garbage that gets washed up on beaches. The oceans around the world are full of plastic – millions of tons of plastic. Unfortunately, plastic doesn't just disappear. It takes centuries to break down. Slat wanted to do something to change all that. So he made it a personal goal to clean up the garbage in the world's oceans.

Slat started with an idea for an extraordinary machine to "catch" the plastic floating in the water using the natural energy of the ocean. He left school in 2013 to begin work on his project, which he called The Ocean Cleanup.

A year later, he was leading a team of 100 scientists and engineers working on the invention. Slat needed money for this, so he started asking people to donate to his project online and raised over $2 million!

Soon after, Slat was named a "Champion of the Earth" by the United Nations. It's the most important title the UN gives to people helping the environment. The Ocean Cleanup also won several awards for having one of the best inventions of 2015. But the dream goes on for Boyan Slat. He hopes that the oceans will be free of plastic in about twenty or thirty years.

B Who do you think this article was written for? Choose (✓) the correct answer.

☐ People who care about the environment
☐ College students who want to be inventors
☐ People on vacation who hate garbage

C Read the article and answer the questions.

1. Where was Boyan Slat when he had his big idea?
2. Why did Slat leave school?
3. What is the problem with plastic?
4. How did Slat get the money for his project?
5. When does Slat hope the oceans will be clean?

D **GROUP WORK** Have you had a personal goal that you achieved? Or do you know someone who achieved an amazing personal goal? What was the goal?

SELF-ASSESSMENT

How well can you do these things? Check (✓) the boxes.

I can . . .	Very well	OK	A little
Discuss future plans and arrangements (Ex. 1)	☐	☐	☐
Make and respond to invitations (Ex. 2)	☐	☐	☐
Understand and pass on telephone messages (Ex. 3)	☐	☐	☐
Ask and answer questions about changes in my life (Ex. 4)	☐	☐	☐
Describe personal goals (Ex. 5)	☐	☐	☐
Discuss and decide how to accomplish goals (Ex. 5)	☐	☐	☐

1 DISCUSSION The weekend

A GROUP WORK Find out what your classmates are doing this weekend.
Ask for details about each person's plans.

Name	Plans	Details

A: What are you going to do this weekend?
B: I'm watching a soccer game on Sunday.
C: Who's playing?

B GROUP WORK Whose weekend plans sound the best? Why?

2 ROLE PLAY Inviting a friend

Student A: Invite Student B to one of the
events from Exercise 1. Say where
and when it is.

Student B: Student A invites you out. Accept
and ask for more information, or
refuse and give an excuse.

Change roles and try the role play again.

3 LISTENING Matthew isn't here.

▶ Listen to the phone conversations. Write down the messages.

1

Message for: _____

Caller: _____

Message: _____

_____

_____

2

Message for: _____

Caller: _____

Message: _____

_____

_____

4 SURVEY Changes

A CLASS ACTIVITY Go around the class and find this information.
Write a classmate's name only once. Ask follow-up questions.

Find someone who . . .	Name
1. doesn't wear glasses anymore	
2. goes out more often these days	
3. got his or her hair cut last month	
4. got married last year	
5. has changed schools recently	
6. has gotten a part-time job recently	
7. has started a new hobby	
8. is happier these days	

B CLASS ACTIVITY Compare your information.
Who in the class has changed the most?

5 SPEAKING Setting goals

Check (✓) the goals you have and add two more. Then choose one goal.
Plan how to accomplish it with a partner.

- ☐ get into a good school
- ☐ have more free time
- ☐ have more friends
- ☐ move to a new city
- ☐ own my own apartment
- ☐ travel a lot more
- ☐ live a long time
- ☐ _____
- ☐ _____

A: I'd like to have more free time.
B: How are you going to do that?

WHAT'S NEXT?

Look at your Self-assessment again. Do you need to review anything?

Interchange activities

INTERCHANGE 1 Getting to know you

A CLASS ACTIVITY Add one more question to the chart. Go around
the class and interview three classmates. Complete the chart.

	Classmate 1	Classmate 2	Classmate 3
What's your first name?			
What's your last name?			
What city are you from?			
When's your birthday?			
What's your favorite color?			
What are your hobbies?			
_____			

B GROUP WORK Compare your information. Then discuss these questions.

Who . . . ?

has a long first name   has the next birthday
has a long last name   likes orange or brown
is not from a big city   has an interesting hobby

A CLASS ACTIVITY Add one more question to the chart. Answer these questions about yourself. Then interview two classmates. Write their names and the times they do each thing.

What time do you . . . ?	Me	Name _____	Name _____
get up during the week			
get up on weekends			
have breakfast			
leave for school or work			
get home during the week			
have dinner			
go to bed during the week			
_____			

B PAIR WORK Whose schedule is similar to yours? Tell your partner.

A: Amir and I have similar schedules. We both get up at 7:00 and have breakfast at 7:30.

B: I leave for work at 7:30, but Nikki leaves for school at . . .

---

useful expressions

We both . . . at . . .

We . . . at different times.

My schedule is different from my two classmates' schedules.

STUDENT A

A You want to sell these things. Write your "asking price" for each item.

TABLET

asking price: _____

sold for: _____

HEADPHONES

asking price: _____

sold for: _____

ARMCHAIR

asking price: _____

sold for: _____

SKATEBOARD

asking price: _____

sold for: _____

STUDENT B

A You want to sell these things. Write your "asking price" for each item.

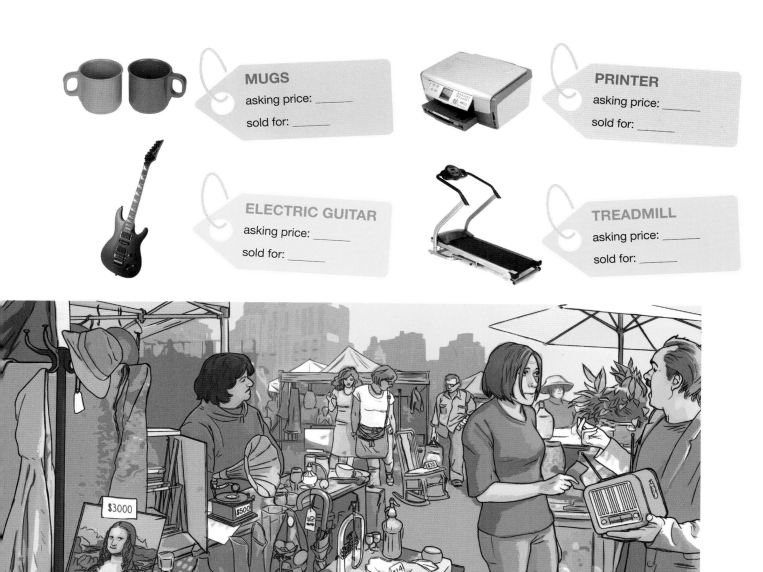

MUGS

asking price: _____

sold for: _____

PRINTER

asking price: _____

sold for: _____

ELECTRIC GUITAR

asking price: _____

sold for: _____

TREADMILL

asking price: _____

sold for: _____

STUDENTS A AND B

B PAIR WORK Now choose three things you want to buy. Get the best price for each one. Then write what each item "sold for" on the price tag.

A: How much is the tablet computer?
B: It's only $70.
A: Wow! That's expensive!
B: Well, how about $35?
A: No. That's still too much. I'll give you $30 for it.
B: Sold! It's yours.

C GROUP WORK Compare your earnings in groups. Who made the most money at the flea market?

go bike riding

go to a street fair

go dancing

do the laundry

clean the house

A Write three things you need to do and three things you want to do this weekend. Include the days of the week and the times.

I need to . . .	I want to . . .

B **PAIR WORK** Invite your partner to do things on the weekend. Accept or decline invitations. If you decline an invitation, explain why. Agree on two activities to do together.

A: Would you like to see a movie on Saturday at 8:00 P.M.?

B: I'd like to, but I need to study for a test. Would you like to go to the park on Sunday at 10:00 A.M.?

A: Yes, I would. And would you like to . . . ?

C **GROUP WORK** Get together with another pair. Can you agree on two things to do together?

D **CLASS WORK** Explain your group's choices to the class.
"Eu-jin wanted to go to the park on Sunday at 10 A.M., but Serhat needs to visit his aunt on Sunday morning, so we're going out for lunch on Sunday at . . ."

CLASS ACTIVITY Go around the class telling your classmates three activities that members of your family are doing these days. Two activities have to be true, but one needs to be false! Can your classmates guess which activity is false with only two questions?

learning a foreign language

raising a child

renovating the house

working in another country

writing a blog

your ideas

learning to drive

going to college

traveling around the world

playing in a band

playing on a team

A: My brother is working in Berlin and his wife is studying German there. My niece is learning three languages at school: German, English, and Spanish.

B: Is your brother really working in Berlin?

A: Yes, he is.

B: Is your niece really learning Spanish?

A: No, she's not! She's learning German and English, but she isn't learning Spanish.

A CLASS ACTIVITY Add two items to the chart. Does anyone in your class do these things? How often and how well? Go around the class and find one person for each activity.

	Name	How often?	How well?
bake cookies			
cook			
cut hair			
do card tricks			
fix things			
play an instrument			
sing			
do yoga			

A: Do you bake cookies?
B: Yes, I do.
A: How often do you bake cookies?
B: Once a month.
A: Really? And how well do you bake?

B GROUP WORK Imagine there's a fundraiser to buy new books for the school library this weekend. Who do you think can help? Choose three people from your class. Explain your choices.

A: Let's ask Lydia to help with the fundraiser.
B: Why Lydia?
A: Because she bakes cookies very well.
C: Yes, she really does. And Mariana is very good at fixing things. Let's ask her, too!

INTERCHANGE 7 Memories

GROUP WORK Play the board game. Follow these instructions.

1. Write your initials on small pieces of paper. These are your game pieces.
2. Take turns by tossing a coin: If the coin lands face up, move two spaces.
   If the coin lands face down, move one space.
3. When you land on a space, answer the question. Answer any follow-up questions.
4. If you land on "Free question," another player asks you any question.

A: I'll go first. OK, one space. Last night, I met my best friend.
B: Oh, yeah? Where did you go?
A: We went to the movies.

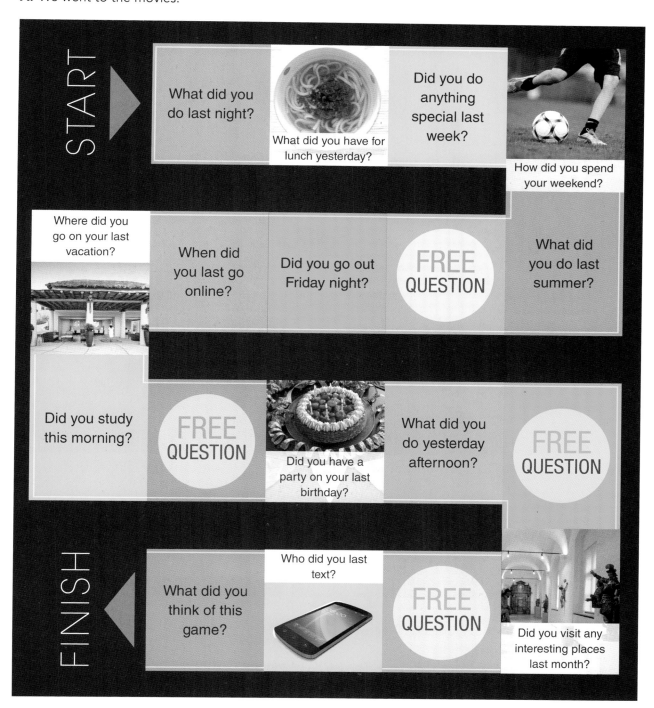

CLASS ACTIVITY Play a guessing game. Follow these instructions.

1. Get into two teams, A and B.
2. Each team chooses one of the locations below. Keep it a secret!
3. Each team chooses a teammate to guess the other team's location. He or she is the guesser.
4. Show your location to all the students on the other team, except their guesser.
5. Take turns giving your guessers one clue at a time until they guess the location. Use *There is/ There are* plus a quantifier. You cannot give more than 10 clues. Your team can get 1 to 10 points, depending on how many clues you need to give your guesser (1 clue = 1 point) before he or she guesses the right location. Remember: you don't want to get many points!
6. At the end of the game, the team with fewer points wins.

an airport | a bank | a bookstore | a café

a clothing store | a drugstore | a grocery store | a gym

a hair salon | a hospital | a movie theater | a newstand

an outdoor market | a park | a shopping mall | a stadium

A: There is a lot of food here. Where are we?
B: You're in a grocery store.
C: No. There aren't any walls here. This isn't a building.
B: You're at an outdoor market!
A: Correct! We're at an outdoor market.

STUDENT A

A PAIR WORK How many differences can you find between your picture here and your partner's picture? Ask questions like these to find the differences.

How many people are standing / sitting / wearing . . . / holding a drink? Who?
What color is . . . 's T-shirt / sweater / hair?
Does . . . wear glasses / have a beard / have long hair?
What does . . . look like?

Picture 1

Leon

Elliott

Daniel

Joanna

Isla

Megan

B CLASS ACTIVITY How many differences are there in the pictures?
"In picture 1, Daniel's T-shirt is . . . In picture 2, it's . . ."

STUDENT B

A PAIR WORK How many differences can you find between your picture here and your partner's picture? Ask questions like these to find the differences.

How many people are standing / sitting / wearing . . . / holding a drink? Who?

What color is . . .'s T-shirt / sweater / hair?

Does . . . wear glasses / have a beard / have long hair?

What does . . . look like?

B CLASS ACTIVITY How many differences are there in the pictures?

"In picture 1, Daniel's shirt is . . . In picture 2, it's . . ."

A PAIR WORK How much fun does your partner have? Interview him or her. Write the number of points using this scale.

never = 1 point
1–3 times = 2 points

4–7 times = 3 points
8 or more times = 4 points

SURVEY

HOW MANY TIMES HAVE YOU . . .	POINTS
1. watched a really good movie or TV show in the last two months?	_____
2. listened to your favorite kind of music in the last week?	_____
3. talked to your best friend in the last two weeks?	_____
4. read something interesting that wasn't for work or school in the last month?	_____
5. eaten your favorite foods in the last three weeks?	_____
6. had a really fun weekend in the last three months?	_____
7. spent at least one hour doing something you like in the last three days?	_____
8. taken a relaxing vacation in the last year?	_____
9. had a good laugh in the last 24 hours?	_____
10. told yourself "This is fun!" in the last 12 hours?	_____

B GROUP WORK Add up your partner's points. Tell the group how much fun your partner has and why.

10–19 = You don't have enough fun. You should try to do things you enjoy more often! Stop and smell the roses!

20–29 = You have fun sometimes, but you need to do it more often. Continue to take time to do the things that you like.

30–40 = You know how to have fun! You know how to have a good time and enjoy life. Keep it up!

"Ellen has fun sometimes. She watches her favorite TV show once a week and takes a vacation twice a year. But she never reads anything she really likes – only the things she has to read for school."

C CLASS ACTIVITY Do you think your partner needs to have more fun? In what way?

"I think Ellen needs to have more fun in her life. She needs to spend more time doing things she likes. And she needs to eat her favorite foods more often. She also . . ."

A PAIR WORK You want to attract more visitors to your city or town. Complete the sentences below and add one more sentence to write a guide for tourists.

WELCOME TO OUR CITY!

LOGIN / REGISTER

It's a really _____ place and you will find _____ to do here.

The weather is _____ and the best times of the year to visit are _____ and _____.

You can _____, _____, and _____, and you shouldn't miss the famous _____!

Don't forget to try our local food! _____ can be a little expensive, though, but you can have a good meal for a reasonable price at _____.

Also, _____.

Enjoy your stay and come back soon!

B CLASS ACTIVITY Read your guide to the class. Ask follow-up questions to learn more.

What is the first place you should visit?

What is an exciting place to have fun on a Saturday night?

What is a relaxing place to visit on a Sunday morning?

What is a quiet place to study or do some work?

What is a really beautiful area that you shouldn't miss?

What is a dangerous area that you should avoid?

What places are usually too crowded?

Where can you exercise outdoors?

What fun things can you do for free?

Where's a popular place to meet?

C CLASS ACTIVITY Which are your two favorite guides? Which details did you find especially interesting about them?

A **GROUP WORK** Play the board game. Follow these instructions.

1. Write your initials on small pieces of paper. These are your game pieces.
2. Take turns by tossing a coin: If the coin lands face up, move two spaces. If the coin lands face down, move one space.
3. When you land on a space, ask two others in your group for advice.
4. The first person to cross the finish line is the winner.

A: I have the hiccups, Hiroto. What should I do?
B: Well, it's sometimes useful to hold your breath.
A: Thanks. What about you, Erica? What's your advice?
C: You should drink some water. That always works for me.

useful expressions
You should . . .
You could . . .
It's a good idea to . . .
It's important to . . .
I think it's useful to . . .

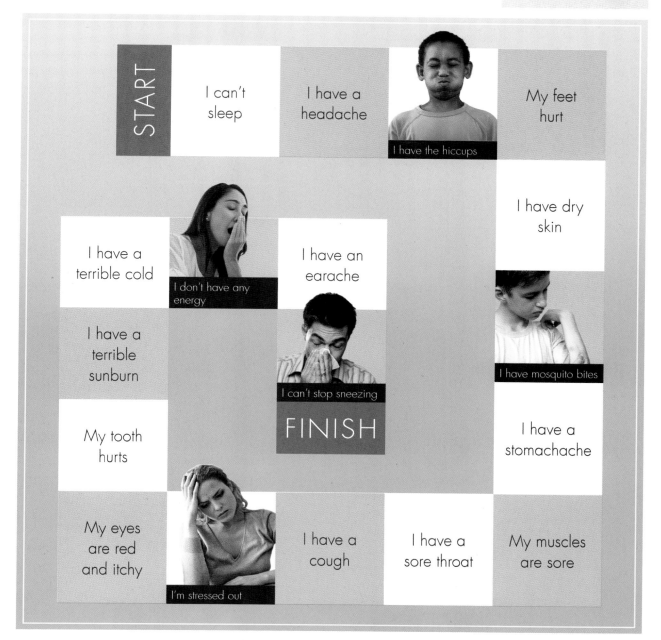

B **CLASS ACTIVITY** Who gave the best advice in your group? Tell the class.

INTERCHANGE 13 Planning a food festival

A PAIR WORK Imagine your class is organizing a food festival with different food trucks. You and your classmate are responsible for one of the trucks. Choose a name for your truck. Write it at the top of the menu. Then, write the food and drinks you'd like to sell at your truck. Then write the prices.

B GROUP WORK Trade your menus with another pair. Order food and drinks from their menu, and then leave some suggestions about the menu on the message board.

____

(write the name of your food truck here)

FOOD	PRICE

DRINKS	PRICE

CUSTOMERS' SUGGESTIONS

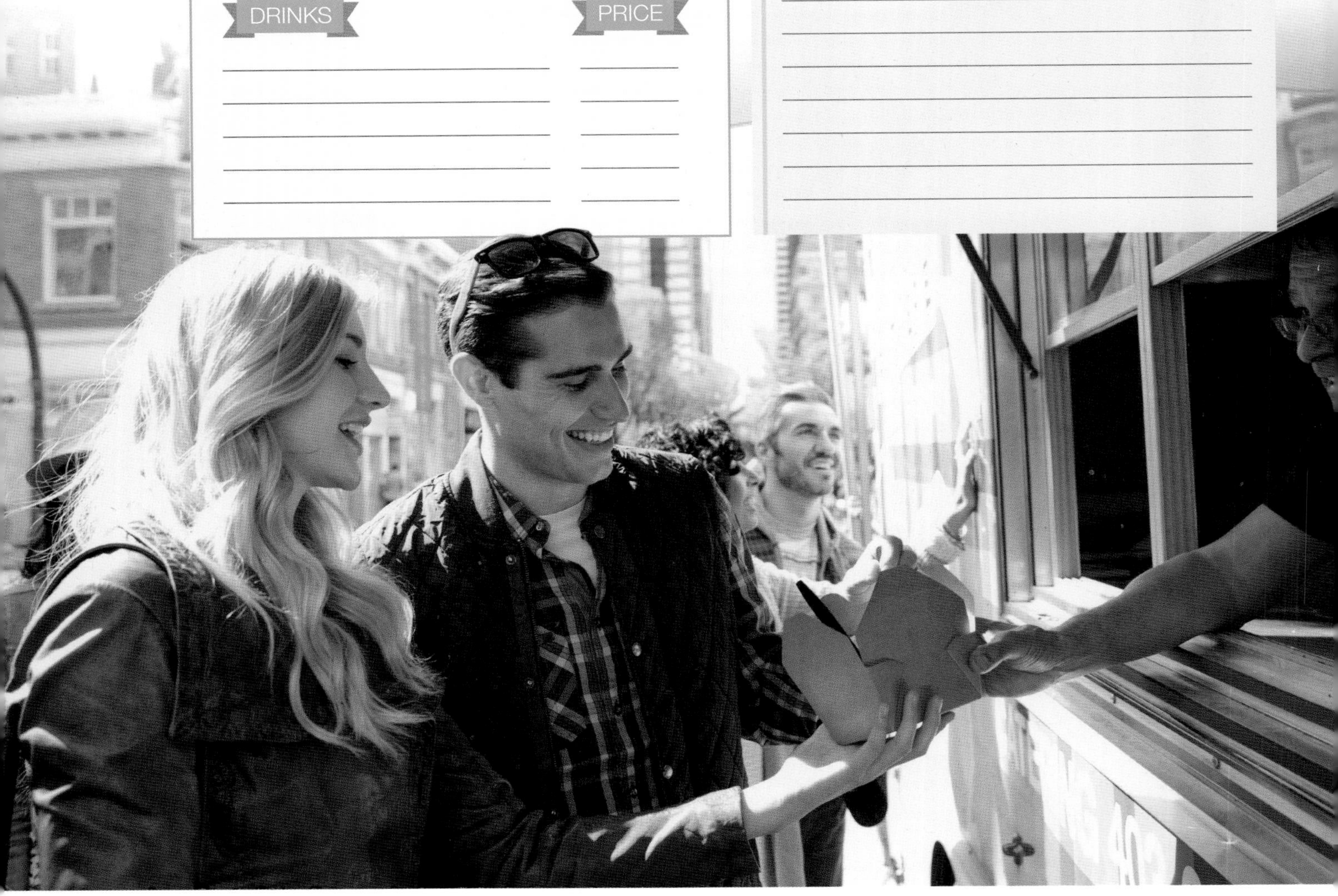

A **PAIR WORK** Take turns asking and answering these questions. Check (✓) the answer you think is correct for each question. Then write two more questions and answers.

World Knowledge Quiz

1. Which place is the wettest?	☐ Kaua'i, Hawai'i	☐ Manaus, Brazil	☐ Emei Shan, China
2. Which country is the hottest?	☐ Algeria	☐ Libya	☐ Somalia
3. Which country is closest to the equator?	☐ Colombia	☐ India	☐ Malaysia
4. Which animal is the biggest?	☐ a bison	☐ an elephant	☐ a blue whale
5. Which animal lives the longest?	☐ an elephant	☐ a tortoise	☐ a green iguana
6. Which mountain range is the longest?	☐ the Andes	☐ the Himalayas	☐ the Rockies
7. Which planet is the smallest?	☐ Earth	☐ Mercury	☐ Venus
8. Which planet is the largest?	☐ Jupiter	☐ Neptune	☐ Saturn
9. Which city is the oldest?	☐ Beijing, China	☐ Luxor, Egypt	☐ Rome, Italy
10. Which metal is the heaviest?	☐ aluminum	☐ gold	☐ silver
11. _____	_____	_____	_____
12. _____	_____	_____	_____

Manaus, Brazil

Emei Shan, China

Kaua'i, Hawai'i

1. Kaua'i, Hawai'i   6. the Andes
2. Lybia   7. Mercury
3. Colombia   8. Jupiter
4. a blue whale   9. Luxor, Egypt
5. a tortoise   10. gold

B **PAIR WORK** Check your answers. You and your partner get a point for every correct answer.

C **CLASS ACTIVITY** Ask your classmates your two questions. Get a point for every question nobody can answer correctly.

CLASS ACTIVITY What are your classmates' plans for the weekend? Add two activities to the list. Then go around the class and find people who are going to do these things. For each question, ask for more information and take notes.

Find someone who's going to . . .	Name	Notes
go to a party		
go out of town		
go shopping		
see a live performance		
see/watch a movie		
see/watch a game		
meet friends		
visit relatives		
clean the house		
study for a test		

A: Samira, are you going to a party this weekend?

B: Yes, I am.

A: Where is the party going to be?

B: At my friend Lila's place. She's having a party to celebrate her birthday.

A PAIR WORK Talk with your partner and complete this chart with two ideas for each question – your idea and your partner's idea.

What is . . .	You	Your partner
something you plan to do next year?		
something you aren't going to do next year?		
something you hope to buy in the next year?		
something you would like to change about yourself?		
something you would like to learn?		
a place you would like to visit someday?		
a city you would like to live in someday?		
a job you would like to have?		
a goal you hope to achieve?		

A: What is something you plan to do next year?
B: Well, I'm going to travel to Morocco.
A: Oh, really? Where in Morocco?
B: I'm not sure yet! What about you?
　　What do you plan to do next year?

A: I'd like to get my own place.
B: Oh, really? Are you planning to rent an apartment?
A: No, actually I'm going to buy one.
B: Good for you!

B GROUP ACTIVITY Compare your information with another pair. Explain your goals and plans.

A: What are two things you plan to do next year?
B: Well, I'm going to visit Morocco, and Helena is going to get her own place.
C: That's right. I'm going to buy a small apartment. And you?
A: Well, I . . .

Grammar plus

1 Statements with *be*; possessive adjectives `page 3`

> ■ Don't confuse contractions of *be* with possessive adjectives: **You're** a student. **Your** class is English 1. (NOT: ~~You're class is English 1.~~) **He's** my classmate. **His** name is Ricardo. (NOT: ~~He's name is Ricardo.~~)

Choose the correct words.

1. This **is** / **are** Dulce Castelo. **She's** / **Her** a new student from Santo Domingo.
2. My name **am** / **is** Sergio. **I'm** / **He's** from Brazil.
3. My brother and I **is** / **are** students here. **Our** / **We're** names are Nate and Chad.
4. **He's** / **His** Kento. **He's** / **His** 19 years old.
5. **They're** / **Their** in my English class. **It's** / **Its** a big class.

2 Wh-questions with *be* `page 4`

> ■ Use *What* to ask about things: **What's** in your bag? Use *Where* to ask about places: **Where's** your friend from? Use *Who* to ask about people: **Who's** your teacher? Use *What . . . like?* to ask for a description: **What's** your friend **like**?

Match the questions with the answers.

1. Who's that? ___f___
2. Where's your teacher? _____
3. What are your friends like? _____
4. Where's she from? _____
5. Who are they? _____
6. What's his name? _____

a. They're really nice.
b. She's from South Korea.
c. They're my brother and sister.
d. His name is Daniel.
e. He's in class.
f. That's our new classmate.

3 Yes/No questions and short answers with *be* `page 5`

> ■ Use short answers to answer yes/no questions. Don't use contractions with short answers with Yes: **Are you** from Mexico? Yes, **I am**. (NOT: ~~Yes, I'm.~~)

Complete the conversations.

1. **A:** ___Are they___ in your class?
    B: No, _____. They're in English 2.
2. **A:** Hi! _____ in this class?
    B: Yes, _____. I'm a new student here.
3. **A:** _____ from the United States?
    B: No, _____. We're from Calgary, Canada.
4. **A:** Hi, Monica. _____ free?
    B: No, _____. I'm on my way to class.
5. **A:** That's the new student. _____ from Paraguay?
    B: No, _____. He's from Uruguay.
6. **A:** _____ from Indonesia?
    B: Yes, _____. She's from Jakarta.

1 Simple present Wh-questions and statements page 10

Statements

- Verbs with *he/she/it* end in –s: He/She **walks** to school. BUT I/You/We/They **walk** to school.
- *Have*, *go*, and *do* are irregular with *he/she/it*: She **has** a class at 1:00. He **goes** to school at night. She **does** her homework before school.

Wh-questions

- Use *does* in questions with *he/she/it* and *do* with all the others: Where does he/she/it live? Where do I/you/we/they live?
- Don't add –s to the verb: Where does she **live**? (NOT: ~~Where does she lives~~?)

Complete the conversations with the correct form of the verbs in parentheses.

1. A: I _____have_____ (have) good news! Mona _____ (have) a new job.
   B: How _____ she _____ (like) it?
   A: She _____ (love) it. The hours are great.
   B: What time _____ she _____ (start)?
   A: She _____ (start) at ten and _____ (finish) at four.
2. A: What _____ you _____ (do)?
   B: I'm a teacher.
   A: What _____ you _____ (teach)?
   B: I _____ (teach) Spanish and English.
   A: Really? My sister _____ (teach) English, too.

2 Time expressions page 12

- Use *in* with *the morning/afternoon/evening.* Use *at* with *night*: He goes to school **in** the afternoon and works **at** night. BUT: **on** Friday night.
- Use *at* with clock times: She gets up **at** 7:00.
- Use *on* with days: He gets up early **on** weekdays. She has class **on** Mondays.

Complete the conversation with time expressions from the box.
You can use some words more than once.

| at | early | in | on | until |

A: How's your new job?
B: I love it, but the hours are difficult. I start work _____ 6:30 A.M., and I work _____ 3:30.
A: That's interesting! I work the same hours, but I work _____ night. I start _____ 6:30 _____ the evening and finish _____ 3:30 _____ the morning.
B: Wow! What time do you get up?
A: Well, I get home _____ 4:30 and go to bed _____ 5:30. And I sleep _____ 2:00. But I only work _____ weekends, so it's OK. What about you?
B: Oh, I work _____ Monday, Wednesday, and Friday. And I get up _____ – around 5:00 A.M.

1 Demonstratives; *one, ones* page 17

■ With singular nouns, use *this* for a thing that is nearby and *that* for a thing that is not nearby: How much is **this** hat here? How much is **that** hat over there?

■ With plural nouns, use *these* for things that are nearby and *those* for things that are not nearby: How much are **these** earrings here? How much are **those** earrings over there?

■ Use *one* to replace a singular noun: I like the red hat. I like the red **one**. Use *ones* to replace plural nouns: I like the green bags. I like the green **ones**.

Choose the correct words.

1. **A:** Excuse me. How much are **this** /**these** shoes?
   B: **It's / They're** $279.
   A: And how much is **this / that** bag over there?
   B: **It's / They're** only $129.
   A: And are the two gray **one / ones** $129, too?
   B: No. **That / Those** are only $119.
   A: Oh! **This / That** store is really expensive.

2. **A:** Can I help you?
   B: Yes, please. I really like **these / those** jeans over there. How much **is it / are they**?
   A: Which **one / ones**? Do you mean **this / these**?
   B: No, the black **one / ones**.
   A: Let me look. Oh, **it's / they're** $35.99.
   B: That's not bad. And how much is **this / that** sweater here?
   A: **It's / They're** only $9.99.

2 Preferences; comparisons with adjectives page 20

■ For adjectives with one syllable or adjectives of two syllables ending in –y, add –er to form the comparative:
cheap → cheaper; nice → nicer; big → bigger, pretty → prettier.

■ For adjectives with two syllables not ending in –y or adjectives of three or more syllables, use *more* + adjective to form the comparative: stylish → more stylish, expensive → more expensive.

A Write the comparatives of these adjectives.

1. attractive   _more attractive_
2. happy   _____
3. exciting   _____
4. friendly   _____

5. interesting   _____
6. reasonable   _____
7. sad   _____
8. warm   _____

B Answer the questions. Use the first word in the parentheses in your answer.
Then write another sentence with the second word.

1. Which pants do you prefer, the cotton ones or the wool ones? (wool / attractive)
   I prefer the wool ones. They're more attractive than the cotton ones.

2. Which ring do you like better, the gold one or the silver one? (silver / interesting)
   _____

3. Which one do you prefer, the silk blouse or the cotton blouse? (silk / pretty)
   _____

4. Which ones do you like more, the black shoes or the purple ones? (purple / cheap)
   _____

1 Simple present questions; short answers page 23

- Use *do* + base form for yes/no questions and short answers with *I/you/we/they*: **Do** I/you/we/they **like** rock? Yes, I/you/we/they **do**. No, I/you/we/they **don't**.
- Use *does* in yes/no questions and short answers with *he/she/it*: **Does** he/she **like** rock? Yes, he/she **does**. No, he/she **doesn't**.
- Use *don't* and *doesn't* + base form for negative statements: I **don't** like horror movies. He **doesn't like** action movies.
- Remember: Don't add *–s* to the base form: Does she **like** rock? (NOT: ~~Does she likes rock?~~)
- Subject pronouns (*I, you, he, she, it, we, they*) usually come before a verb. Object pronouns (*me, you, him, her, it, us, them*) usually come after a verb: He likes **her**, but she doesn't like **him**.

A Complete the questions and short answers.

1. A: _Do you play_ (play) a musical instrument?
B: Yes, _I do_____. I play the guitar.

2. A: _____ (like) Carrie Underwood?
B: No, _____. John doesn't like country music.

3. A: _____ (like) talk shows?
B: Yes, _____. Lisa is a big fan of them.

4. A: _____ (watch) the news on TV?
B: Yes, _____. Kevin and I watch the news every night.

5. A: _____ (like) hip-hop?
B: No, _____. But I love R&B.

6. A: _____ (listen to) jazz?
B: No, _____. But my parents listen to a lot of classical music.

B Complete the sentences with object pronouns.

1. We don't listen to hip-hop because we really don't like ___it___.

2. We love your voice. Please sing for _____.

3. These sunglasses are great. Do you like _____?

4. Who is that man? Do you know _____?

5. Beth looks great in green. It's a really good color for _____.

2 *Would; verb + to + verb* page 26

- Don't use a contraction in affirmative short answers with *would*: **Would** you **like to go to** the game? Yes, I **would**. (NOT: ~~Yes, I'd.~~)

Unscramble the questions and answers to complete the conversation.

A: tonight   to see   would you like   with me   a movie

_____?

B: I would.   yes,   what   to see   would you like

_____?

A: the new Matt Damon movie   to see   I'd like

_____.

B: OK. That's a great idea!

1 Present continuous page 32

> ■ Use the present continuous to talk about actions that are happening now: What **are** you **doing (these days)**? I**'m studying** English.
> ■ The present continuous is present of *be* + *–ing*. For verbs ending in *e*, drop the *e* and add *–ing*: have → having, live → living.
> ■ For verbs ending in vowel + consonant, double the consonant and add *–ing*: sit → sitting.

Write questions with the words in parentheses and the present continuous.
Then complete the responses with short answers or the verbs in the box.

| live   study   take   ✓ teach   work |

1. **A:** (what / your sister / do / these days) <u>What's your sister doing these days?</u>
   B: <u>She's teaching</u> English.
   A: Really? (she / live / abroad) _____
   B: Yes, _____. She _____ in South Korea.
2. **A:** (how / you / spend / your summer) _____
   B: I _____ part-time. I _____ two classes also.
   A: (what / you / take) _____
   B: My friend and I _____ photography and Japanese. We like our classes a lot.

2 Quantifiers page 34

> ■ Use *a lot of, all, few, nearly all* before plural nouns: **A lot of/All/Few/Nearly all** families are small. Use *no one* before a verb: **No one** gets married before the age of 18.
> ■ *Nearly all* means "almost all."

Read the sentences about the small town of Monroe. Rewrite the sentences using the quantifiers in the box. Use each quantifier only once.

| a lot of   all   few   nearly all   ✓ no one |

1. In Monroe, 0% of the people drive before the age of 16.
   <u>In Monroe, no one drives before the age of 16.</u>
2. Ninety-eight percent of students finish high school.
   _____
3. One hundred percent of children start school by the age of six.
   _____
4. Eighty-nine percent of couples have more than one child.
   _____
5. Five percent of families have more than four children.
   _____

1 Adverbs of frequency page 37

- Adverbs of frequency (*always, almost always, usually, often, sometimes, hardly ever, almost never, never*) usually come before the main verb: She **never plays** tennis. I **almost always eat** breakfast. BUT Adverbs of frequency usually come after the verb *be*: I**'m always** late.

- *Usually* and *sometimes* can begin a sentence: **Usually** I walk to work. **Sometimes** I exercise in the morning.

- Some frequency expressions usually come at the end of a sentence: *every day, once a week, twice a month, three times a year*: Do you exercise **every day**? I exercise **three times a week**.

Put the words in order to make questions. Then complete the answers with the words in parentheses.

1. you   what   weekends   usually   do   do   on
   Q: _What do you usually do on weekends?_
   A: I _____ (often / play sports)

2. ever   you   go jogging   do   with a friend
   Q: _____
   A: No, _____ (always / alone)

3. you   play   do   basketball   how often
   Q: _____
   A: I _____ (four times a week)

4. do you   what   in the evening   usually   do
   Q: _____
   A: My family and I _____ (almost always / go online)

5. go   how often   you   do   to the gym
   Q: _____
   A: I _____ (never)

2 Questions with *how*; short answers page 40

- Don't confuse *good* and *well*. Use the adjective *good* with *be* and the adverb *well* with other verbs: How **good** are you at soccer? BUT How **well** do you play soccer?

Complete the questions with *How* and a word from the box.
Then match the questions and the answers.

good	long	often	well

1. _____ do you lift weights? _____   **a.** Not very well, but I love it.
2. _____ do you play basketball? _____   **b.** About six hours a week.
3. _____ are you at volleyball? _____   **c.** Not very often. I prefer martial arts.
4. _____ do you spend at the gym? _____   **d.** Pretty good, but I hate it.

1 Simple past   page 45

- Use *did* with the base form – not the past form – of the main verb in questions: How **did** you **spend** the weekend? (NOT: How did you spent . . .?)
- Use *didn't* with the base form in negative statements: We **didn't go** shopping. (NOT: We didn't went shopping.)

Complete the conversation.

A: _____ Did _____ you _____ have _____ (have) a good weekend?

B: Yes, I _____ . I _____ (have) a great time. My sister and I _____ (go) shopping on Saturday. We _____ (spend) all day at the mall.

A: _____ you _____ (buy) anything special?

B: I _____ (buy) a new laptop. And I _____ (get) some new clothes, too.

A: Lucky you! What clothes _____ you _____ (buy)?

B: Well, I _____ (need) some new boots. I _____ (get) some great ones at Great Times Department Store. What about you? What _____ you _____ (do) on Saturday?

A: I _____ (not, do) anything special. I _____ (stay) home and _____ (work) around the house. Oh, but I _____ (see) a really good movie on TV. And then I _____ (make) dinner with my mother. I actually _____ (enjoy) the day.

2 Past of *be*   page 47

Present		Past
am/is	→	**was**
are	→	**were**

Rewrite the sentences. Find another way to write each sentence using *was*, *wasn't*, *were*, or *weren't* and the words in parentheses.

1. Bruno didn't come to class yesterday. (in class)
   <u>Bruno wasn't in class yesterday.</u>

2. He worked all day. (at work)
   _____

3. Bruno and his co-workers worked on Saturday, too. (at work)
   _____

4. They didn't go to work on Sunday. (at work)
   _____

5. Did Bruno stay home on Sunday? (at home)
   _____

6. Where did Bruno go on Sunday? (on Sunday)
   _____

7. He and his brother went to a baseball game. (at a baseball game)
   _____

8. They stayed at the park until 7:00. (at the park)
   _____

1 There is, there are; one, any, some page 51

> ■ Don't use a contraction in a short answer with *Yes*: Is there a hotel near here? Yes, **there is**. (NOT: ~~Yes, there's.~~)
>
> ■ Use *some* in affirmative statements and *any* in negative statements: There are **some** grocery stores in my neighborhood, but there aren't **any** restaurants. Use *any* in most questions: Are there **any** nice stores around here?

Complete the conversations. Choose the correct words.

1. A: **Is** / **Are** there any supermarkets in this neighborhood?
   B: No, there **isn't** / **aren't**, but there are **one** / **some** on Main Street.
   A: And **is** / **are** there a post office near here?
   B: Yes, **there's** / **there is**. It's across from the bank.

2. A: **Is** / **Are** there a gas station around here?
   B: Yes, **there's** / **there are** one behind the shopping center.
   A: Great! And are there **a** / **any** coffee shops nearby?
   B: Yes, there's a good **one** / **some** in the shopping center.

2 Quantifiers; *how many* and *how much* page 54

> ■ Use *a lot* with both count and noncount nouns: Are there many traffic lights on First Avenue? Yes, there are **a lot**. Is there much traffic? Yes, there's **a lot**.
>
> ■ Use *any* – not *none* – in negative statements: How much traffic is there on your street? There **isn't any**. = There's **none**. (NOT: ~~There isn't none.~~)
>
> ■ Use *How many* with count nouns: **How many books** do you have?
>
> ■ Use *How much* with noncount nouns: **How much traffic** is there?

A Complete the conversations. Choose the correct words.

1. A: Is there **many** / **much** traffic in your city?
   B: Well, there's **a few** / **a little**.

2. A: Are there **many** / **much** Wi-Fi hotspots around here?
   B: No, there aren't **many** / **none**.

3. A: **How many** / **How much** restaurants are there in your neighborhood?
   B: There **is** / **are** a lot.

4. A: **How many** / **How much** noise **is** / **are** there in your city?
   B: There's **much** / **none**. It's very quiet.

B Write questions with the words in parentheses. Use *much* or *many*.

1. A: _Is there much pollution in your neighborhood?_ (pollution)
   B: No, there isn't. My neighborhood is very clean.

2. A: _____ (parks)
   B: Yes, there are. They're great for families.

3. A: _____ (crime)
   B: There's none. It's a very safe part of the city.

4. A: _____ (laundromats)
   B: There aren't any. A lot of people have their own washing machines.

UNIT 9

1 Describing people page 59

■ Use *have* or *is* to describe eye and hair color: I **have** brown hair. = My hair **is** brown.
He **has** blue eyes. = His eyes **are** blue.

■ Don't confuse *How* and *What* in questions: **How** tall are you? (NOT: ~~What tall are you?~~)
What color is your hair? (NOT: ~~How color is your hair?~~)

Unscramble the questions. Then write answers using the phrases in the box.

blond	brown eyes	contact lenses
✓ tall and good-looking	6 foot 2	26 – two years older than me

A: brother   like   look   what   your   does
<u>What does your brother look like?</u>

B: <u>He's tall and good-looking.</u>

A: tall   is   how   he

_____

B: _____

A: he   does   glasses   wear

_____

B: _____

A: what   hair   color   his   is

_____

B: _____

A: he   does   blue   have   eyes

_____

B: _____

A: old   he   how   is

_____

B: _____

2 Modifiers with participles and prepositions page 62

■ Don't use a form of *be* in modifiers with participles: Sylvia is the woman **standing**
near the window. (NOT: ~~Sylvia is the woman is standing near the window.~~)

Rewrite the conversations. Use the words in parentheses and *one* or *ones*.

1. **A:** Who's Carla?
   B: She's the woman in the red dress.

2. **A:** Who are your neighbors?
   B: They're the people with the baby.

3. **A:** Who's Jeff?
   B: He's the man wearing glasses.

A: <u>Which one is Carla?</u> (which)
B: _____ (wearing)
A: _____ (which)
B: _____ (walking)
A: _____ (which)
B: _____ (with)

1 Present perfect; *already, yet* page 65

- Use the present perfect for actions that happened some time in the past.
- Use *yet* in questions and negative statements: Have you checked your email **yet**? No, I haven't turned on my computer **yet**. Use *already* in affirmative statements: I've **already** checked my email.

A Complete the conversations with the present perfect of the verbs in parentheses and short answers.

1. **A:** _____Has_____ Leslie _____called_____ (call) you lately?
   B: No, she _____ (not call) me, but I _____ (get) some emails from her.
2. **A:** _____ you and Jan _____ (have) lunch yet?
   B: No, we _____. We're thinking of going to Tony's. _____ you _____ (try) it yet? Come with us.
   A: Thanks. I _____ (not eat) there yet, but I _____ (hear) it's pretty good.

B Look at things Matt said. Put the adverb in the correct place in the second sentence.

1. I'm very hungry. I haven't eaten. (yet)   *yet*
2. I don't need any groceries. I've gone shopping. (already)
3. What have you done? Have you been to the zoo? (yet)
4. I called my parents before dinner. I've talked to them. (already)

2 Present perfect vs. simple past page 66

- Don't mention a specific time with the present perfect: I've **been** to a jazz club. Use the simple past to say when a past action happened: I **went** to a jazz club **last night**.

Complete the conversation using the present perfect or the simple past of the verbs in parentheses and short answers.

1. **A:** _____Did_____ you _____see_____ (see) the game last night? I really _____ (enjoy) it.
   B: Yes, I _____. It _____ (be) an amazing game. _____ you ever _____ (go) to a game?
   A: No, I _____. I _____ never _____ (be) to the stadium. But I'd love to go!
   B: Maybe we can go to a game next year.
2. **A:** _____ you ever _____ (be) to Franco's Restaurant?
   B: Yes, I _____. My friend and I _____ (eat) there last weekend. How about you?
   A: No, I _____. But I _____ (hear) it's very good.
   B: Oh, yes – it's excellent!

3 *For* and *since* page 67

- Use *for* + a period of time to describe how long a present condition has been true: We've been in New York **for two months**. (= We arrived two months ago.)
- Use *since* + a point in time to describe when a present condition started: We've been here **since August**. (= We've been here from August to now.)

Choose the correct word.

1. I bought my car almost 10 years ago. I've had it **for** / **since** almost 10 years.
2. The Carters moved to Seattle six months ago. They've lived there **for** / **since** six months.
3. I've wanted to see that movie **for** / **since** a long time. It's been in theaters **for** / **since** March.

1 Adverbs before adjectives _page 73_

> ■ Use *a/an* with (adverb) + adjective + singular noun: It's **a very modern city**. It's **an expensive city**. Don't use *a/an* with (adverb) + adjective: It's **really interesting**. (NOT: ~~It's a really interesting.~~)

Read the sentences. Add *a* or *an* where it's necessary to complete the sentences.

          an
1. Brasília is ∧ extremely modern city.

2. Seoul is very interesting place.

3. Santiago is pretty exciting city to visit.

4. Montreal is beautiful city, and it's fairly old.

5. London has really busy airport.

2 Conjunctions _page 73_

> ■ Use *and* for additional information: The food is delicious, **and** it's not expensive.
> ■ Use *but*, *though*, and *however* for contrasting information: The food is delicious, **but** it's very expensive./The food is delicious. It's expensive, **though/however**.

Choose the correct word.

1. Spring in my city is pretty nice, **and / but** it gets extremely hot in summer.
2. There are some great museums. They're always crowded, **and / however**.
3. There are a lot of interesting stores, **and / but** many of them aren't expensive.
4. There are many amazing restaurants, **and / but** some are closed in August.
5. My city is a great place to visit. Don't come in summer, **but / though**!

3 Modal verbs *can* and *should* _page 75_

> ■ Use *can* to talk about things that are possible: Where **can** I get some nice souvenirs? Use *should* to suggest things that are good to do: You **should** try the local restaurants.
> ■ Use the base form with *can* and *should* – not the infinitive: Where **can I get** some nice souvenirs? (NOT: ~~Where can I to get . . ?~~) **You should try** the local restaurants. (NOT: ~~You should to try . . .~~)

Complete the conversation with *can*, *can't*, *should*, or *shouldn't*.

A: I _____*can't*_____ decide where to go on vacation. _____ I go to Costa Rica or Hawaii?
B: You _____ definitely visit Costa Rica.
A: Really? What can I see there?
B: Well, San Jose is an exciting city. You _____ miss the Museo del Oro. That's the gold museum, and you _____ see beautiful animals made of gold.
A: OK. What else _____ I do there?
B: Well, you _____ visit the museum on Mondays. It's closed then. But you _____ definitely visit the rain forest. It's amazing!

1 Adjective + infinitive; noun + infinitive   page 79

> ■ In negative statements, *not* comes before the infinitive: With a cold, it's important **not to exercise** too hard. (NOT: ~~With a cold, it's important **to don't exercise** too hard.~~)

Rewrite the sentences using the words in parentheses. Add *not* when necessary.

1. For a bad headache, you should relax and close your eyes. (a good idea)
   <u>It's a good idea to relax and close your eyes when you have a headache.</u>

2. You should put some cold tea on that sunburn. (sometimes helpful)
   _____

3. For a backache, you should take some pain medicine. (important)
   _____

4. For a cough, you shouldn't drink milk. (important)
   _____

5. For a cold, you should take a hot bath. (sometimes helpful)
   _____

6. When you feel stressed, you shouldn't drink a lot of coffee. (a good idea)
   _____

2 Modal verbs *can*, *could*, and *may* for requests; suggestions   page 81

> ■ In requests, *can*, *could*, and *may* have the same meaning. *May* is a little more formal than *can* and *could*.

Number the lines of the conversation. Then write the conversation below.

_____ Hi. Yes, please. What do you suggest for itchy skin?

_____ Here you are. Can I help you with anything else?

_____ Sure I can. You should see a dentist!

___1___ Hello. May I help you?

_____ You should try this lotion.

_____ Yes. Can you suggest something for a toothache?

_____ OK. And could I have a bottle of pain medicine?

A: <u>Hello. May I help you?</u> _____

B: _____

A: _____

B: _____

A: _____

B: _____

A: _____

UNIT 13

1 So, too, neither, either page 87

> - Use *so* or *too* after an affirmative statement: I'm crazy about sushi. **So** am I./I am, **too**.
> - Use *neither* or *not either* after a negative statement: I don't like fast food. **Neither** do I./I don't **either**.
> - With *so* and *neither*, the verb comes before the subject: **So am I**. (NOT: ~~So I am.~~) **Neither do I**. (NOT: ~~Neither I do.~~)

A Choose the correct response to show that B agrees with A.

1. **A:** I'm in the mood for something salty.
   B: (I am, too.)/ I do, too.
2. **A:** I can't stand fast food.
   B: Neither do I. / I can't either.
3. **A:** I really like Korean food.
   B: So do I. / I am, too.
4. **A:** I don't eat French food very often.
   B: I do, too. / I don't either.
5. **A:** I'm not crazy about chocolate.
   B: I am, too. / Neither am I.

B Write responses to show agreement with these statements.

1. **A:** I'm not a very good cook.
   B: _____
2. **A:** I love french fries.
   B: _____
3. **A:** I can't eat very spicy food.
   B: _____
4. **A:** I never eat bland food.
   B: _____
5. **A:** I can make delicious desserts.
   B: _____

2 Modal verbs *would* and *will* for requests page 89

> - Don't confuse *like* and *would like*. *Would like* means "want."
> - You can also use *I'll have . . .* when ordering in a restaurant to mean *I will have . . .*

Complete the conversation with *would*, *I'd*, or *I'll*.

A: _____Would_____ you like to order now?

B: Yes, please. _____ have the shrimp curry.

A: _____ you like noodles or rice with that?

B: Hmm, _____ have rice.

A: And _____ you like a salad, too?

B: No, thanks.

A: _____ you like anything else?

B: Yes, _____ like a cup of green tea.

1 Comparisons with adjectives *page 93*

- Use the comparative form (adjective + *-er* or *more* + adjective) to compare two people, places, or things: Which river is **longer**, the Nile or the Amazon? The Nile is **longer than** the Amazon. Use the superlative form (*the* + adjective + *-est* or *the most* + adjective) to compare three or more people, places, or things: Which river is **the longest**: the Nile, the Amazon, or the Mississippi? The Nile is **the longest** river in the world.

- You can use a comparative or superlative without repeating the noun: Which country is **larger**, Canada or China? Canada is **larger**. What's the highest waterfall in the world? Angel Falls is **the highest**.

Write questions with the words. Then look at the underlined words, and write the answers.

1. Which desert / dry / the Sahara or <u>the Atacama</u>?
   Q: <u>Which desert is drier, the Sahara or the Atacama?</u>
   A: <u>The Atacama is drier than the Sahara.</u>

2. Which island / large / <u>Greenland</u>, New Guinea, or Honshu?
   Q: _____
   A: _____

3. Which island / small / New Guinea or <u>Honshu</u>?
   Q: _____
   A: _____

4. Which U.S. city / large / Los Angeles, Chicago, or <u>New York</u>?
   Q: _____
   A: _____

5. Which ocean / deep / the Atlantic or <u>the Pacific</u>?
   Q: _____
   A: _____

2 Questions with *how* *page 96*

- Use *high* to describe mountains and waterfalls: How **high** is Mount Fuji? Angel Falls is 979 meters **high**. Use *tall* to describe buildings: How **tall** is the Empire State Building? (NOT: ~~How high is the Empire State Building?~~)

Complete the questions with the phrases in the box. There is one extra phrase.

How big	How cold	✓ How deep	How high	How tall

1. **Q:** _How deep_ is Lake Baikal?   **A:** It's 1,642 meters (5,387 feet) at its deepest point.
2. **Q:** _____ is Alaska?   **A:** It's 1,717,900 square kilometers (663,300 square miles).
3. **Q:** _____ is Denali?   **A:** It's 6,190 meters (20,310 feet) high.
4. **Q:** _____ is the Tokyo Skytree?   **A:** It is 634 meters (2,080 feet) tall.

1 Future with present continuous and *be going to*   page 101

- Use the present continuous to talk about something that is happening now: What **are** you **doing**? I**'m studying**. You can also use the present continuous with time expressions to talk about the future: What **are** you **doing tomorrow**? I**'m working**.

- Use *be going to* to talk about the future: I**'m going to** see an old school friend tomorrow.

A Read the sentences. Are they present or future? Write **P** or **F**.

1. Why are you wearing shorts? It's cold. ___P___
2. What are you wearing to the party on Friday? _____
3. What are you doing this weekend? _____
4. What are you doing? Can you please see who's at the door? _____
5. Are you going to see a movie tonight? _____

B Complete the conversations. Use *be going to*.

1. **A:** What _____are_____ you and Tony going to _____do_____ (do) tonight?
   B: We _____ (try) the new Chinese restaurant. Do you want to come?
   A: I'd love to. What time _____ you _____ (go)?
   B: We _____ (meet) at Tony's house at 7:00. And don't forget an umbrella. The weather forecast says it _____ (rain) tonight.

2. **A:** Where _____ you _____ (go) on vacation this year?
   B: I _____ (visit) my cousins in Paris. It _____ (be) great!
   A: Well, I _____ (not go) anywhere this year. I _____ (stay) home.
   B: That's not so bad. Just think about all the money you _____ (save)!

2 Messages with *tell* and *ask*   page 103

- In messages with a request, use the infinitive of the verb: Please ask her **to meet** me at noon. (NOT: Please ask her meet me at noon.)

- In messages with negative infinitives, *not* goes before *to* in the infinitive: Could you ask him **not to be** late? (NOT: Could you ask him to don't be late?)

Read the messages. Ask someone to pass them on. Use the words in parentheses.

1. Message: Patrick – We don't have class tomorrow. (please)
   *Please tell Patrick that we don't have class tomorrow.*_____

2. Message: Ana – Wait for me after class. (would)
   _____

3. Message: Alex – The concert on Saturday has been canceled. (would)
   _____

4. Message: Sarah – Don't forget to return the book to the library. (could)
   _____

1 Describing changes page 107

■ You can use several tenses to describe change – present tense, past tense, and present perfect.

A Complete the sentences with the information in the box. Use the present perfect of the verbs given.

buy a house	change her hairstyle	join a gym	start looking for a new job

1. Chris and Brittany _____. Their apartment was too small.
2. Josh _____. The one he has now is too stressful.
3. Shawna _____. Everyone says it's more stylish.
4. Max _____. He feels healthier now.

B Rewrite the sentences using the present tense and the words in parentheses.

1. Holly doesn't wear jeans anymore. _She wears dresses._____ (dresses)
2. They don't live in the city anymore. _____ (in the suburbs)
3. Jackie isn't so shy anymore. _____ (more outgoing)
4. I don't eat greasy food anymore. _____ (healthier food)

2 Verb + infinitive page 109

■ Use the infinitive after a verb to describe future plans or things you want to happen:
I **want to learn** Spanish.

Complete the conversation with the verbs in parentheses in the correct form.

A: Hey, Zach. What _are you going to do_____ (go / do) after graduation?
B: Well, I _____ (plan / stay) here in the city for a few months.
A: Really? I _____ (want / go) home. I'm ready for my mom's cooking.
B: I understand that, but my boss says I can keep my job for the summer. So
I _____ (want / work) a lot of hours because I
_____ (hope / make) enough money for a new car.
A: But you don't need a car in the city.
B: I _____ (not plan / be) here for very long. In the
fall, I _____ (go / drive) across the country. I really
_____ (want / live) in California.
A: California? Where in California _____ (like / live)?
B: In Hollywood, of course. I _____ (go / be) a movie star!

Grammar plus answer key

Unit 1

1 Statements with *be*; possessive adjectives
1. This **is** Dulce Castelo. **She's** a new student from Santo Domingo.
2. My name **is** Sergio. **I'm** from Brazil.
3. My brother and I **are** students here. **Our** names are Nate and Chad.
4. **He's** Kento. **He's** 19 years old.
5. **They're** in my English class. **It's** a big class.

2 Wh-questions with *be*
2. e 3. a 4. b 5. c 6. d

3 Yes/No questions and short answers with *be*
1. A: **Are they** in your class?
   B: No, **they're not / they aren't**. They're in English 2.
2. A: Hi! **Are you** in this class?
   B: Yes, **I am**. I'm a new student here.
3. A: **Are you** from the United States?
   B: No, **we're not / we aren't**. We're from Calgary, Canada.
4. A: Hi, Monica. **Are you** free?
   B: No, **I'm not**. I'm on my way to class.
5. A: That's the new student. **Is he** from Paraguay?
   B: No, **he's not / he isn't**. He's from Uruguay.
6. A: **Is she** from Indonesia?
   B: Yes, **she is**. She's from Jakarta.

Unit 2

1 Simple present Wh-questions and statements
1. A: I **have** good news! Mona **has** a new job.
   B: How **does** she **like** it?
   A: She **loves** it. The hours are great.
   B: What time **does** she **start**?
   A: She **starts** at ten and **finishes** at four.
2. A: What **do** you **do**?
   B: I'm a teacher.
   A: What **do** you **teach**?
   B: I **teach** Spanish and English.
   A: Really? My sister **teaches** English, too.

2 Time expressions
B: I love it, but the hours are difficult. I start work **at** 6:30 A.M., and I work **until** 3:30.
A: That's interesting! I work the same hours, but I work **at** night. I start **at** 6:30 **in** the evening and finish **at** 3:30 **in** the morning.
B: Wow! What time do you get up?
A: Well, I get home **at** 4:30 and go to bed **at** 5:30. And I sleep **until** 2:00. But I only work **on** weekends, so it's OK. What about you?
B: Oh, I work **on** Monday, Wednesday, and Friday. And I get up **early** – around 5:00 A.M.

Unit 3

1 Demonstratives; *one*, *ones*
1. A: Excuse me. How much are **these** shoes?
   B: **They're** $279.
   A: And how much is **that** bag over there?
   B: **It's** only $129.
   A: And are the two gray **ones** $129, too?
   B: No. **Those** are only $119.
   A: Oh! **This** store is really expensive.
2. A: Can I help you?
   B: Yes, please. I really like **those** jeans over there. How much **are they**?
   A: Which **ones**? Do you mean **these**?
   B: No, the black **ones**.
   A: Let me look. Oh, **they're** $35.99.
   B: That's not bad. And how much is **this** sweater here?
   A: **It's** only $9.99.

2 Preferences; comparisons with adjectives
A
2. happier
3. more exciting
4. friendlier
5. more interesting
6. more reasonable
7. sadder
8. warmer
B
2. I like the silver one (better). It's more interesting.
3. I prefer the silk one. It's prettier.
4. I like the purple ones (more). They're cheaper.

Unit 4

1 Simple present questions; short answers
A
2. A: **Does John like** Carrie Underwood?
   B: No, **he doesn't**. John doesn't like country music.
3. A: **Does Lisa like** talk shows?
   B: Yes, **she does**. Lisa is a big fan of them.
4. A: **Do you / you and Kevin watch** the news on TV?
   B: Yes, **we do**. Kevin and I watch the news every night.
5. A: **Do you like** hip-hop?
   B: No, **I don't**. But I love R&B.
6. A: **Do your parents listen to** jazz?
   B: No, **they don't**. But my parents listen to a lot of classical music.
B
2. us 3. them 4. him 5. her

2 *Would*; verb + *to* + verb
A: Would you like to see a movie with me tonight?
B: Yes, I would. What would you like to see?
A: I'd like to see the new Matt Damon movie.

Unit 5

1 Present continuous
1. A: Really? **Is she living abroad**?
   B: Yes, **she is**. She**'s living / is living** in South Korea.
2. A: **How are you spending your summer**?
   B: **I'm working** part-time. **I'm taking** two classes also.
   A: **What are you taking**?
   B: My friend and I **are studying** photography and Japanese. We like our classes a lot.

2 Quantifiers
2. Nearly all students finish high school.
3. All children start school by the age of six.
4. A lot of couples have more than one child.
5. Few families have more than four children.

Unit 6

1 Adverbs of frequency
1. A: **I often play sports.**
2. Q: **Do you ever go jogging with a friend?**
   A: No, **I always jog / go jogging alone.**
3. Q: **How often do you play basketball?**
   A: I **play (basketball) four times a week.**
4. Q: **What do you usually do in the evening?**
   A: My family and I **almost always go online.**
5. Q: **How often do you go to the gym?**
   A: I **never go (to the gym).**

2 Questions with *how*; short answers
1. **How often** do you lift weights? c
2. **How well** do you play basketball? a
3. **How good** are you at volleyball? d
4. **How long** do you spend at the gym? b

Unit 7

1 Simple past
B: Yes, I **did**. I **had** a great time. My sister and I **went** shopping on Saturday. We **spent** all day at the mall.
A: **Did** you **buy** anything special?
B: I **bought** a new laptop. And I **got** some new clothes, too.
A: Lucky you! What clothes **did** you **buy**?
B: Well, I **needed** some new boots. I **got** some great ones at Great Times Department Store. What about you? What **did** you **do** on Saturday?
A: I **didn't do** anything special. I **stayed** home and **worked** around the house. Oh, but I **saw** a really good movie on TV. And then I **made** dinner with my mother. I actually **enjoyed** the day.

2 Past of *be*
2. He was at work all day.
3. Bruno and his co-workers were at work on Saturday, too.
4. They weren't at work on Sunday.
5. Was Bruno at home on Sunday?
6. Where was Bruno on Sunday?
7. He and his brother were at a baseball game.
8. They were at the park until 7:00.

Unit 8

1 *There is, there are; one, any, some*
1. A: **Are** there any supermarkets in this neighborhood?
   B: No, there **aren't**, but there are **some** on Main Street.
   A: And **is** there a post office near here?
   B: Yes, **there is**. It's across from the bank.
2. A: **Is** there a gas station around here?
   B: Yes, **there's** one behind the shopping center.
   A: Great! And are there **any** coffee shops nearby?
   B: Yes, there's a good **one** in the shopping center.

2 Quantifiers; *how many* **and** *how much*
A
1. A: Is there **much** traffic in your city?
   B: Well, there's a **little**.
2. A: Are there **many** Wi-Fi hotspots around here?
   B: No, there aren't **many**.
3. A: **How many** restaurants are there in your neighborhood?
   B: There **are** a lot.
4. A: **How much** noise **is** there in your city?
   B: There's **none**. It's very quiet.
B
2. A: Are there many parks (in your neighborhood)?
3. A: Is there much crime (in your neighborhood)?
4. A: Are there many laundromats (in your neighborhood)?

Unit 9

1 Describing people
A: How tall is he?
B: He's 6 foot 2.
A: Does he wear glasses?
B: No, he doesn't. He wears contact lenses.
A: What color is his hair?
B: He has blond hair.
A: Does he have blue eyes?
B: No, he has brown eyes.
A: How old is he?
B: He's 26 – two years older than me.

2 Modifiers with participles and prepositions
1. B: She's the one wearing a red dress.
2. A: Which ones are your neighbors?
   B: They're the ones walking with the baby.
3. A: Which one is Jeff?
   B: He's the one with glasses.

Unit 10

1 Present perfect; *already, yet*
A
1. B: No, she **hasn't called** me, but I**'ve gotten** some emails from her.
2. A: **Have** you and Jan **had** lunch yet?

B: No, we **haven't**. We're thinking of going to Tony's. **Have** you **tried** it yet? Come with us.
A: Thanks. I **haven't eaten** there yet, but I**'ve heard** it's pretty good.
B
2. I've **already** gone shopping.
3. Have you been to the zoo **yet**?
4. I've **already** talked to them./I've talked to them **already**.

2 Present perfect vs. simple past
1. A: Did you see the game last night? I really **enjoyed** it.
   B: Yes, I **did**. It **was** an amazing game. **Have** you ever **gone** to a game?
   A: No, I **haven't**. I**'ve** never **been** to the stadium. But I'd love to go!
   B: Maybe we can go to a game next year.
2. A: **Have** you ever **been** to Franco's Restaurant?
   B: Yes, I **have**. My friend and I **ate** there last weekend. How about you?
   A: No, I **haven't**. But I**'ve heard** it's very good.
   B: Oh, yes – it's excellent!

3 *For* and *since*
1. I've had it **for** almost 10 years.
2. They've lived there **for** six months.
3. I've wanted to see that movie **for** a long time. It's been in theaters **since** March.

Unit 11

1 Adverbs before adjectives
2. Seoul is **a** very interesting place.
3. Santiago is **a** pretty exciting city to visit.
4. Montreal is **a** beautiful city, and it's fairly old.
5. London has **a** really busy airport.

2 Conjunctions
1. Spring in my city is pretty nice, **but** it gets extremely hot in summer.
2. There are some great museums. They're always crowded, **however**.
3. There are a lot of interesting stores, **and** many of them aren't expensive.
4. There are many amazing restaurants, **but** some are closed in August.
5. My city is a great place to visit. Don't come in summer, **though**!

3 Modal verbs *can* **and** *should*
A: I **can't** decide where to go on vacation. **Should** I go to Costa Rica or Hawaii?
B: You **should** definitely visit Costa Rica.
A: Really? What can I see there?
B: Well, San Jose is an exciting city. You **shouldn't** miss the Museo del Oro. That's the gold museum, and you **can** see beautiful animals made of gold.
A: OK. What else **can / should** I do there?
B: Well, you **can't** visit the museum on Mondays. It's closed then. But you **should** definitely visit the rain forest. It's amazing!

Unit 12

1 Adjective + infinitive; noun + infinitive
Possible answers:
2. For a sunburn, **it's sometimes helpful to put** some cold tea on it.
3. For a backache, **it's important to take** some pain medicine.
4. For a cough, **it's important not to drink** milk.
5. For a cold, **it's sometimes helpful to take** a hot bath.
6. When you feel stressed, **it's a good idea not to drink** a lot of coffee.

2 Modal verbs *can, could,* **and** *may* **for requests; suggestions**
2. Yes, please. What do you suggest for itchy skin?
3. You should try this lotion.
4. OK. And could I have a bottle of pain medicine?
5. Here you are. Can I help you with anything else?
6. Yes. Can you suggest something for a toothache?
7. Sure I can. You should see a dentist!

Unit 13

1 *So, too, neither, either*
A
2. B: I can't either.
3. B: So do I.
4. B: I don't either.
5. B: Neither am I.

B
1. B: I'm not either./Neither am I.
2. B: I do, too./So do I.
3. B: I can't either./Neither can I.
4. B: I don't either./Neither do I.
5. B: I can, too./So can I.

2 Modal verbs *would* and *will* for requests
B: I'll
A: Would
B: I'll
A: would
A: Would
B: I'd

Unit 14

1 Comparisons with adjectives
2. Q: Which island is the largest: Greenland, New Guinea, or Honshu?
   A: Greenland is the largest.
3. Q: Which island is smaller, New Guinea or Honshu?
   A: Honshu is smaller than New Guinea.
4. Q: Which U.S. city is the largest: Los Angeles, Chicago, or New York?
   A: New York is the largest.
5. Q: Which ocean is deeper, the Atlantic or the Pacific?
   A: The Pacific is deeper than the Atlantic.

2 Questions with *how*
2. How big
3. How high
4. How tall

Unit 15

1 Future with present continuous and *be going to*
A
2. F
3. F
4. P
5. F

B
1. B: We**'re going to try** the new Chinese restaurant. Do you want to come?
   A: I'd love to. What time **are** you **going to go**?
   B: We**'re going to meet** at Tony's house at 7:00. And don't forget an umbrella. The weather forecast says it**'s going to rain** tonight.
2. A: Where **are** you **going to go** on vacation this year?
   B: I**'m going to visit** my cousins in Paris. It**'s going to be** great!
   A: Well, I**'m not going to go** anywhere this year. I**'m going to stay** home.
   B: That's not so bad. Just think about all the money you**'re going to save**!

2 Messages with *tell* and *ask*
2. Would you ask Ana to wait for me after class?
3. Would you tell Alex (that) the concert on Saturday has been canceled?
4. Could you tell Sarah not to forget to return the book to the library?

Unit 16

1 Describing changes
A
1. Chris and Brittany **have bought a house**.
2. Josh **has started looking for a new job**.
3. Shawn **has changed her hairstyle**.
4. Max **has joined a gym**.

B
2. They live in the suburbs.
3. Jackie/She is more outgoing.
4. I eat healthier food now.

2 Verb + infinitive
B: Well, I **plan to stay** here in the city for a few months.
A: Really? I **want to go** home. I'm ready for my mom's cooking.
B: I understand that, but my boss says I can keep my job for the summer. So I **want to work** a lot of hours because I **hope to make** enough money for a new car.
A: But you don't need a car in the city.
B: I **don't plan to be** here for very long. In the fall, I**'m going to drive** across the country. I really **want to live** in California.
A: California? Where in California **would you like to live**?
B: In Hollywood, of course. I**'m going to be** a movie star!

Credits

The authors and publishers acknowledge the following sources of copyright material and are grateful for the permissions granted. While every effort has been made, it has not always been possible to identify the sources of all the material used, or to trace all copyright holders. If any omissions are brought to our notice, we will be happy to include the appropriate acknowledgements on reprinting and in the next update to the digital edition, as applicable.

Keys: E = Exercise; T = Top, B = Below, TR = Top Right, TL = Top Left, BR = Below Right, BL = Below Left, C = Centre, CR = Centre Right, CL = Centre Left, L = Left, R = Right, BC = Below Centre, B/G = Background.

Illustrations

337 Jon (KJA Artists): 17(T); **Mark Duffin**: 17(B), 80; **Thomas Girard** (Good Illustration): 50, 64, 66, 78(B), 108, 116–117; **Daniel Gray-Barnett**: 51, 57, 92; **Quino Marin** (The Organisation): 17(C), 18, 56, 70, 120; **Gavin Reece** (New Division): 2, 3, 5, 61, 123, 124; **Paul Williams** (Sylvie Poggio Artists): 60, 78(T).

Photos

Back cover (woman with whiteboard): Jenny Acheson/Stockbyte/GettyImages; Back cover (whiteboard): Nemida/GettyImages; Back cover (man using phone): Betsie Van Der Meer/Taxi/GettyImages; Back cover (woman smiling): PeopleImages.com/DigitalVision/GettyImages; Back cover (name tag): Tetra Images/GettyImages; Back cover (handshake): David Lees/Taxi/GettyImages; p. v: Caiaimage/Chris Ryan/GettyImages; p. 2 (header), p. vi (Unit 1): M G Therin Weise/Photographer's Choice RF/GettyImages; p. 4 (photo 1): Hill Street Studios/Tobin Rogers/Blend Images/GettyImages; p. 4 (photo 2): Steve Debenport/E+/GettyImages; p. 4 (photo 3): Monty Rakusen/Cultura/GettyImages; p. 4 (photo 4): Jose Luis Pelaez Inc/Blend Images/GettyImages; p. 4 (photo 5): Peter Cade/Iconica/GettyImages; p. 4 (photo 6): Sofia Bagdasarian/EyeEm/GettyImages; p. 4 (photo 7): Jon Feingersh/Blend Images/GettyImages; p. 4 (photo 8): Echo/Cultura/GettyImages; p. 6 (T): Caiaimage/Sam Edwards/Caiaimage/GettyImages; p. 6 (B): DragonImages/iStock/Getty Images Plus/GettyImages; p. 7 (T): Jamie McCarthy/Getty Images Entertainment/GettyImages; p. 7 (B): Pool/Samir Hussein/WireImage/GettyImages; p. 8 (header), p. vi (Unit 2): Hero Images/GettyImages; p. 8 (babysitter): Jonas unruh/E+/GettyImages; p. 8 (fitness instructor): Jutta Klee/Canopy/GettyImages; p. 8 (office assistant): Sturti/E+/GettyImages; p. 8 (sales associate): Matthias Tunger/DigitalVision/GettyImages; p. 8 (social media assistant): Tim Robberts/Taxi/GettyImages; p. 8 (tutor): Prasit photo/Moment/GettyImages; p. 9 (T): Hero Images/GettyImages; p. 9 (C): Westend61/GettyImages; p. 9 (B): Westend61/GettyImages; p. 10: Steve Debenport/E+/GettyImages; p. 11 (T): Marc Romanelli/Blend Images/GettyImages; p. 11 (B): Yellow Dog Productions/Iconica/GettyImages; p. 11 (taxi driver): Monty Rakusen/Cultura/GettyImages; p. 11 (Kristina): Yellow Dog Productions/Iconica/GettyImages; p. 13 (Danny): tulpahn/iStock/Getty Images Plus/GettyImages; p. 13 (Carla): Image Source/DigitalVision/GettyImages; p. 13 (Nico): Golero/E+/GettyImages; p. 13 (Lisa): Portishead1/E+/GettyImages; p. 14: Fabrice LEROUGE/ONOKY/GettyImages; p. 15 (engineer): B Busco/Photographer's Choice/GettyImages; p. 15 (caregiver): Maskot/GettyImages; p. 15 (electrician): Pamela Moore/E+/GettyImages; p. 15 (IT worker): Echo/Cultura/GettyImages; p. 15 (B): i love images/Cultura/GettyImages; p. 16 (header), p. vi (Unit 3): John Fedele/Blend Images/GettyImages; p. 16 (white mug): Steve Gorton/Dorling Kindersley/GettyImages; p. 16 (blue mug): Dorling Kindersley/GettyImages; p. 16 (green mug): Denis Gladkiy/iStock/Getty Images Plus/GettyImages; p. 16 (yellow mug): serggn/iStock/Getty Images Plus/GettyImages; p. 16 (orange mug): Markus Guhl/Stockbyte/GettyImages; p. 16 (red mug): ampols/iStock/Getty Images Plus/GettyImages; p. 16 (pink mug): Pavlo Vakhrushev/Hemera/Getty Images Plus/GettyImages; p. 16 (purple mug): Ozii45/iStock/Getty Images Plus/GettyImages; p. 16 (brown mug): spaxiax/iStock/Getty Images Plus/GettyImages; p. 16 (black mug): DaddyBit/iStock/Getty Images Plus/GettyImages; p. 16 (gray mug): ambassador806/iStock/Getty Images Plus/GettyImages; p. 17 (B): londoneye/E+/GettyImages; p. 17: Nick David/Iconica/GettyImages; p. 17: londoneye/Vetta/GettyImages; p. 19 (tie): Phil Cardamone/E+/GettyImages; p. 19 (bracelet): Elnur Amikishiyev/Hemera/Getty Images Plus/GettyImages; p. 19 (ring): frender/iStock/Getty Images Plus/GettyImages; p. 19 (shirt): gofotograf/iStock/Getty Images Plus/GettyImages; p. 19 (belt): clark_fang/iStock/Getty Images Plus/GettyImages; p. 19 (earrings): Tarzhanova/iStock/Getty Images Plus/GettyImages; p. 19 (flip flops): subjug/E+/GettyImages; p. 19 (socks): Gary Ombler/Dorling Kindersley/GettyImages; p. 19 (B): Klaus Vedfelt/Iconica/GettyImages; p. 20 (jacket): White Packert/The Image Bank/GettyImages; p. 20 (coat): Steve Gorton/Dorling Kindersley/GettyImages; p. 20 (orange sweater): ARSELA/iStock/Getty Images Plus/GettyImages; p. 20 (grey sweater): popovaphoto/iStock/Getty Images Plus/GettyImages; p. 20 (gold rings): Tarek El Sombati/E+/GettyImages; p. 20 (silver rings): Burazin/Photographer's Choice/GettyImages; p. 21 (TR): Ivo Peer/EyeEm/GettyImages; p. 21 (TL): martinedoucet/E+/GettyImages; p. 21 (BR): Richard Boll/Photographer's Choice/GettyImages; p. 21 (BL): Al Freni/The LIFE Images Collection/GettyImages; p. 22 (header), p. vi (Unit 4): Westend61/GettyImages; p. 22 (T): Philip Othberg/EyeEm/GettyImages; p. 23 (T): Mark Metcalfe/Getty Images Entertainment/GettyImages; p. 23 (C): Leon Bennett/WireImage/GettyImages; p. 23 (Seth): Halfpoint/iStock/Getty Images Plus/GettyImages; p. 23 (Leanne): Caiaimage/Martin Barraud/Caiaimage/GettyImages; p. 23 (B): Ollie Millington/WireImage/GettyImages; p. 24 (Adele): Joern Pollex/Getty Images Entertainment/GettyImages; p. 24 (Steph Curry): TPG/Getty Images Entertainment/GettyImages; p. 24 (Star Wars): Bravo/NBCUniversal/GettyImages; p. 24 (Top chef): Atlaspix/Alamy; p. 25 (Alexis): Todor Tsvetkov/E+/GettyImages; p. 25 (Jacob): Neustockimages/E+/GettyImages; p. 25 (Tyler): fotostorm/E+/GettyImages; p. 25 (Andrew): panic_attack/iStock/Getty Images Plus/GettyImages; p. 25 (B): Henrik Sorensen/Iconica/GettyImages; p. 25 (Connor): Hero Images/GettyImages; p. 25 (Camila): Tetra Images/Brand X Pictures/GettyImages; p. 27 (B): STAN HONDA/AFP/GettyImages; p. 27 (C): Noel Vasquez/GC Images/GettyImages; p. 27 (T): Michael Tran/FilmMagic/GettyImages; p. 28 (leather jacket): deniztuyel/iStock/Getty Images Plus/GettyImages; p. 28 (wool jacket): Leonid Nyshko/iStock/Getty Images Plus/GettyImages; p. 28 (silk shirt): popovaphoto/iStock/Getty Images Plus/GettyImages; p. 28 (cotton shirt): gofotograf/iStock/Getty Images Plus/GettyImages; p. 28 (laptop): MyImages_Micha/iStock/Getty Images Plus/GettyImages; p. 28 (desktop computer): Ryan McVay/Photodisc/GettyImages; p. 29: Chad Slattery/The Image Bank/GettyImages; p. 30 (header), p. vi (Unit 5): eli_asenova/E+/GettyImages; p. 30 (James): alvarez/E+/GettyImages; p. 30 (Betty): Image Source/GettyImages; p. 30 (Robert): Siri Stafford/Stone/GettyImages; p. 30 (Patricia): Courtney Keating/E+/GettyImages; p. 30 (Deborah): Juanmonino/E+/GettyImages; p. 30 (Arturo): Kevin Dodge/Blend Images/GettyImages; p. 30 (Joseph): Izabela Habur/E+/GettyImages; p. 30 (Keiko): Paul Simcock/Blend Images/GettyImages; p. 30 (Joshua): Liam Norris/Cultura/GettyImages; p. 30 (Nicole): Westend61/Brand X Pictures/GettyImages; p. 30 (Veronica): lukas_zb/iStock/Getty Images Plus/GettyImages; p. 30 (Andrew): BDLM/Cultura/GettyImages; p. 30 (Emily): Robert Daly/Caiaimage/GettyImages; p. 30 (Alyssa): Westend61/GettyImages; p. 30 (Ethan): Compassionate Eye Foundation/Photodisc/GettyImages; p. 31 (Quincy Jones): Jason LaVeris/FilmMagic/GettyImages; p. 31 (Rashida Jones): Barry King/FilmMagic/GettyImages; p. 31 (Ashton Kutcher): JB Lacroix/WireImage/GettyImages; p. 31 (Mila Kunis): Vera Anderson/WireImage/GettyImages; p. 31 (Emma Roberts): Noam Galai/Getty Images North America/GettyImages; p. 31 (Julia Roberts): Dan MacMedan/WireImage/GettyImages; p. 31 (Cameron Diaz): Jason LaVeris/FilmMagic/GettyImages; p. 31 (Nicole Richie): Jeffrey Mayer/WireImage/GettyImages; p. 31 (BL): Vladimir Serov/Blend Images/GettyImages; p. 31 (Max): Flashpop/DigitalVision/GettyImages; p. 31 (Tina): Michael Blann/Iconica/GettyImages; p. 31 (BR): Oliver Strewe/Lonely Planet Images/GettyImages; p. 32 (man calling): Jed Share/Kaoru Share/Blend Images/GettyImages; p. 32 (woman calling): Justin Lambert/DigitalVision/GettyImages; p. 32 (woman chatting): Johnny Greig/iStock/Getty Images Plus/GettyImages; p. 32 (girl chatting): Tim Robberts/The Image Bank/GettyImages; p. 33 (T): Stuart Fox/Gallo Images/GettyImages; p. 33 (B): David Sacks/DigitalVision/GettyImages; p. 33 (C): Aping Vision/STS/Photodisc/GettyImages; p. 33 (Luis): yellowdog/Image Source/GettyImages; p. 33 (Vicky): XiXinXing/GettyImages; p. 34 (T): Robert Daly/Caiaimage/GettyImages; p. 34 (B): Nerida McMurray Photography/DigitalVision/GettyImages; p. 35 (TR): Hero Images/GettyImages; p. 35 (TL): Francesco Ridolfi/Cultura/GettyImages; p. 35 (BR): Compassionate Eye Foundation/Natasha Alipour Faridani/DigitalVision/GettyImages; p. 35 (BL): Edgardo Contreras/Taxi/GettyImages; p. 36 (header), p. vi (Unit 6): Thomas Barwick/DigitalVision/GettyImages; p. 36 (TL): Thomas Barwick/Stone/GettyImages; p. 36 (TR): RuslanDashinsky/iStock/Getty Images Plus/GettyImages; p. 36 (swimming fins): Bluemoon Stock/Stockbyte/GettyImages; p. 36 (shoes): yasinguneysu/E+/GettyImages; p. 36 (golf ball): Duncan Babbage/E+/GettyImages; p. 36 (volley ball): pioneer111/iStock/Getty Images Plus/GettyImages; p. 36 (karate uniform): Comstock/Stockbyte/GettyImages; p. 36 (fitness ball): ayzek/iStock/Getty Images Plus/GettyImages; p. 36 (yoga mat): Serg Myshkovsky/E+/GettyImages; p. 36 (soccer ball): Creative Crop/DigitalVision/GettyImages; p. 36 (bicycle): Comstock/Stockbyte/GettyImages; p. 37 (TR): Mike Kemp/Blend Images/GettyImages; p. 37 (TL): Tim Kitchen/The Image Bank/GettyImages; p. 39 (TR): Jon Bradley/The Image Bank/GettyImages; p. 39 (BR): Studio J Inc/GettyImages; p. 39 (Steph): ATELIER CREATION PHOTO/iStock/Getty Images Plus/GettyImages; p. 39 (Mick): ATELIER CREATION PHOTO/iStock/Getty Images Plus/GettyImages; p. 40 (T): ImagesBazaar/GettyImages; p. 40 (Ex 12.1): Ann Summa/Photolibrary/GettyImages; p. 40 (Ex 12.2): Portra Images/Iconica/GettyImages; p. 40 (Ex 12.3): mediaphotos/E+/GettyImages; p. 40 (Ex 12.4): T.T/Stone/GettyImages; p. 41 (T): Maximilian Stock Ltd./The Image Bank/GettyImages; p. 41 (BR): Gary Burchell/DigitalVision/GettyImages; p. 42: Hero Images/GettyImages; p. 43: Diana Mulvihill/The Image Bank/GettyImages; p. 44 (header), p. vi (Unit 7): edwardolive/iStock/Getty Images Plus/GettyImages; p. 44 (social media): sturti/iStock/Getty Images Plus/GettyImages; p. 44 (go dancing): Tom Merton/Caiaimage/GettyImages; p. 44 (listen to music): Sam Edwards/Caiaimage/GettyImages; p. 44 (play video games): Robert Deutschman/DigitalVision/GettyImages; p. 44 (read): John Lund/Marc Romanelli/Blend Images/GettyImages; p. 44 (relax): SolStock/E+/GettyImages; p. 44 (spend time): Image Source/GettyImages; p. 44 (watch TV): Dan Dalton/Caiaimage/GettyImages; p. 44 (CR): Caiaimage/Paul Bradbury/OJO+/GettyImages; p. 44 (BR): Hero Images/GettyImages; p. 44 (Cara): Caiaimage/Paul Bradbury/OJO+/GettyImages; p. 44 (Neil): Ezra Bailey/Taxi/GettyImages; p. 45: Westend61/GettyImages; p. 46: chinaface/E+/GettyImages; p. 47 (T): AleksandarNakic/E+/GettyImages; p. 47 (B): Songquan Deng/iStock/Getty Images Plus/GettyImages; p. 48: Elena Elisseeva/iStock/Getty Images Plus/GettyImages; p. 49 (T): AYOTOGRAPHY/iStock/Getty Images Plus/GettyImages; p. 49 (C): Gato Desaparecido/Alamy; p. 49 (B): simon's photo/Moment/GettyImages; p. 50 (header), p. vi (Unit 8): GARDEL Bertrand/hemis.fr/GettyImages; p. 50: Miles Ertman/All Canada Photos/GettyImages; p. 52: Chris Bennett/GettyImages; p. 53 (downtown): Anne Sophie Dhainaut/EyeEm/GettyImages; p. 53 (suburb): Bob O'Connor/Stone/GettyImages; p. 53 (shopping district): Busà Photography/Moment/GettyImages; p. 53 (college campus): Witold Skrypczak/Lonely Planet Images/GettyImages; p. 53 (business district): Julian Elliott Photography/Photolibrary/GettyImages; p. 53 (theatre district): Jerry Driendl/Stone/GettyImages; p. 53 (industrial district): ULTRA.F/Taxi Japan/GettyImages; p. 53 (small town): Barry Winiker/Photolibrary/GettyImages; p. 53 (BR): UpperCut Images/Stockbyte/GettyImages; p. 53 (Alana): UpperCut Images/Stockbyte/GettyImages; p. 53 (Barry): franckreporter/E+/GettyImages; p. 54: Guillermo Murcia/Moment/GettyImages; p. 55 (T): Noriko Hayashi/Bloomberg/GettyImages; p. 55 (C): Alessandra Santorelli/REX/Shutterstock; p. 55 (B): migstock/Alamy; p. 58 (header), p. viii (Unit 9): Tom Merton/Caiaimage/GettyImages; p. 58 (long hair): Portra Images/DigitalVision/GettyImages; p. 58 (short hair): KidStock/Blend Images/GettyImages; p. 58 (straight hair): Rick Gomez/Blend Images/GettyImages; p. 58 (curly hair): Rainer Holz/Westend61/GettyImages; p. 58 (bald): wickedpix/iStock/Getty Images Plus/GettyImages; p. 58 (mustache and beard): shapecharge/E+/GettyImages; p. 58 (young): RedChopsticks/GettyImages; p. 58 (middle aged): Caiaimage/Chris Ryan/OJO+/GettyImages; p. 58 (elderly): David Sucsy/E+/GettyImages; p. 58 (handsome): Yuri_Arcurs/iStock/Getty Images Plus/GettyImages; p. 58 (good looking): Wavebreakmedia Ltd/Getty Images Plus/GettyImages; p. 58 (pretty): AntonioGuillem/iStock/Getty Images Plus/GettyImages; p. 58 (short): Ana Abejon/E+/GettyImages; p. 58 (fairly short): DRB Images, LLC/E+/GettyImages; p. 58 (medium height): 4x6/E+/GettyImages; p. 58 (pretty tall): momentimages/GettyImages; p. 58 (very tall): Photodisc/Stockbyte/GettyImages; p. 59: Tim Robberts/Taxi/GettyImages; p. 61 (Boho): Christian Vierig/WireImage/GettyImages; p. 61 (Classic): aleksle/E+/GettyImages; p. 61 (Hipster): SeanShot/E+/GettyImages; p. 61 (Streetwear): Peter Muller/Cultura/GettyImages; p. 63 (TL): Robert Cornelius/Hulton Archive/GettyImages; p. 63 (BL): Dougal Waters/DigitalVision/GettyImages; p. 63 (TR): NASA/Getty Images North America/GettyImages; p. 63 (BR):

interchange
FIFTH EDITION

1

Video Activity Worksheets

Jack C. Richards
Revised by Deborah B. Gordon

CAMBRIDGE
UNIVERSITY PRESS

Credits

Illustration credits

Andrezzinho: 6 (*bottom*), 34; Mark Collins: 8 (*top*), 18, 30 (*bottom*), 58; Carlos Diaz: 4 (*center*), 48, 60, 62 (*bottom*); Chuck Gonzales: 2, 16 (*top*), 26, 54; Jim Haynes: 12 (*top*), 20, 24, 36, 46 (*top*), 57, 62 (*top*); Dan Hubig: 53, 61; Trevor Keen: 4 (*bottom*), 6 (*top*), 18 (*bottom*), 38, 65; Joanna Kerr: 12 (*bottom*), 30 (*top*), 32; KJA-artists.com: 23, 49, 64 (*bottom*); Monika Melnychuk/i2iart.com: 46 (*bottom*); Karen Minot: 50; Rob Schuster: 16 (*bottom*); James Yamasaki: 10 (*bottom*), 22 (*bottom*); Rose Zgodzinski: 22 (*top*)

Photo Acknowledgements

The authors and publishers acknowledge the following sources of copyright material and are grateful for the permissions granted. While every effort has been made, it has not always been possible to identify the sources of all the material used, or to trace all copyright holders. If any omissions are brought to our notice, we will be happy to include the appropriate acknowledgements on reprinting and in the next update to the digital edition, as applicable.

Key: T = Top, B = Below, TL = Top Left, TC = Top Centre, TR = Top Right, CL = Centre Left, C = Centre, CR = Centre Right, BL = Below Left, BCL = Below Centre Left, BC = Below Centre, BCR = Below Centre Right, BR = Below Right.

p. 14 (BCL): Weinstein/Everett/REX/Shutterstock; p. 14 (BCR): Dimension Films/Everett/REX/ Shutterstock; p. 14 (BL): Everett Collection/REX/ Shutterstock; p. 14 (BR): Warner Br/Everett/ REX/Shutterstock; p. 14 (CR): Courtesy Everett Collection/REX/Shutterstock; p. 14 (popcorn): Oleksandr Staroseltsev/Hemera/Getty Images; p. 14 (Ticket): Christophe Testi/Hemera/Getty Images; p. 14 (TR): Rafa Irusta/Shutterstock; p. 20: UpperCut Images/SuperStock; p. 26 (CL): Worakit Sirijinda/ Shutterstock; p. 26 (C): Maksym Gorpenyuk/ Shutterstock; p. 26 (CR): Etienne/age fotostock; p. 26 (BL): simongurney/iStock/Getty Images; p. 26 (BC): Simon James/Shutterstock; p. 26 (BR): Samot/ Shutterstock; p. 27 (TL): Wright/Relaximages/ age fotostock; p. 27 (BL): Julian Love/AWL/Getty Images; p. 27 (TR): Stockbyte/Getty Images; p. 27 (BR): claudiodivizia/iStock/Getty Images; p. 28 (TC): Worakit Sirijinda/Shutterstock; p. 28 (TL): Maksym Gorpenyuk/Shutterstock; p. 28 (BC): Etienne/ age fotostock; p. 28 (TR): simongurney/iStock/ Getty Images; p. 28 (BL): Wright/Relaximages/ age fotostock; p. 28 (BR): Travelshots/SuperStock; p. 42 (TR): Anna Shakina/Shutterstock; p. 42 (CL): Hoberman Collection/SuperStock; p. 42 (C): Mitchell Funk/Photographer's Choice/Getty Images; p. 42 (CR): Ruth Tomlinson/Robert Harding Picture Library/age fotostock; p. 42 (BL): © Ron Koeberer/Aurora Photos/Alamy; p. 42 (BC): John Elk III/Lonely Planet Images/Getty Images; p. 42 (BR): Novastock/F1online/age fotostock; p. 43 (BL): mcrosno/iStock/Getty Images; p. 43 (CL): Barry Winiker/Getty Images; p. 43 (CR): LimeWave - inspiration to exploration/Moment/Getty Images; p. 43 (TL): fStop/SuperStock; p. 43 (TC): Matt Payne of Durango, Colorado/Getty Images; p. 43 (TR): rramirez125/iStock/Getty Images; p. 43 (BR): Pietro Scozzari/age fotostock; p. 44 (TL): Mitchell Funk/Photographer's Choice/Getty Images; p. 44 (TC): © Travel Division Images/Alamy; p. 44 (BL): © Lee Foster/Alamy; p. 44 (BC): © Roberta Allen/ Alamy; p. 44 (TR): © Ed Rhodes/Alamy; p. 44 (BR): Bob Thomason/Stone/Getty Images; p. 51 (CL): © T.M.O.Buildings/Alamy; p. 52 (T): © Image Source/ Alamy; p. 53 (C): Comstock Images/Getty Images; p. 53 (B): Kongsak/Shutterstock; p. 54 (TR): Paul Harris/AWL Images/Getty Images; p. 54 (TL): © FrèdÈric Soltan/Sygma/Corbis; p. 54 (BL): Jochen Schlenker/robertharding/Getty Images; p. 54 (BR): Corbis/SuperStock; p. 55 (TR): Hisham Ibrahim/ Photographer's Choice/Getty Images; p. 55 (TL): © David Sailors/Terra/Corbis; p. 64 (Clipboard): Beboy_ltd/istockphoto.com; p. 64 (Pencil): t_kimura/Getty Images; p. 65 (CR): volare2004/ iStock/Getty Images.

Plan of Video 1

1 Are you Evan Chu? The wrong name tag at a conference causes confusion.

Functional Focus Introducing oneself; asking for and giving personal information
Grammar Present tense of *be*; Wh-questions with *be*
Vocabulary Greetings; personal information

2 I love my job! Lisa, a film student, interviews several people about their jobs for a school project.

Functional Focus Talking about work
Grammar Wh-questions with *do*
Vocabulary Occupations; time expressions

3 Yard sale Todd and Mariela have different opinions about things at a yard sale.

Functional Focus Asking for and discussing prices of things; expressing opinions
Grammar Questions with *how*; demonstratives
Vocabulary Yard sale items

4 Movies Lisa, a film student, interviews people about movies, how they watch them, and how often they watch them.

Functional Focus Expressing likes and dislikes; giving reasons
Grammar Object pronouns, questions with *do*
Vocabulary Kinds of movies; movie venues

5 A family picnic Beth introduces her family members during their picnic in the country.

Functional Focus Talking about family and family relationships
Grammar Present continuous vs. simple present
Vocabulary Family members

6 I like to stay in shape. Tim tries to impress Anne by telling her about his fitness routine.

Functional Focus Talking about routines
Grammar Adverbs of frequency
Vocabulary Words related to sports and exercise

7 My trip to London Melissa tells Lili about her trip to London.

Functional Focus Describing past events; expressing opinions
Grammar Past tense
Vocabulary Sights to see in London, England; verbs for sightseeing

8 Nice neighborhood Carmen and Luis learn about their new neighborhood.

Functional Focus Describing neighborhoods
Grammar *There is/There are*; quantifiers
Vocabulary Places in a neighborhood

9 Suspicious visitors Sarah and George are relaxing at home when they are surprised by visitors.

Functional Focus Describing physical appearance
Grammar Modifiers with participles and prepositions
Vocabulary Terms for physical appearance

10 What took you so long? On his way to meet Linda, Jacob has some problems.

Functional Focus Telling a story; apology and forgiveness
Grammar Present perfect tense; sequencing words: *first, then, after that, . . .*
Vocabulary Verbs in different tenses

11 San Francisco! Dr. and Mrs. Smith get directions and advice about what to do and see in San Francisco.

Functional Focus Asking and telling about places; giving advice
Grammar *Should* and *shouldn't*
Vocabulary Sights to see in San Francisco, California; describing tourist sights

12 Onion soup and chocolate People discuss their home remedies for colds.

Functional Focus Talking about health problems; giving advice
Grammar Infinitive complements
Vocabulary Cold remedies

13 How about a pizza? Carmen and Luis decide to try something new – in a way.

Functional Focus Agreeing and disagreeing; ordering food
Grammar *So, too, neither, either*; requests with *would* and *will*
Vocabulary Types of foods

14 Around the World Marlene, Ted, and Lili are contestants on a game show about geography.

Functional Focus Asking and answering questions about geography
Grammar Adjective comparisons; questions with *how*
Vocabulary Geographical terms

15 String cheese Mariela is throwing a party for Todd and asks for help from her guests.

Functional Focus Making phone calls and leaving messages
Grammar Requests with *tell* and *ask*
Vocabulary Telephone expressions

16 Life changes Three young people describe how their lives have changed since they finished school and started working.

Functional Focus Describing changes and plans for the future
Grammar Verb forms to describe change; verb + infinitive for future plans
Vocabulary Verb and noun pairs to describe changes

Are you Evan Chu?

☰ Preview

1 CULTURE

In North America, people go to conferences to learn more about their work, their hobbies, and other interests. At conferences, people usually don't know each other. They wear name tags to make it easier to meet each other and to help them remember new names. People at conferences usually use each other's first names.

Where do people wear name tags in your country?
When people meet new people at places like conferences, do they use first names or titles (Ms., Mrs., Mr., Professor) with last names?

2 VOCABULARY *At a conference*

PAIR WORK Here are some conference words and phrases.
Write the words and phrases under the pictures.

| clerk | name tag | introducing yourself | ✓participant |

1. participant   2. ....   3. ....   4. ....

3 GUESS THE STORY

Watch the first minute of the video with the sound off.
What do you think happens to Mike? Check (✓) your answer.

☐ Mike uses the wrong name tag.
☐ Mike changes his name to Evan Chu.
☐ Mike doesn't use any name tag.

4 *GET THE PICTURE*

A Check your answer to Exercise 3. Did you guess correctly?

B Put the pictures in the correct order (1 to 4). Then write the correct sentence from the video under each picture. Compare with a partner.

"Excuse me. This isn't mine."
"Good to see you! How's it going?"
"Hi. I'm Evan Chu."
"Hi, Rachel. Good to meet you."

....
....

5 *WATCH FOR DETAILS*

Check (✓) the correct answers. Then compare with a partner.

1. Mike's last name is ....
   - ✓ O'Neill
   - ☐ Chu
   - ☐ Anderson

2. Linda and Mike are probably ....
   - ☐ friends
   - ☐ family
   - ☐ strangers

3. The clerk gives Evan ....
   - ☐ no name tag
   - ☐ a new name tag
   - ☐ Linda's name tag

4. Mike is wearing ....
   - ☐ his name tag
   - ☐ Bill's name tag
   - ☐ Evan's name tag

5. There are .... name tags for Evan Chu.
   - ☐ three
   - ☐ two
   - ☐ zero

6 WHAT'S YOUR OPINION?

Check (✓) your opinion. Then compare with a partner.

1. When the clerk can't find Evan's name tag, how does she feel?
   - ☐ angry
   - ☐ amused
   - ☐ confused

2. When Evan meets Rachel and Mike, how does he feel?
   - ☐ pleased
   - ☐ amused
   - ☐ surprised

3. When Mike realizes he has Evan's name tag, how does he feel?
   - ☐ angry
   - ☐ embarrassed
   - ☐ pleased

angry　　　　**confused**　　　　**embarrassed**　　　　**pleased**

Follow-up

7 ROLE PLAY At a conference

A Imagine you are at a conference. Choose your name, hometown, and job. Write them below. Make a name tag for yourself.

My name is ....

I am from ....

I am a/an ....

B CLASS ACTIVITY Now walk around the room and introduce yourself. Have conversations like this:

A: Hello, my name's Sidney.
B: Hi, I'm Michelle.
A: Where are you from, Michelle?
B: I'm from Paris, France. What about you?

Where are you from?

I'm from Ontario.

8 WHAT DID THEY SAY?

Watch the video and complete the conversation. Then practice it.

Mike, Bill, and Rachel introduce themselves.

Mike: Hi, ...I'm.......... Mike ....O'Neill.......... .
Bill: What did you say your name was .... ?
Mike: .... Mike. Mike O'Neill.
Bill: .... I'm Bill. Bill ....
.... to meet you, . . . Mike.
Mike: Good to .... you, ...
Rachel: Hi. ....
Bill: Hi. .... me.
Rachel: Hi, I'm Rachel Stevens. .... to the conference.
Mike: Hi, Rachel. .... to meet you. And, ...
do you do?
Rachel: I, um, I have .... own business. I'm an interior
.... , but I volunteer with the ....
History Association. Are you from .... here?
Mike: Oh, no. I'm .... Chicago.
Rachel: Chicago. Nice ....
Mike: .... you.

9 QUESTIONS WITH BE

A Complete the questions with **is** or **are**.

1. ....Is.......... Mike's last name Chu?
2. .... Mike and Evan conference participants?
3. .... Evan and Bill friends?
4. .... Rachel a participant?
5. .... Mike an interior designer?

B **PAIR WORK** Take turns asking and answering the questions.

A: Is Mike's last name Chu?
B: No, it isn't. It's O'Neill.

10 WH-QUESTIONS *Getting to know people*

A Complete these questions with **is, are, do,** or **does**.

1. What ....is.......... Evan's last name?
2. Where .... Mike from?
3. Who .... the participants?
4. What .... Rachel do?
5. Where .... Evan's first name tag?

B **PAIR WORK** Take turns asking and answering the questions above.

C **CLASS ACTIVITY** Now find out about your classmates. Write three more questions. Then go around the class and ask them.

1. What's your first name? ....
2. ....
3. ....
4. ....

I love my job!

1 CULTURE

In North America, people with full-time jobs usually work eight hours a day. The hours of a typical office job are 9:00 A.M. to 5:00 P.M. Many people also work part time. Some people work two or more part-time jobs. People in North America usually change jobs several times in their lives. The average person also changes careers – not just jobs – two or three times.

How many hours a day do people work in your country?
What are typical office hours? Do people also work part time?
Do people often change jobs or careers?

2 VOCABULARY *Occupations*

PAIR WORK Who works inside, who works outside, and who works in both places? Put the words in the chart. Can you add three more words?

chef

Inside	Outside	Inside and Outside
......	......	......
......	......	......
......	......	......
......	......	......
......	......	......
......	......	......

cab driver

dance instructor

construction worker

waiter

mover

3 GUESS THE STORY

Watch the first 25 seconds of the video.
Which jobs is Lisa going to focus on?

- ☐ cab driver
- ☐ chef
- ☐ construction worker
- ☐ dance instructor
- ☐ mover
- ☐ waiter

▤ Watch the video

4 GET THE PICTURE

Match the pictures of the people with their names and their jobs.

| 1. Sasha | 2. Brian | 3. Tim | 4. Chris |

| waiter | mover | dance instructor | cab driver |

5 WATCH FOR DETAILS

Check (✓) **True** or **False.** Then correct the false statements.
Compare with a partner.

	True	False	
1. Tim doesn't like his job.	☐	✓	Tim likes his job.
2. Tim doesn't drive the truck.	☐	☐	
3. Sasha works five hours a day.	☐	☐	
4. Chris works long hours.	☐	☐	
5. Chris works at night.	☐	☐	
6. Brian starts work at 9:00.	☐	☐	

6 GIVING REASONS

PAIR WORK Read the sentences below. Then use them to complete the chart.

Reasons Tim likes his job	Reasons Chris doesn't like his job
....	....
....	....
....	....
....	....

Reasons Sasha likes her work	Reasons Brian's job is important
....	....
....	....
....	....
....	....

It helps people get fit and be healthy.

It's fun to drive a big truck.

It's necessary to work long hours.

It's fun to teach people new moves.

People are hungry.

People don't have time to cook.

There is traffic.

There are different problems to solve.

Follow-up

7 ROLE PLAY Jobs

PAIR WORK Imagine you are one of the people in the video. Don't tell anyone who you are. Walk around the room and use these questions to ask about each other's jobs. Guess people's jobs.

Do you like your job?
What do you like or not like about your job?

8 WHAT DID THEY SAY?

Watch the video and complete the conversation. Then practice it.

Lisa is talking to Chris.

Lisa: Hi. Do you ....*have*.......... a minute?

Chris: ....

Lisa: What's your name, and what ....

.... ?

Chris: My name is Chris, and I ....

a ....

Lisa: .... you .... your job?

Chris: Most .... , yes.

Lisa: What .... you .... about your job?

Chris: I work .... I work ....

.... , too. And .... is the ....

9 QUESTIONS WITH DO; PRESENT TENSE VERBS

A Complete the *questions* in the present tense. Complete the *answers* with the correct verb. Then practice the conversation.

Tim: I'm a mover. I .... people .... their entire lives from their old home to their new home.

Lisa: How .... you .... about your job?

Tim: I really .... my job.

Lisa: How .... you .... your day?

Tim: I .... boxes, ... items, and .... the truck.

Sometimes I .... the truck. That's the easy part.

B (PAIR WORK) Now have similar conversations using your own information. (If you don't work, choose a job from the book.)

10 ASKING ABOUT JOBS

(PAIR WORK) Brian's friend is a chef in his restaurant. Think of three different questions Lisa could ask him about his job. Then work with your partner to ask and answer these questions.

1. How do you like your job? ....

2. ....

3. ....

4. ....

Yard sale

Preview

1 CULTURE

In North America, people often sell old things like furniture, jewelry, or clothing at a garage sale or yard sale. They decide on prices, put the things on tables in their garage or yard, and then they put a sign in front of their house to advertise the sale. People come to look and maybe to buy. Some things at yard sales are antiques and are worth a lot of money.

Do people have garage sales or yard sales in your country?
What old things do you have at home?
What things would you like to sell at a yard sale?

GARAGE SALE
Saturday 9-5; children's clothes, books, toys, kitchen items, TV. 257 Maple Ave.

YARD SALE
Saturday/Sunday 8-4; exercise equipment, furniture, CDs, DVDs. 89 Oak St.

2 VOCABULARY *Yard sale items*

PAIR WORK Put the words in the chart. Can you add six more words? Add things from your home.

Kitchen items	Jewelry	Other
		books

snorkeling equipment

a bracelet

a watch

a necklace

books

dishes

cups and saucers

a camera

3 GUESS THE STORY

A *Watch the video with the sound off.* Which things from Exercise 2 do you see at the yard sale? Circle the things you see.

B What do you think the man wants to buy? What does the woman want to buy? Make a list.

....
....
....
....

....
....
....
....

Watch the video

4 WHAT'S YOUR OPINION?

In the end, do you think Todd and Mariela buy any of these things at the yard sale? Check (✓) **Yes** or **No**. Then compare your answers with a partner.

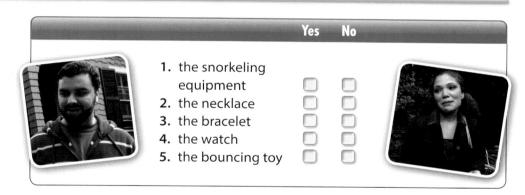

	Yes	No
1. the snorkeling equipment	☐	☐
2. the necklace	☐	☐
3. the bracelet	☐	☐
4. the watch	☐	☐
5. the bouncing toy	☐	☐

5 MAKING INFERENCES

PAIR WORK Check (✓) the best answers.

1. Mariela thinks Todd
....
the snorkeling equipment.
☐ really wants
☐ really doesn't want

2. Todd thinks the snorkeling equipment is
....
☐ cheap
☐ expensive

3. Todd thinks the necklace and bracelet are
....
☐ a good price
☐ too expensive

4. Todd thinks the watch is
....
☐ not very nice
☐ too old

6 ROLE PLAY *Shop at a Yard Sale*

A **PAIR WORK** Imagine you are at a yard sale. Number the sentences
(1 to 6) to make conversations. Then practice the conversations.

1. .... And how much are these earrings?
   ....1.... Hello. Can I help you?
   .... It's twelve dollars.
   .... Yes, how much is this ring?
   .... They're twenty dollars.
   .... Thanks. I'll think about it.

2. .... Can I help you?
   .... Oh, that's pretty expensive.
   .... OK. I'll take it.
   .... Yes, how much is this MP3 player?
   .... Well, how about thirty dollars?
   .... It's forty dollars.

B **CLASS ACTIVITY** Plan a class yard sale. Form two groups.
Make a list of things your group will sell, and give each item a price.

Items for sale	Price
....	....
....	....
....	....
....	....
....	....
....	....

Now have the yard sale:

Group A: You are the sellers. Try to sell everything on
your list to Group B. Then change roles and decide
what to buy from Group B.

Group B: You are the buyers.
Ask questions and decide what to buy.
Then change roles and try to sell
everything on your list to Group A.

7 WHAT DID THEY SAY?

Watch the video and complete the conversation. Then practice it.

Mariela and Todd are looking at things at the yard sale.

Todd: Hey, Mariela, how do you ....like........... this?

Mariela: Oh, ... , Todd.

Todd: Oh, come on. It's only a ....

Mariela: .... you really .... it, Todd?

Todd: No. I guess .... right.

Sarah: Hi. Can I .... you?

Todd: No, thanks .... We're just ....

Mariela: Oh! Todd, ... over here. Just look at this lovely old ....

Todd: Yeah, it's ....

Mariela: It's .... just "OK," Todd. It's very ....

8 EXPRESSING OPINIONS

Todd says these sentences. What do they mean in the video? Check (✓) the correct answer. Then compare with a partner.

1. How do you like this?
   ☐ Can you believe how little this costs?
   ☐ What do you think of this?

2. Oh, come on.
   ☐ Please let me [buy it].
   ☐ Are you kidding?

3. Yeah, it's OK.
   ☐ I like it a little.
   ☐ The price is reasonable.

4. That's not bad.
   ☐ It's nice.
   ☐ The price is reasonable.

5. Mariela, are you kidding?
   ☐ I don't believe it!
   ☐ Let's go!

9 HOW MUCH AND HOW OLD

A Complete the conversations with **how much is (are)** or **how old is (are)**. Complete the answers with the correct verb.

1. A: How much is .... this necklace?
   B: It's only $10.
   A: .... it?
   B: It's 20 years old.

2. A: .... these books?
   B: They're $2 each.
   A: And .... they?
   B: They're about 10 years old.

3. A: .... these shoes?
   B: About two years old, I think.
   A: .... they?
   B: They're $20.

B **PAIR WORK** Practice the conversations in Exercise 9. Use items of your own.

4 Movies

Preview

1 CULTURE

In North America, most people live close to at least one movie theater. Movies are popular with people on dates, families, young people in groups, or just about anyone. Most movie theaters in North America have more than one screen. Some have as many as 20 or 25 screens! There are lots of different kinds of food and drinks to buy at movie theaters, but the most popular snack is popcorn.

Number of U.S. Movie Screens in 2009

Indoor   Drive-In
38,605   628

TOTAL
39,233

Who likes to go to movies in your country?
What kinds of movies are popular?
What kinds of snacks do people buy?

2 VOCABULARY Kinds of movies

What kinds of movies or videos do you like? Check (✓) your opinions.
Then compare answers in groups.

classic

WHAT'S YOUR OPINION?				
	I love them.	I like them.	I don't like them very much.	I don't like them at all.
romance movies	☐	☐	☐	☐
classic films	☐	☐	☐	☐
comedies	☐	☐	☐	☐
horror films	☐	☐	☐	☐
science-fiction movies	☐	☐	☐	☐
historical dramas	☐	☐	☐	☐

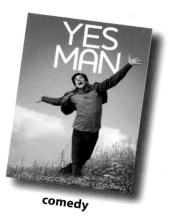

comedy

science fiction

historical drama

horror

3 GUESS THE STORY

Watch the first 45 seconds of the video.
Then answer these questions:

1. What different ways to watch movies does Lisa talk about?
2. What is Lisa's main question?
3. How many people is she going to interview?

Watch the video

4 GET THE PICTURE

A Circle the correct answers. Then compare with a partner.

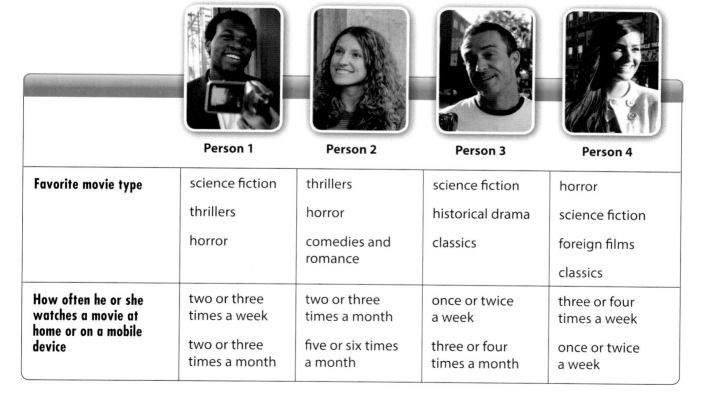

	Person 1	Person 2	Person 3	Person 4
Favorite movie type	science fiction thrillers horror	thrillers horror comedies and romance	science fiction historical drama classics	horror science fiction foreign films classics
How often he or she watches a movie at home or on a mobile device	two or three times a week two or three times a month	two or three times a month five or six times a month	once or twice a week three or four times a month	three or four times a week once or twice a week

B Circle which people gave these opinions.

1. Special effects are better on the big screen.   Person 1   Person 2   Person 3   Person 4
2. All movies are better on the big screen.   Person 1   Person 2   Person 3   Person 4
3. It's a night on the town.   Person 1   Person 2   Person 3   Person 4
4. Watching movies is more fun in a group.   Person 1   Person 2   Person 3   Person 4

5 INTERVIEW QUESTIONS

A How often does Lisa ask each of these questions, or questions that are very similar to these? Make a slash mark (/) each time you hear one of these questions. Then compare with a partner.

.... 1. Do you like movies?
.... 2. What type of movies do you like?
.... 3. How often do you watch movies on your television, computer, or mobile device?
.... 4. How often do you go to a movie theater to watch a movie?
.... 5. What makes going to the movie theater so special for you?

B What other Wh-question word does Lisa use?

Follow-up

6 CLASS INTERVIEW

A **CLASS ACTIVITY** Use the questions in Exercise 5 to interview at least three classmates. Have conversations like this:

A: What types of movies do you like?
B: (*movie types*)
A: How often do you watch movies on your computer?
B: About twice a week.

B Now report the results of your interviews. What types of movies are the most popular? Least popular? How often do your classmates go to movie theaters? How often do they watch movies at home or on their mobile devices?

7 MAKING PLANS

GROUP WORK Plan to see a movie with your group. Also decide where to watch the movie. Give your opinions with statements and questions like these:

There's a great movie on tonight at ....
Do you really like .... ?
That sounds good. How about you, ... ?
I don't really like ....
Well, what kind of .... do you like?

8 WHAT DID THEY SAY?

Watch the video and complete the conversation. Then practice it.

Lisa is interviewing Person 4.

Lisa: What ....type........ of movies ....do............ you like?

Woman: I like .... films. I like to see .... in other cultures.

Lisa: Do you like .... movies?

Woman: Yes, I do.

Lisa: .... ?

Woman: I like to see the .... black-and-white movies.

Lisa: How often .... you watch movies on your television, computer, or .... device?

Woman: I watch movies on my .... quite frequently .... I take the train to work. I probably see one or two a ....

Lisa: And how .... do you go to the theater to .... a movie?

Woman: I go pretty frequently. I would probably say, ... or twice a month.

Lisa: .... makes the theater so .... for you?

Woman: The special effects are much .... in the movie theater.

9 OBJECT PRONOUNS

A Fill in the blanks with **him**, **her**, **it**, or **them**.

1. A: Do you like horror films?
   B: No, I can't stand ......them...... .

2. A: Who's your favorite actor?
   B: Leonardo DiCaprio. I liked .... in *Inception*.

3. A: What do you think of Keira Knightley?
   B: I don't know .... What was she in?

4. A: What do you think of science fiction?
   B: I like .... a lot, too.

5. A: What do you think about romantic comedies?
   B: I like .... because they make me laugh.

6. A: Do you like 3-D?
   B: Yes, I like .... a lot, especially in action movies.

B Take turns asking and answering the questions above. Give your own opinions.

10 GIVING REASONS

PAIR WORK Take turns giving your opinions about movies, actors, and actresses. Use these sentences to start your conversations.

1. A: I don't like historical dramas.
   B: Why not?
   A: I think they're dull.

2. A: I love horror movies.
   B: Really? Why?
   A: I like feeling scared.

3. A: I don't like thrillers at all.
   B: Why not?
   A: Because I don't like to feel scared.

4. A: I love going to movie theaters.
   B: What makes movie theaters so special for you?
   A: Because the special effects are better on a big screen.

A family picnic

1 CULTURE

In North America, 97 percent of people say that their family is the most important part of their life. But people in North America move often, and many children leave home at age 18. Many families only see each other on important holidays or at family parties.

- Six percent of all families move every year.
- On an average day, 116,438 people move.
- People often live far away from their parents and grandparents.
- Only 36 percent of families see their relatives once a week.

RENT A TRUCK

In your country, when do children leave home?
Do families move often?
How often do families see each other?

2 VOCABULARY *Family*

PAIR WORK How are these people related to Jane? Fill in the blanks in her family tree.

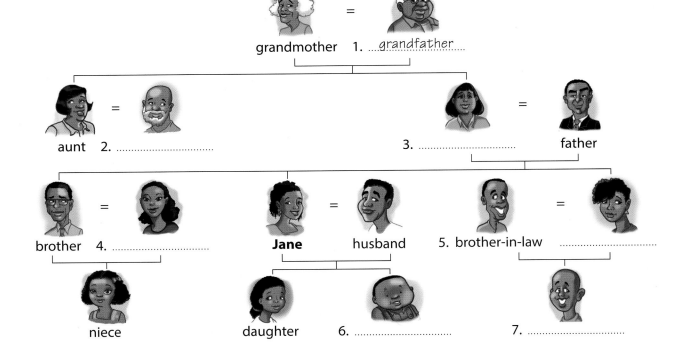

grandmother 1. grandfather

aunt 2. .... 3. .... father

brother 4. .... Jane husband 5. brother-in-law ....

niece daughter 6. .... 7. ....

3 GUESS THE STORY

Watch the first 45 seconds of the video with the sound off.
The young woman is Beth. Who do you think these people are?

1. Beth's husband
2. ....
3. ....
4. ....

 Watch the video

4 GET THE PICTURE

Who's at the picnic? Check (✓) **Yes** or **No**. Then compare with a partner.

	Yes	No
Beth's parents	☐	☐
Beth's uncle and aunt	☐	☐
Beth's brother	☐	☐
Beth's sister	☐	☐
Beth's nephew	☐	☐
Beth's brother-in-law	☐	☐
Beth's niece	☐	☐
Beth's cousin	☐	☐
Beth's grandparents	☐	☐

5 WATCH FOR DETAILS

Check (✓) the correct answer. Then compare with a partner.

1. Kathleen and Jerry are Beth's
   .... parents.
   ☐ mother's
   ☐ father's

2. .... likes to fish.
   ☐ Beth's father
   ☐ Beth's brother-in-law

3. Kathleen and Jerry are looking
   for ....
   ☐ birds
   ☐ Ted

4. Beth's mother, aunt, and uncle are
   getting ready to ....
   ☐ play a game
   ☐ cook lunch

5. Beth's niece is ....
   ☐ Kimberley
   ☐ Megan

6. At every family picnic, Beth's
   husband ....
   ☐ walks in the woods
   ☐ takes a photograph

6 WHAT'S YOUR OPINION?

PAIR WORK Read the culture note on page 18 again. Do you think Beth's family is like most families in North America? How is it the same and how is it different?

☰ Follow-up

---

7 YOUR FAMILY

A PAIR WORK Is your family like Beth's? Tell about your family and find out about your partner's. Ask questions like these:

Are you living with your parents right now?
   If not, do you live near your parents?
Do you live near or far from your brothers, sisters,
   aunts, uncles, and grandparents?
Are you married?
Do you have children? If so, how old are they?
Do you have brothers and sisters?
Are they going to school or working?

B Draw a simple picture (or show your partner a photo) of your family. Your partner will ask questions about each person.

Is this your sister?
What does she do?
Is she studying English, too?

---

8 AN INTERESTING PERSON

A PAIR WORK Find out about your partner's most interesting relative or friend. Ask questions like these:

Who's your most interesting relative or friend?
What's his or her name?
What does he or she do?
Where is he or she living now?
How old is he or she?
Is he or she married?

B Now tell another classmate about your partner's relative like this:

Yong-su has an interesting cousin.
Her name is Son-hee.
She works at a zoo.
She's from Seoul.
She's working in New York now.
She's 30 years old.

9 WHAT DID SHE SAY?

Watch the video and complete Beth's description. Then practice it.

Beth describes her family members.

Hi, I'm Beth, and ....this............ is my husband, Chris. We're
.... for a family picnic. ....
the picnic in the country.

That's my .... , Ted. He .... to fish.
And .... my mom, Angela, ...
.... She's talking to my Aunt Helen and
Uncle James. Helen .... my mom's sister, and
James is Helen's ....

And that's my sister, Kimberley. Jake's .... in
the woods. He's .... years old and very
....

Kimberley .... Jake's mom. So Jake is my ....

10 PRESENT CONTINUOUS VS. SIMPLE PRESENT

A Complete the conversation using the present continuous
or simple present. Then practice with a partner.

1. A: Do all of your relatives live in the United States?
   B: No, I .....have..... (have) relatives in Mexico. My grandparents and older sister
      .... (live) there.

2. A: What does your sister do? Does she have a job?
   B: No, she .... (work) right now. She .... (go) to school.

3. A: What is she studying?
   B: She .... (study) English literature. She .... (love) it.

4. A: What about your grandparents? Do they still work or are they retired?
   B: They .... (work) anymore, but they love to travel. Right now, they're
      .... (visit) China!

B **CLASS ACTIVITY** Write similar questions of your own. Then go
around the class and interview your classmates about their families.
Write some of your questions below.

1. Do your parents live in ....? ....
2. ....
3. ....
4. ....

I like to stay in shape.

1 CULTURE

In North America, most people think regular exercise is important, although not everyone does it. People exercise outdoors, at home, or at a gym or health club. Many people play sports after school, after work, or on weekends. They also bicycle, walk, swim, or jog. People exercise for different reasons: to lose weight, to stay in shape, or just to relax.

Do you exercise or play sports?
What sports are popular in your country?
What percentage of people in your country do you think exercise regularly?

In the U.S. and Canada

 Thirty-five percent of people exercise every day.

 Eighteen percent of people play team sports regularly.

2 VOCABULARY *Sports and exercise*

A **PAIR WORK** Write the activities under the correct pictures.

| stretching | basketball | ✓jogging | soccer | weight lifting | volleyball |

1. jogging

2. ....

3. ....

4. ....

5. ....

6. ....

B Write the words from part A in the chart. Can you add two more words?

Individual activities		Team sports	
jogging	....	....	....
....	....	....	....

3 GUESS THE STORY

Watch the first 40 seconds of the video.
What do you think happens next?

- ☐ The man talks about his exercise routine.
- ☐ The woman talks about her exercise routine.
- ☐ The man and woman compare their exercise routines.

▤ Watch the video

4 GET THE PICTURE

Check (✓) **True** or **False**. Correct the false statements. Then compare with a partner.

	True	False	
1. Tim and Anne are friends.	☐	☐	....
2. Tim really likes to exercise.	☐	☐	....
3. Anne is more energetic and fit than Tim.	☐	☐	....

5 WATCH FOR DETAILS

A Check (✓) the activities Tim talks about doing.

B Circle the activities you think he *really* does. Then compare your responses with a partner.

☐ jogging

☐ stretching

☐ bicycling

☐ lifting weights

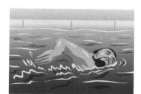
☐ swimming

☐ sit-ups

☐ taking walks

☐ playing tennis

☐ team sports

6 WHAT'S YOUR OPINION?

PAIR WORK What kind of person is Anne? What kind of person is Tim? Choose at least one word for each person.

Anne	Tim
....	....
....	....
....	....

friendly

intelligent

polite

lazy

Follow-up

7 INTERVIEW

A Add three questions to the list about sports and exercise.

1. What kinds of sports do you play?
2. What kinds of exercise do you do?
3. Are you in good shape?

4. ....
5. ....
6. ....

B **PAIR WORK** Take turns asking and answering your questions. Your partner will answer playing the role of the woman or the man in the video.

8 HOW ABOUT YOU?

A Complete the chart. Then compare with a partner.

Things you sometimes do	Things you don't usually do
I sometimes . . . . after school.	I don't usually . . . on the weekend.
....	....
....	....

Things you never do	Things you would like to start doing
I never go . . . . in the morning.	I'd like to start . . . .
....	....
....	....

B **CLASS ACTIVITY** Who in the class likes to exercise? Who doesn't? Make a class chart.

9 *WHAT DID THEY SAY?*

Watch the video and complete the conversation. Then practice it.

Anne stops to tie her shoe and talks to Tim.

Tim: It's a ......*beautiful*...... morning, huh? ....
always come out here this early?

Anne: Yes, I .... I .... get up around
.... o'clock. What about you? Do you come
.... a lot?

Tim: Yeah, I do. I .... stay in shape.

Anne: You .... ?

Tim: Yes.

Anne: How often do you .... ?

Tim: .... day.

Anne: .... ?

Tim: Yeah, I usually .... my day with ....
stretches. Then, I .... do some .... ,
lift .... , and, when the weather's .... ,
my .... and I are never too far apart.

10 *ADVERBS OF FREQUENCY*

A Rewrite the sentences with the adverbs in the correct place.

1. I get up before 5 A.M. (never)
   I never get up before 5 A.M.

2. I don't have a big breakfast. (usually)
   ....

3. I play tennis after work. (sometimes)
   ....

4. I take a long walk on the weekend. (often)
   ....

5. I watch TV. (never)
   ....

6. I jog in the morning. (always)
   ....

B Imagine you are the man in the video. Change the frequency adverbs in the sentences where necessary. Compare with a partner.

C How often do you do these things? Use the phrases below or your own ideas. Then compare with a partner.

every evening	twice a week	very often
once a year	about three times a month	every day

1. go to sleep by 10 P.M.
   ....

2. work late
   ....

3. ride a bicycle
   ....

4. lift weights
   ....

My trip to London

1 CULTURE

Each year, 27 million people visit London, England. London is one of the most popular tourist destinations in the world. London is famous for its beautiful historic buildings, parks and gardens, museums, multinational restaurants, double-decker buses, and shops. London is also famous for rainy weather and fog. It rains more than 100 days a year.

There are more than 5,500 restaurants in London!

Do you know anything else about London?
Would you like to visit London?
What cities in the world would you like to visit?

2 VOCABULARY *Places in London*

PAIR WORK How much do you know about London? Write the captions under the correct pictures.

a boat trip on the River Thames	Buckingham Palace	St. Paul's Cathedral
the Tower of London	✓ the London Eye	Big Ben

the London Eye

....

....

....

....

....

GUESS THE STORY

Watch the video with the sound off. Then look at the pictures in Exercise 2. Number them in the order the woman talks about them.

☰ Watch the video

 GET THE PICTURE

In the video, Melissa mentions three more places she saw in London. Look at the pictures and cross out the place that she did NOT see.

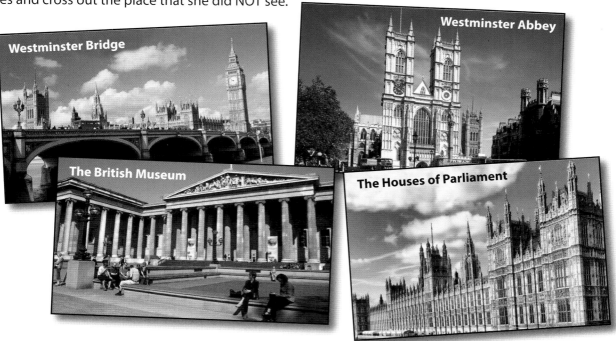

Westminster Bridge

Westminster Abbey

The British Museum

The Houses of Parliament

5 WATCH FOR DETAILS

A What did Melissa say about these places? Check (✓) the correct answers. Then compare with a partner.

1. The London Eye
   - ☐ The views were great.
   - ☐ The ride was fun.

2. The boat trip on the River Thames
   - ☐ The weather was rainy.
   - ☐ It was interesting.

3. Buckingham Palace
   - ☐ She took a tour.
   - ☐ The queen wasn't there.

4. The guards at Buckingham Palace
   - ☐ The guards ignore tourists.
   - ☐ The guards like the tourists.

B What did Melissa do on Sunday? Number the statements in the correct order.

.... She saw Westminster Abbey.

.... She saw Big Ben and Parliament.

.... She went to the airport.

.... She walked around.

.... She walked across Westminster Bridge.

6 A DAY IN LONDON

A **GROUP WORK** Which London sights are most interesting to you?
Number them from 1 to 6 (1 = the most interesting).

St. Paul's Cathedral · The London Eye · The Tower of London

Westminster Bridge · A boat on the River Thames · Buckingham Palace

B **PAIR WORK** Tell another person why two of these places interest you.

7 WHAT'S YOUR OPINION?

A **PAIR WORK** What do you like to do when you visit a new city? Add three
more things to the list. Then number them from 1 to 8.

.... go sightseeing

.... eat at local restaurants

.... buy souvenirs

.... take photographs

.... go shopping

....

....

....

B **PAIR WORK** Now compare answers with another person. Have conversations like this:
A: Do you like to go shopping?
B: No, I don't. I prefer sightseeing.

Language close-up

8 WHAT DID THEY SAY?

Watch the video and complete the conversation. Then practice it.

Melissa is telling Lili about her trip.

Lili: How was your ...._trip_........ to London? Did you have .... free time between meetings?

Melissa: London was .... We were very .... all week, but I had some .... on Saturday and Sunday morning. I flew .... on Sunday evening.

Lili: Did you .... any pictures?

Melissa: Better than .... I have ....

Lili: Excellent!

Melissa: I did .... on Saturday. First, I .... to the London Eye. Here it ....

Lili: Did you .... on .... ?

Melissa: Yes, I .... The .... were fantastic. Then, I went .... a boat .... the River Thames.

Lili: What was the weather .... ? Doesn't it rain a lot in England?

Melissa: The weather was .... It didn't .... all the time.

9 PAST TENSE *Describing a trip*

A Fill in the blanks with the correct past tense of the verbs in parentheses. Then practice the conversation.

Lili: Tell me about your trip to London.

Melissa: Well, I ......_did_...... (do) a lot of interesting things. I .... (go) on the London Eye and I .... (take) a boat trip on the Thames.

Lili: What .... (do) you see on the boat trip?

Melissa: It .... (be) really interesting. I .... (see) Tower Bridge and the Tower of London.

Lili: .... (do) you go in the Tower of London?

Melissa: No, I .... (do / not) have time. But after the boat trip, I .... (go) to Buckingham Palace.

Lili: .... (be) the Queen there?

Melissa: No, she .... (be / not).

Lili: .... (do) you take a tour?

Melissa: No, I .... (do / not). But I .... (see) many other places!

B PAIR WORK Have similar conversations about a real or an imaginary trip of your own. Start like this:

A: I went to . . .
B: Really! Tell me about your trip.

8 Nice neighborhood

Preview

1 CULTURE

People in North America move often. When they look for a new home, they consider many factors. People with children, for example, think about the quality of the local schools. Others consider the number of restaurants, shops, and supermarkets nearby, the availability of public transportation, and how quiet the neighborhood is. People can use real estate agents to help them find a new home, or they can look in the newspaper or online for available places to live. Most people walk around the neighborhood and talk to the neighbors before they make a decision.

In your country, do people use real estate agents to help them find new homes?
Do they talk to the neighbors before deciding on an apartment or house in a new neighborhood?
What else do people think about before they decide on a new home?

2 VOCABULARY Questions about neighborhoods

PAIR WORK Write the correct question under each picture.

Is it noisy?
Are there places to eat nearby?

✓ Is there any crime?
  Is there shopping nearby?

Is there public transportation nearby?
Is there enough street parking?

1. _Is there any crime?_

2. ....

3. ....

4. ....

5. ....

6. ....

3 GUESS THE STORY

Watch the first minute of the video with the sound off.
Then answer the questions:

1. Who is the woman with the couple?
   - ☐ a friend
   - ☐ a real estate agent
   - ☐ a neighbor

2. What do you think the couple is going to do?
   - ☐ go back into the apartment building
   - ☐ go with the woman
   - ☐ look around the neighborhood

☰ Watch the video

4 GET THE PICTURE

A Look at your answers to Exercise 3. Did you guess correctly?

B Check (✓) **True** or **False**. Then correct the false statements. Compare with a partner.

	True	False	
1. The neighborhood is quiet and safe now.	☐	☐	....
2. The neighborhood is far from downtown.	☐	☐	....
3. There aren't many restaurants.	☐	☐	....
4. They like the neighborhood.	☐	☐	....

5 MAKING INFERENCES

Check (✓) the best answers. Compare with a partner.

1. Carmen likes the apartment ....
   - ☐ more than Luis likes it
   - ☐ as much as Luis likes it

2. .... is happy to find a good bookstore.
   - ☐ Carmen
   - ☐ Luis

3. Luis likes the neighborhood because of the ....
   - ☐ different types of restaurants
   - ☐ music store

4. Luis and Carmen decide to ....
   - ☐ keep looking at apartments
   - ☐ take the apartment

6 A GOOD NEIGHBORHOOD

GROUP WORK What do you look for in a neighborhood? Number these neighborhood features from 1 to 6 (1 = the most important).

shopping malls

supermarkets

restaurants and coffee shops

parks

good neighbors

public transportation

7 WHAT'S YOUR OPINION?

A PAIR WORK List three more features of a good neighborhood.

1. ....

2. ....

3. ....

B Now think about your own neighborhood. Put a check (✓) beside the features in Exercises 6 and 7 that are true for your neighborhood. Then compare with a partner. Have conversations like this:

A: My neighborhood has a great grocery store. Does yours?
B: No, it doesn't. And the supermarket is far away. My neighborhood has . . .

8 WHAT DID THEY SAY?

Watch the video and complete the conversation. Then practice it.

Carmen and Luis explore the neighborhood.

Carmen: ....There's.......... a furniture store.

Luis: Uh-huh. ....

Carmen: And .... a jewelry store.

My .... coming up . . .

Both: . . . . month.

Luis: Yeah, I ....

Carmen: .... , Luis. .... a really nice grocery store.

Luis: Yeah, that's a nice .... store.

Carmen: And .... are a lot of really good .... shops.

I .... like this neighborhood!

Luis: Yes, it's really .... Wow! .... an amazing guitar!

Carmen: So, ... we .... the apartment?

Luis: .... Why .... ? Let's go for it.

9 QUANTIFIERS *Describing a neighborhood*

A Fill in the blanks with **many** or **much**. Then practice the conversation.

A: Is there .... crime in this neighborhood?

B: Oh no. There isn't .... crime at all. Not anymore.

A: How about noise? How .... street noise is there?

B: Well, there aren't .... major roads in this neighborhood.

A: Are there .... students in the neighborhood?

B: Yes. It's very close to the university, so .... students live here.

A: I see. How .... parking spaces come with the apartment?

B: I'm afraid there aren't any parking spaces. You have to park on the street.

A: How about supermarkets? Is there .... shopping nearby?

B: Oh, yes. There's a big supermarket just down the street. And there

are .... other shops nearby, too.

A: OK. I'll have a look around and call you later. Thanks!

B **PAIR WORK** Practice the conversation again, but this time use neighborhood features of your own. Be sure to include sentences with the words *many* and *much*.

Suspicious visitors

Preview

1 CULTURE

To protect their homes against crime, people in North America sometimes do one or more of the following:

- keep their doors locked
- leave lights on when they go out
- have a "peephole" (or hole in the door) to see who's outside
- have an alarm system that makes noise if someone tries to open a door or window
- buy a dog to guard their home

Which types of neighborhoods have more crime in your country: suburbs, rural areas, or cities?
How do people protect their homes in your country?

2 VOCABULARY *Physical appearance*

A **PAIR WORK** Write the words and phrases in the chart. (One word can go in two places.) Can you add two more words or phrases?

average	blond	✓early forties	late thirties	middle-aged	tall
bald	curly	elderly	long	short	teens

Age	Height	Hair
early forties		

B List two words or phrases that describe the man and the woman.

The man	The woman
late forties	

3 GUESS THE STORY

Watch the first minute of the video with the sound off.
Answer the questions.

1. Who do you think is in the car?
2. Do you think the couple is expecting visitors?

Watch the video

4 GET THE PICTURE

A Look at your answers to Exercise 3. Did you guess correctly?

B What really happens? Check (✓) your answer.
Then compare with a partner.

☐ Sarah is afraid of the police.
☐ The people in the car are escaped prisoners.
☐ The people outside are driving Sarah's car.
☐ The people outside are George's relatives.

5 WATCH FOR DETAILS

Put the pictures in order (1 to 6). Then write the correct sentence under each picture.
Compare with a partner.

George is calling the police.   ✓ Sarah is writing, and George is pouring coffee.
Sarah and George are greeting their visitors.   The visitors are getting out of the SUV.
Sarah is looking at the SUV.   The visitors are standing outside their SUV.

....
....

Sarah is writing, and George is
pouring coffee.   ....
                                             ....

6 DESCRIBING SOMEONE

A Circle the correct answers. Then compare with a partner.

1. Age	twenties	forties	twenties	forties
2. Hair color	light	dark	light	dark
3. Hair description	short	long	short	long
	straight	curly	straight	curly
4. Height	tall	short	tall	short
5. Other	baseball cap	no hat	baseball cap	no hat
	glasses	no glasses	glasses	no glasses

B What else can you add about Harry and Alexis? Compare your descriptions.

Follow-up

7 THE RIGHT DECISION?

PAIR WORK Sarah and George decide to call the police. What do you think is the best thing to do in a situation like this?

- ☐ Call the police.
- ☐ Don't open the door, but ask, "Who is it?"
- ☐ Run and hide.
- ☐ other ....

8 WHAT HAPPENS NEXT?

A **GROUP WORK** What do you think happens when the police arrive? Write out the conversation between Sarah, George, Harry, Alexis, and the police. Start like this:

Officer: Is there a problem here?
George: Well, actually, . . .

B **CLASS ACTIVITY** Act out your conversation for the class.

9 WHAT DID THEY SAY?

Watch the video and complete the conversation. Then practice it.

Sarah describes the visitors to George.

George: Sarah, would you ....*like*............ another cup of .... ?

Sarah: .... thanks. . . . Honey, ...
we know .... who has an SUV?

George: An SUV? The Thompsons .... an
SUV. A .... one.

Sarah: This .... not green.

George: .... not? What .... is it?

Sarah: I .... tell. It's red, or brown. It's ....

George: .... is it?

Sarah: It's parked in front of the ....
And .... are two .... inside.

George: .... ?

Sarah: Uh-huh. .... now they're getting out of it.

George: .... do they .... like?

Sarah: One man's .... , and he's got ....
hair, and he's .... sunglasses.

George: And .... about the .... one?

 10 MODIFIERS WITH PARTICIPLES AND PREPOSITIONS

A Look at the picture. Match the information in columns A, B, and C.

A	B	C
Sarah	is the heavier man	wearing an open jacket.
George	is the young one	wearing a red sweater.
Harry	is the older woman	wearing a blue shirt.
Alexis	is the tall one	wearing a baseball cap.

B **PAIR WORK** What else do you remember about the people in the video?
Write sentences of your own.

1. .... 3. ....
2. .... 4. ....

 11 DESCRIBING SOMEONE

A **PAIR WORK** Take turns asking and answering questions about a classmate. Try to guess who the person is.

A: Is it a tall person with curly hair?
B: No, the person is short and has . . .

B Write five sentences describing your classmates. Two of your sentences should be false. Then read your sentences. Your partner should say "True" or "False" and correct the false sentences.

A: Steve's the tall guy wearing a blue shirt.
B: False. He's wearing a white shirt.

What took you so long?

1 CULTURE

In North America, people usually like others to be on time, but for some occasions it's OK to be a little late. For example, people should always arrive on time or a little early for a business appointment, work, or a class. However, when they meet a friend or when someone invites them to dinner, it's OK to arrive 5 to 10 minutes late. For an informal party, it's OK to arrive 15 to 30 minutes late.

Are people usually on time for appointments, work, or a class in your country?

Is it OK to arrive late when you meet a friend for dinner or go to an informal party?

When are some other times when it is OK to arrive a little late? How late is too late?

2 VOCABULARY Past tense of verbs

PAIR WORK Complete the chart with the past tense of these verbs.

Present	Past	Present	Past
call	called	lock	....
cost	cost	open	....
do	....	pay	....
find	....	put	....
get	....	remember	....
go	....	see	....
have	....	take	....
leave	....	try	....

3 GUESS THE STORY

Watch the first 30 seconds of the video with the sound off.
What do you think happened? Check (✓) your answer.

- The woman arrived very early.
- The man arrived very late.

4 GET THE PICTURE

What really happened? Check (✓) the correct answers. Then compare with a partner.

1. What was the problem with Jacob's car?
   - ☐ It didn't start.
   - ☐ He locked his keys in it.
   - ☐ It was the wrong car.

2. What was the problem with Jacob's wallet?
   - ☐ He left it in the car.
   - ☐ He lost it.
   - ☐ He had no money in it.

3. What did Jacob forget?
   - ☐ He forgot his cell phone.
   - ☐ He forgot to bring his neighbor.
   - ☐ He forgot where he parked.

5 WATCH FOR DETAILS

A Put the pictures in order (1 to 6). Then write the correct sentence under each picture. Compare with a partner.

✓ Jacob noticed that his neighbor needed help.
Jacob paid the locksmith.
Jacob realized he didn't have his wallet.

Jacob saw his keys inside the car.
Jacob told Linda the story.
Jacob tried to call Linda.

....
....

....
....

....
....

Jacob noticed that his neighbor needed help.

....
....

....
....

B **PAIR WORK** What else happened in the video? Can you add two things?

1. ....
2. ....

6 WHAT'S YOUR OPINION?

PAIR WORK Complete the chart. Check (✓) the words that describe Jacob and Linda.

	Forgetful	Upset	Helpful	Embarrassed	Understanding	Worried
Jacob	☐	☐	☐	☐	☐	☐
Linda	☐	☐	☐	☐	☐	☐

☰ Follow-up

7 QUESTION GAME

A Write three more questions about the story. Use the past tense and *how, why, how much, who,* or *where.*

1. Why did Jacob get out of his car?
2. When did Jacob lock his keys in the car?
3. ....
4. ....
5. ....

B **PAIR WORK** Answer your partner's questions. If you don't think the answer was in the video, say, "It didn't say."

8 TELL THE STORY

PAIR WORK Write out the story using *first, after that, next, then,* and *finally.* Include one mistake. Then read your story to another pair. Can they find the mistake?

First, Jacob was late, so he ran to his car. ....
....
....
....
....
....
....
....
....
....

Interchange VRB 1 © Cambridge University Press 2012   Photocopiable

9 WHAT DID THEY SAY?

Watch the video and complete the conversation. Then practice it.

Jacob has just arrived at the restaurant.

Jacob: Linda, I'm really ...... sorry ....

Linda: It's .... , Jacob. I've only .... here for a little .... Is .... all right?

Jacob: Yes, it is .... , but you won't .... what just happened to me.

Linda: .... happened?

Jacob: Well, ... of all, I was .... leaving my apartment, so I had to .... Then, just .... I got in my car, I .... my neighbor, Mrs. Flanagan. She had a heavy trash .... , and she couldn't move it very easily. So, I .... her.

Linda: That was .... of you.

Jacob: Yeah, but, ... after, there was a problem. .... I went back to my .... , I couldn't get ....

Linda: Did you lock your .... in the car?

Jacob: .... you believe it?

Linda: Oh, no. What happened .... ?

Jacob: First, I .... to call you, but I got your voicemail. Then, I called a locksmith.

10 PRESENT PERFECT

A **PAIR WORK** Write questions using **Have you ever...?** and the correct forms of the verbs in parentheses. Can you add three questions to the list?

1. Have you ever locked .... (lock) your keys in the car?
2. .... (call) a locksmith?
3. .... (leave) your wallet in the car?
4. .... (arrive) late for an important appointment?
5. .... (go) to a restaurant without money?
6. .... (wait) a long time for someone in a restaurant?
7. ....
8. ....
9. ....

B **CLASS ACTIVITY** Go around the class and interview at least three classmates. Try to find out who answered "yes" to the most questions.

San Francisco!

Preview

1 CULTURE

San Francisco attracts more than sixteen million visitors a year. There are many things to do in the city, from shopping at Fisherman's Wharf to walking over the Golden Gate Bridge. While visitors come all year, the summer is the most popular time. It never gets extremely cold or hot in San Francisco, but it can be fairly cool much of the time.

Have you heard of any other interesting places to visit in or around San Francisco?
What is one of the most interesting cities to visit in your country?
What do tourists do there?

2 VOCABULARY *Taking a trip*

PAIR WORK Match the pictures with the words in the glossary below.

1. architectural details

2. ....

3. ....

4. ....

5. ....

6. ....

aquarium a museum for fish and other animals and plants that live under or near water
✓**architectural details** the things that make buildings special
bay an area of water that is partly enclosed by land, but is open to the sea

cable car a type of public transportation that is pulled by a moving cable under a track on the street
monuments buildings or structures built to remember an important person or event in history
wharf a structure that is built on the water for boats, fishing, business, or tourism

Interchange VRB 1 © Cambridge University Press 2012   Photocopiable

3 GUESS THE STORY

Watch the video with the sound off. What do you think Dr. Smith is most interested in seeing?

1. Alamo Square

2. Golden Gate Bridge

3. Japanese Tea Garden

Watch the video

4 GET THE PICTURE

What places does the hotel clerk tell Dr. and Mrs. Smith about? Circle them.
Then compare with a partner.

Alamo Square

Alcatraz

Coit Tower

Fisherman's Wharf

Ghirardelli Square

Golden Gate Park

Japanese Tea Garden

Lombard Street

Muir Woods

5 WATCH FOR DETAILS

Why does the clerk say the Smiths should go to the places below? Complete the sentences.
Then compare with a partner.

1. You should visit Fisherman's ....
   You can find a little bit of .... there.

2. Alamo Square is a small .... surrounded by
   really wonderful ....
   We call them Painted ....

3. Lombard Street is a very steep ....
   with a lot of ....

4. The most .... way to drive to San Francisco
   is across the .... Bridge.

6 COMPLETE THE STORY

Complete the paragraph below. Choose words from the list.
Then compare with a partner.

Alamo Square
Alcatraz Island
boat ride
cable car

Fisherman's Wharf
Golden Gate Bridge
Golden Gate Park
Highway 101

Lombard Street
✓ Northern California
Painted Ladies
Tea Garden

The Smiths arrived in San Francisco from ..Northern California.. . They entered the city by driving
over the .... They decided to start their visit with a ride on a ....
Next, they took a boat ride to .... Then, they walked through ....
and saw the Japanese .... After that, they went to .... to do
some shopping. The next day, they drove down curvy .... very slowly, and then
they went to .... to see the colorful Victorian Houses.

☰ Follow-up

7 SAN FRANCISCO

GROUP WORK Imagine you have two days in San Francisco. Plan your itinerary.
You can use these tourist attractions and any other places from this unit.

Chinatown

The Asian Art Museum

A bus tour of the city

A San Francisco
Giants baseball game

Shopping around
Union Square

The chocolate festival
at Ghirardelli Square

8 YOUR CITY

A GROUP WORK Now, imagine the Smiths are
visiting your city. Plan their itinerary. Give at
least six suggestions, like this:

A: First, I think they should go to . . .
B: Yes, and they should also visit the . . .

B CLASS ACTIVITY Share your
information with the class.

9 WHAT DID THEY SAY?

Watch the video and complete the conversation. Then practice it.

The Smiths are checking out of their Northern California hotel.

Clerk: Thank you. ....Here........ is your card and a copy of
the ....

Mrs. Smith: ....

Clerk: .... you enjoy your stay with .... ?

Dr. Smith: Yeah, it was .... , thank you.

Clerk: .... are you traveling to .... ?

Dr. Smith: We're heading .... , to San Francisco.

Clerk: San Francisco is .... !

Mrs. Smith: We're going to .... there for just a couple of
....

Clerk: .... you .... there before?

Dr. Smith: Well, I've been .... once, when I was a
.... , but Mona, she's .... been there.

Clerk: What are you .... to do .... you're there?

Mrs. Smith: No plans. We just want to .... I want to see all the ....

10 SHOULD *AND* SHOULDN'T *Giving advice*

A Complete these sentences with **should** or **shouldn't**. Then compare with a partner.

1. When you visit a foreign country, you .....should.... learn
   a few words of the local language.

2. You .... find out about the weather before you travel.

3. To be safe, you .... carry a lot of cash when you travel.

4. You .... do some research on interesting places to visit.

5. You .... be afraid to ask local people questions.

B **PAIR WORK** Give advice for things visitors to your city should or
shouldn't do. Write three suggestions in each column.

They should . . .	They shouldn't . . .
1.	1.
2.	2.
3.	3.

Onion soup and chocolate

1 CULTURE

In North America, people spend more on health care than in other parts of the world. In drugstores and health-food stores, people can buy over-the-counter medicines for colds, coughs, and sore throats, as well as vitamins and other supplements. Home remedies for common illnesses, such as colds and sore throats, are also popular.

What types of medicines are available over the counter for colds and sore throats in your country?

Do people usually take medicine or use home remedies when they have a cold?

2 VOCABULARY *Cold remedies*

PAIR WORK Write the remedies in the chart. Can you add two more to each category?

aspirin

chicken soup

steam

onions and garlic

cough medicine and sore throat lozenges

tea with lemon and honey

Home remedies		Over-the-counter drugs	
chicken soup			

3 GUESS THE STORY

Watch the video with the sound off.
What remedies in Exercise 2 does the host try?

4 GET THE PICTURE

Answer the questions with the correct person's name. Then compare with a partner.

The host

Henry

Anna

Roberto

Kathleen

1. Who hates colds? ....

2. Who never gets a cold? ....

3. Who has a cold right now? ....

4. Who just caught a cold? ....

5 WATCH FOR DETAILS

Match the person with the remedy he or she suggests. Then compare with a partner.

.... Henry   A. Rest.

.... Anna   B. Drink hot lemon and honey, and rest.

.... Kathleen   C. Take vitamin C and drink coffee.

.... Roberto   D. Eat onion soup and chocolate, and keep warm.

6 WHAT'S YOUR OPINION?

PAIR WORK Answer these questions.

1. Which of the remedies have you tried?
2. Which of the remedies do you think works best?
3. Are there any remedies from the video that you will try in the future?
   If so, which ones?
4. What other home or drugstore remedies for a cold do you know about?
   Do you use them?

☰ Follow-up

7 HEALTH PROBLEMS

A GROUP WORK What do you do for these problems? Add two more remedies
for each one. Then compare around the class. Who has the best remedies?

1. a backache

It's a good idea to lie
on the floor. Also, get
some ....
....
....
....

2. a headache

Take some aspirin. It's
also helpful to ....
....
....
....
....

3. a stomachache

You should eat some
yogurt. Also, try
some ....
....
....
....

4. the flu

You should stay home
from school or work. It's
also important to ....
....
....
....

B PAIR WORK Take turns role-playing a person with one of the problems
in part A and a friend giving advice.

A: Hi, ... How are you?
B: I'm not doing too well. I have . . .
A: That's terrible! Listen. I've got the perfect remedy . . .

C Do you need advice for a problem of your own? Have a similar conversation,
using personal information and asking for someone else's home remedies.

Language close-up

8 WHAT DID THEY SAY?

Watch the video and complete the conversation. Then practice it.

The host is interviewing Kathleen about what to do for a cold.

Host: What should you do ....**when**............ you get a cold?

Kathleen: Oh, I .... get a cold.

Host: .... ?

Kathleen: Yes, ... when I feel a cold coming
.... , I know it's .... to eat lots of
homemade .... soup.

Host: ....

Kathleen: Oh, and it's a good idea to eat .... of
.... , too!

Host: At the .... as the onion soup?

Kathleen: No, ... The onion soup ....
you vitamins, and the chocolate gives you ....
That .... the cold virus. Oh, uh, it's a good
.... to keep very .... , too. It's not
a good idea to hang around on the street.

Host: OK. ....

Kathleen: Bye!

9 REQUESTS AND SUGGESTIONS

A Complete the conversations with **may** or **could** to make requests and **should**, **try**, or
suggest to give suggestions. Then compare with a partner.

1. *At work*

A: Here's the perfect cold remedy: garlic juice, onions,
and carrots. You ...**should**..... drink a cup every two hours.

B: But I don't like carrots.

A: Well, then I .... an old-fashioned bowl of chicken
soup! And .... to get some rest, too.

2. *At a drugstore*

A: .... I help you?

B: Yes. .... I have something for a cold? It's a bad one.

A: Yes. I have these pills. They're a little strong. Just don't drive
after you take them.

B: Hmm. I drive to work. .... I have something else?

A: Well, ... these other pills then. They won't
make you sleepy.

B **PAIR WORK** Act out the conversations. First, act them out as written. Then, change the
problems and the remedies.

How about a pizza?

Preview

1 CULTURE

Most U.S. and Canadian cities have restaurants that serve food from many different countries and cultures. Chinese, Italian, and Mexican restaurants have been very popular in North America for a long time, but now there are also Japanese, Thai, and Indian restaurants in most cities and small towns. Many people like to order food from restaurants for delivery to their homes. Chinese food and pizza are common home-delivery types of food.

What types of foreign food are available in your town?
Which ones are the most popular with you and your friends and family?

2 VOCABULARY *Food*

PAIR WORK Here are some foods from several different cultures.
Where can you find these foods? Write the foods under the pictures.

egg rolls	prawns in coconut milk	tacos
✓ pizza	sushi	vegetable curry

1. .... pizza ....

2. ....

3. ....

4. ....

5. ....

6. ....

3 GUESS THE STORY

Watch the first minute of the video with the sound off. Which type of restaurant do you think they choose?

Watch the video

4 GET THE PICTURE

A Put the restaurants in the order that Carmen and Luis see them (1–4). Then compare with a partner.

B (PAIR WORK) Which two types of food do Carmen and Luis say they *don't* want?

5 WATCH FOR DETAILS

A Complete the names of the foods in the video with words from the list. Then circle the items Carmen and Luis order. Compare with a partner.

coconut milk   ginger   smoothie
✓ curry   pizza   tea

1. Seafood or green ......curry......

2. Prawns in ....

3. Chicken with ....

4. Thai ....

5. Ginger and honey ....

6. Jasmine ....

B What items do both Carmen and Luis say they like?

....

6 HOW ABOUT YOU?

GROUP WORK Answer these questions.
1. How often do you eat in restaurants?
2. What's your favorite kind of restaurant?
3. What do you usually order?
4. When is the last time you ate something for the first time? Describe it. Did you like it?
5. Which of the foods and drinks from the video have you tried or would you like to try?

7 IN A RESTAURANT

GROUP WORK Role-play ordering lunch at one of the restaurants in the video. Two students order, while the third student plays the waiter or waitress. Then switch roles until each student has been the waiter or waitress. Use this model:

A: Do you have any questions about the menu?
B: . . .
A: Oh, that's very good. It's one of the most popular dishes. Are you ready to order?
C: . . .
A: OK. What would you like?
B: . . .
C: . . .
A: What do you want to drink?
B: . . .
C: . . .
A: OK. I'll be right back with your food and your drinks.

8 WHAT DID THEY SAY?

Watch the video and complete the conversation. Then practice it.
Carmen and Luis are trying to decide what to eat.

Luis: You know, I'm beginning to ....*feel*............ hungry.

Carmen: .... am I. I really could eat ....

Luis: .... pizza?

Carmen: Hmm. I'm not .... I'm not really in the

.... for a pizza.

Luis: You know, ... am I.

Carmen: OK. Let's .... for something ....

But I want to eat. .... !

Luis: No .... I do, too.

Carmen: I .... Japanese food a ....

Luis: .... do I, but . . .

Carmen: We .... get some sushi.

Luis: Yeah, I'm just not .... that's ....

I want.

Carmen: But Luis, I'm ....

9 WOULD AND WILL Ordering food

A Rewrite these questions using **Would you like . . . ?**
Then compare with a partner.

1. What do you want to eat?

   What would you like to eat?

2. Do you want salad or soup with that?

   ....

3. Do you want something to drink?

   ....

4. What do you want for dessert?

   ....

B PAIR WORK Now answer the questions with **I'll have . . .**
A: What would you like to eat?
B: I'll have . . .

14 Around the World

1 CULTURE

In North America, game shows are one of the most popular types of TV programs. There are several different game shows on at various times of the day. In most game shows, players test their knowledge on different subjects. Sometimes the questions are quite easy, and sometimes they are very difficult. But other game shows are games of chance. The winner must be lucky, but doesn't have to know a lot of facts.

What are some game shows on TV in your country?
Which ones are the most popular?
Which ones do you like to watch?

2 GUESS THE FACTS

PAIR WORK How is your knowledge of geography?
Check (✓) the correct answers.

1. Which is longer?
   ☐ the Nile River
   ☐ the Amazon River

2. Which is higher?
   ☐ Mt. McKinley
   ☐ Mt. Kilimanjaro

3. What's the largest desert in Asia?
   ☐ the Great Indian Desert
   ☐ the Gobi Desert

the Nile River

the Amazon River

Mt. McKinley

Mt. Kilimanjaro

4. Which is the largest city in North America?
   ☐ Los Angeles
   ☐ Mexico City

5. Which country is called the "island continent"?
   ☐ Antarctica
   ☐ Australia

Mexico City

Los Angeles

3 GUESS THE STORY

Watch the first minute of the video. Which contestant do you think is going to win?

☰ Watch the video

4 CHECK THE FACTS

Correct your answers to Exercise 2. Did you guess correctly? Compare with a partner.

5 WATCH FOR DETAILS

Check (✓) the correct answers. Then compare with a partner.

1. Marlene is from
   ☐ Seattle, Washington.
   ☐ Washington, D.C.

2. Marlene is a
   ☐ computer programmer.
   ☐ computer engineer.

3. Ted is from
   ☐ Cambridge, Massachusetts.
   ☐ Boston, Massachusetts.

4. Ted is a
   ☐ high school teacher.
   ☐ college teacher.

5. Lili is from
   ☐ Vero Beach, Florida.
   ☐ Miami Beach, Florida.

6. Lili is a
   ☐ café owner.
   ☐ chef.

6 WHO WINS THE GAME?

A What is each person's score at the end of the game? Write the number.
Then compare with a partner.

Marlene ....   Ted ....   Lili ....

B Is the winner happy with the prize? Why or why not?

☰ Follow-up

7 AROUND THE WORLD

A GROUP WORK Write three questions in each category for the game
"Around the World." Give one question 25 points, one question 50 points,
and one question 75 points. (You can also add categories of your own.)

Mountains	Islands
....	....
....	....
....	....
Rivers	**Cities**
....	....
....	....
....	....

B CLASS ACTIVITY Now play "Around the World." Half the class
is in Group A. The other half is in Group B.

Group A: Choose one student to be the host.

Group B: Take turns choosing a category for 25, 50, or 75 points.
Then answer the host's questions. Play for five minutes.

Begin your conversation like this:

A: Are you ready?
B: Yes, I'll try (*name of category*) for 25 points.
A: OK. (*Asks question.*)
B: (*Answers question.*)
A: That's right! **or** Sorry, that's not correct.

Now change roles. Group B should choose a host and Group A
should answer the questions. Play for five more minutes.
Which group wins the game?

   Interchange VRB 1 © Cambridge University Press 2012   Photocopiable

Language close-up

8 WHAT DID HE SAY?

Watch the video and complete the host's comments. Then practice it.

The host introduces the contestants.

Hi, ...*again*........ , folks. And .... back to the Final Round of our

show. I'm your host, Richard Darien, and .... are our contestants:

A computer .... from Seattle, Washington: Marlene Miller!

Marlene has .... points.

And next to you we have a high school .... from Boston,

Massachusetts: Ted Simmons! Ted currently has .... points,

and he is .... the .... !

And our .... contestant is a café .... from Vero Beach,

Florida: Lili Chen! Lili has .... points, so she's currently .... with Marlene.

Oh boy, this is going to be an .... game, ... get on to the Final

Round. Our .... are Cities, Deserts, ... , Mountains, and ....

9 COMPARISONS WITH ADJECTIVES

A Write questions using the comparative or superlative form of each adjective in parentheses. Then add three questions of your own.

1. city: New York – Tokyo? (cold)
   Which city is colder, New York or Tokyo?

2. planet: Earth – Saturn – Mars? (big)
   ....

3. structure: the Eiffel Tower – the Statue of Liberty? (tall)
   ....

4. building: the Houses of Parliament – the Empire
   State Building? (old)
   ....
   ....

5. country: Brazil – Canada – Argentina? (large)
   ....

6. ....
7. ....
8. ....

B **PAIR WORK** Take turns asking and answering the questions.
Who answered the most questions correctly?

String cheese

1 CULTURE

Many people in the United States and Canada celebrate their birthdays with a party. These parties can be dinner parties, dance parties, or just parties where people have snacks and chat with one another. Typical snacks at parties include chips and dip, cheese and crackers, nuts, cookies, and other snacks that people eat with their fingers.

Are birthday parties common for adults as well as for children in your country?

What kinds of foods do you often have at birthday parties?

2 VOCABULARY *Asking for favors*

Match the requests for favors with the responses.

.... 1. May I ask you for a favor?

.... 2. Could you please pick me up on your way to the party?

.... 3. Could you bring some soda to the party?

.... 4. Would you ask Claire to call me when she gets home?

.... 5. Would you please call me when your class is finished?

a. Sorry, but I won't be able to. I'm riding with someone else.

b. Sure. That should be about 9:30.

c. No problem. I'll leave her a message.

d. Sure. What is it?

e. I'd be happy to. How many bottles should I get?

3 GUESS THE STORY

Watch the first 30 seconds of the video with the sound off.
Answer the questions.

1. What is Mariela doing?
2. Why do you think Mariela is upset?
3. What do you think Olivia does to help her?

 Watch the video

4 CHECK YOUR GUESSES

Now check your answers to the questions in Exercise 3. Did you guess correctly? Compare with a partner.

5 WATCH FOR DETAILS

Answer the questions with a number. Then compare with a partner.

How many . . .

1. people does Olivia call? ....

2. messages does Olivia leave? ....

3. people does Olivia talk to on the phone? ....

4. people does Olivia ask to bring cheese to the party? ....

5. people bring cheese to the party? ....

6 MAKING INFERENCES

Check (✓) the best answers. Then complete the last item with your opinion. Check with a partner.

1. .... cheese is necessary for the party.
   - [ ] Both Mariela and Olivia think
   - [ ] Only Mariela thinks
   - [ ] Only Olivia thinks

2. Olivia asks everyone to get different kinds of cheese because ....
   - [ ] she can't remember the kinds Mariela mentioned
   - [ ] she wants everyone to buy different kinds of cheese
   - [ ] Todd likes all kinds of cheese

3. In the end, there is probably .... cheese at the party.
   - [ ] too much
   - [ ] the right amount of
   - [ ] not enough

4. Melanie gives Todd a ball of string because ....

Follow-up

7 HAVING A PARTY

A **GROUP WORK** Use this chart to plan a party. Then make invitations for your party.

Choose an occasion.	Choose a location and time.
....	....
....	....
Choose things to do at the party.	**Choose the foods and drinks you want at the party.**
....	....
....	....

B **CLASS ACTIVITY** Walk around the class inviting students to your party. Show them your invitation.

Begin your conversations like this:

A: Hi, would you like to come to my party? It's (*say a date and time*).
B: Thanks. I'd love to. What's the occasion?
A: It's for (*give a reason for the party*).
B: That sounds fun. Can I bring anything?
A: Thanks for offering. You could bring (*suggest something*).
B: OK. See you then.
A: Bye.

Interchange VRB 1 © Cambridge University Press 2012   Photocopiable

8 WHAT DID THEY SAY?

Watch the video and complete the conversation. Then practice it.

Olivia is asking Carlos for a favor.

Olivia: Hi, Carlos? ....It's....... Olivia. How are you?

Carlos: Olivia, hi. I'm .... , thanks. ....
seeing you at Todd's .... party, ... ?

Olivia: Yeah, that's right. .... , Carlos, could you
.... some cheese to the party?

Carlos: Cheese?

Olivia: Todd really .... cheese, and Mariela didn't get
.... , and now she's in a panic .... it.

Carlos: Yeah, sure. What .... of cheese?

Olivia: Camembert, I .... , or Roquefort, and some
Gorgonzola. Oh, and some .... cheese.

Carlos: OK, Olivia. .... do it. Don't ....

Olivia: Thanks, Carlos. It's so .... of you
to .... us.

9 REQUESTING A FAVOR

PAIR WORK Practice the conversation in Exercise 8 again. This time make a request
for something different. Then switch roles and ask for other things. Choose from the
list below or use your own ideas.

Things for the party:

1. different types of music
2. different types of drinks
3. different types of decorations
4. different types of desserts
5. different types of snack food

16 Life changes

1 CULTURE

After high school, many students in the United States and Canada don't go straight to college. They get a job or take time off to travel before continuing their education. Most students are not sure what they want to do with their lives just after high school. Their goals and plans become clearer as they gain more life experience.

What were your goals and plans when you were younger?
How have they changed over the years?

2 VOCABULARY *Career goals*

A Here are some people's dreams for their future. What does each person hope to do or be? Write the sentences under the pictures.

I'm going to be a chef.
I'd really love to perform on Broadway.
✓ I hope to have a family.

I'd like to be a reporter.
I plan to practice law.
I hope to be a teacher.

1. *I hope to have a family.*

2. ....

3. ....

4. ....

5. ....

6. ....

B **CLASS ACTIVITY** Walk around the room talking to people. Use these expressions to talk about what you hope to do or be.

Begin your conversation like this:

A: I'd love to be a (*occupation*). How about you?
B: I plan to (*work verb*).

3 GUESS THE STORY

Watch the video with the sound off. What do you think each person does for a living?

1. Reza is a / an ....
2. Kim is a / an ....
3. Robert is a / an ....

Reza

Kim

Robert

☰ Watch the video

4 CHECK YOUR GUESSES

A Check your answers to Exercise 3. Did you guess correctly? Compare with a partner.

B Check (✓) the level of education each person finished.

	High School	College	Graduate School
1. Reza	☐	☐	☐
2. Kim	☐	☐	☐
3. Robert	☐	☐	☐

5 WATCH FOR DETAILS

Check (✓) **True** or **False**. Correct the false statements. Then compare with a partner.

	True	False	
1. Reza worked in politics before going to law school.	☐	☐	....
2. Reza is married and has children.	☐	☐	....
3. Kim always hoped to be a reporter.	☐	☐	....
4. Kim was interested in writing about theater.	☐	☐	....
5. Kim works for a large newspaper.	☐	☐	....
6. Robert didn't go to college.	☐	☐	....
7. Robert teaches and performs comedy.	☐	☐	....
8. Robert would love to own a comedy club.	☐	☐	....

6 A JOB QUIZ

A Check (✓) five things you like to do or you are good at.

What do you like to do?

.... work with people

.... work alone

.... build or create things

.... fix things

.... help people

.... listen to people

.... talk to people

.... solve problems

.... work with my hands

.... work with my mind

.... work inside

.... work outside

.... work with numbers

.... with ideas

.... work with children

.... work with animals

.... my idea:

....

B CLASS ACTIVITY Walk around the room and find another student who checked at least three of the same things as you did. Sit down with the student or students and make a list of jobs that might be good for these categories.

1. ....

2. ....

3. ....

7 CAREER AND LIFE ADVICE

PAIR WORK Take turns being a career or life coach for each other. What advice would you give? Use the information in Exercise 6 and phrases in the box. You can begin your conversations like this:

A: I'd love to work with children.
B: What else do you like to do?
A: I like . . .
B: And what are you good at?
A: I'm good at . . .
B: Well, I think you should . . .

> You could . . .
> You should . . .
> It would be a good idea/useful for you to . . .

Interchange VRB 1 © Cambridge University Press 2012   Photocopiable

☰ Language close-up

 VIDEO ACTIVITIES

8 WHAT DID HE SAY?

Watch the video and complete the description.

Reza is talking about his life before and after law school.

In ....college........ , I was a political science major. And ....
college, I went to Washington, D.C., to .... in ....
I worked on Capitol Hill for .... two years, which is ....
the government is, and it's also the .... of the ....

.... in government, I .... more about the law.
And I .... to get more .... in the law. I decided
I wanted to come .... and go to law school ....
Boston. When I .... , I had a job .... for me, and I started
work right away at the ....

The .... level now is a lot .... than when I was
in .... school. In law school, you're stressing ....
your academics, but when you're .... law, as a lawyer, you're
.... about doing the best job you .... on those projects
you're working on for .... clients.

9 TELLING YOUR STORY

A Choose verbs from the box to complete the story.
Then compare with a partner.

bought	had	registered
✓ finished	knew	save
found	looked for	started
got	moved back	wanted

1. When I ....finished....... high school, I didn't know what I
   .... to do.
2. I .... I wanted to improve my English, so I went online
   and .... an English school in an English-speaking country.
3. I .... a great school in London, England.
4. To .... money, I .... a job and
   .... home with my parents.
5. After six months, I .... enough money.
6. I .... a plane ticket, and I .... at the school.
   I .... taking classes the day after I arrived.

B Change the sentences in part A so they tell your story. Then tell your
story to another student.

Interchange VRB 1 © Cambridge University Press 2012   Photocopiable

Unit 16 ▪ 65

This page is intentionally left blank

interchange

FIFTH EDITION

1

Workbook

Jack C. Richards
with Jonathan Hull and Susan Proctor

CAMBRIDGE
UNIVERSITY PRESS

This page is intentionally left blank

Contents

Credits

Illustrations

Pablo Gallego (Beehive Illustration): 42, 53, 65, 78, 91; **Thomas Girard** (Good Illustration): 3, 25, 50, 72, 92; **Quino Marin** (The Organisation): 2, 47, 54, 66; **Gavin Reece** (New Division): 15, 48, 52(B); **Paul Williams** (Sylvie Poggio Artists): 51.

Photos

Back cover (woman with whiteboard): Jenny Acheson/Stockbyte/GettyImages; Back cover (whiteboard): Nemida/GettyImages; Back cover (man using phone): Betsie Van Der Meer/Taxi/GettyImages; Back cover (woman smiling): PeopleImages.com/DigitalVision/GettyImages; Back cover (name tag): Tetra Images/GettyImages; Back cover (handshake): David Lees/Taxi/GettyImages; p. 1: Jon Feingersh/Blend Images/Brand X Pictures/GettyImages; p. 4 (TL): Juanmonino/iStock/GettyImages Plus/GettyImages; p. 4 (BL): Caiaimage/Chris Ryan/OJO+/GettyImages; p. 4 (TR): XiXinXing/GettyImages; p. 4 (BR): powerofforever/E+/GettyImages; p. 5: PeopleImages/DigitalVision/GettyImages; p. 6: Martin Barraud/Caiaimage/GettyImages; p. 7 (photo 1): Jetta Productions/Blend Images/GettyImage; p. 7 (photo 2): Oleksandr Rupeta/NurPhoto/GettyImages; p. 7 (photo 3): Hill Street Studios/Blend Images/GettyImages; p. 7 (photo 4): Jupiterimages/Photolibrary/GettyImages; p. 8: Monty Rakusen/Cultura/GettyImages; p. 9: Matt Hage/Design Pics/First Light/GettyImages; p. 10 (TL): Digital Vision/DigitalVision/GettyImages; p. 10 (TR): Hybrid Images/Cultura/GettyImages; p. 10 (BR): kali9/E+/GettyImages; p. 11: kali9/E+/GettyImages; p. 12 (T): Hybrid Images/Cultura/GettyImages; p. 12 (BL): Visage/Stockbyte/GettyImages; p. 12 (BC): segawa7/iStock/GettyImages Plus/GettyImages; p. 12 (BR): asterix0597/E+/GettyImages; p. 13: Westend61/GettyImages; p. 14: Robert Niedring/Alloy/GettyImages; p. 16 (silver earrings): JohnGollop/iStock/GettyImages Plus/GettyImages; p. 16 (gold earrings): cobalt/iStock/GettyImages Plus/GettyImages; p. 16 (leather coat): bonetta/iStock/GettyImages Plus/GettyImages; p. 16 (wool coat): DonNichols/E+/GettyImages; p. 16 (orange shirt): rolleiflextlr/iStock/GettyImages Plus/GettyImages; p. 16 (gray shirt): popovaphoto/iStock/GettyImages Plus/GettyImages; p. 16 (cotton dresses): Evgenii Karamyshev/Hemera/GettyImages Plus/GettyImages; p. 16 (silk dresses): Paolo_Toffanin/iStock/GettyImages Plus/GettyImages; p. 17 (gold ring): Image Source/GettyImages; p. 17 (silver ring): ProArtWork/E+/GettyImages; p. 17 (tablet): luismmolina/E+/GettyImages; p. 17 (laptop computer): Howard Kingsnorth/The Image Bank/GettyImages; p. 17 (hiking boots): AlexRaths/iStock/GettyImages Plus/GettyImages; p. 17 (sneakers): badmanproduction/iStock/GettyImages Plus/GettyImages; p. 17 (wool gloves): popovaphoto/iStock/GettyImages Plus/GettyImages; p. 17 (leather gloves): Hugh Threlfall/Stockbyte/GettyImages; p. 17 (black sunglasses): Vladimir Liverts/Hemera/GettyImages Plus/GettyImages; p. 17 (white sunglasses): Dimedrol68/iStock/GettyImages Plus/GettyImages; p. 18 (photo 3): csfotoimages/iStock/GettyImages Plus/GettyImages; p. 18 (photo 1): Donald Iain Smith/Moment/GettyImages; p. 18 (photo 4): goir/iStock/GettyImages Plus/GettyImages; p. 18 (photo 2): Marc Romanelli/Blend Images/GettyImages; p. 19 (T): Larry Busacca/GettyImages Entertainment/GettyImages North America/GettyImages; p. 19 (B): Steve Granitz/WireImage/GettyImages; p. 20 (photo 1): Brian Bahr/GettyImages North America/GettyImages; p. 20 (photo 2): Phillip Faraone/GettyImages North America/GettyImages; p. 20 (photo 3): Anthony Harvey/GettyImages Entertainment/GettyImages Europe/GettyImages; p. 20 (photo 4): Taylor Hill/FilmMagic/GettyImages; p. 20 (BR): Jon Kopaloff/FilmMagic/GettyImages; p. 21 (R): DianaHirsch/E+/GettyImages; p. 21 (L): ILM/Universal Studios/GettyImages; p. 23 (T): Shirlaine Forrest/WireImage/GettyImages; p. 23 (B): Moof/Cultura/GettyImages; p. 24 (T): Mike Windle/GettyImages Entertainment/GettyImagesNorth America/GettyImages; p. 24 (B): Donald Miralle/DigitalVision/GettyImages; p. 26: Copyright Anek/Moment/GettyImages; p. 27 (photo 1): Echo/Cultura/GettyImages; p. 27 (photo 2): Juice Images/Cultura/GettyImages; p. 27 (photo 3): Christopher Hope-Fitch/Moment/GettyImages; p. 27 (photo 4): sjenner13/iStock/GettyImages Plus/GettyImages; p. 27 (photo 5): Hero Images/GettyImages; p. 30 (L): Soumen Nath Photography/Moment Open/GettyImages; p. 30 (R): Chaos/The Image Bank/GettyImages; p. 31 (L): Tetra Images/GettyImages; p. 31 (R): John Freeman/Dorling Kindersley/GettyImages; p. 33 (T): Westend61/GettyImages; p. 33 (B): Adam Gault/Photodisc/GettyImages; p. 34 (T): Camilla Watson/AWL Images/GettyImages; p. 34 (C): Stephen McCarthy/Sportsfile/GettyImages; p. 34 (B): PhotoAlto/Laurence Mouton/PhotoAlto Agency RF Collections/GettyImages; p. 35: Koji Aoki/Aflo/GettyImages; p. 36: PeopleImages/DigitalVision/GettyImages; p. 37: Jan Speiser/EyeEm/GettyImages; p. 38 (L): PeopleImages/DigitalVision/GettyImages; p. 38 (R): asiseeit/E+/GettyImages; p. 40 (T): PRASIT CHANSAREEKORN/Moment/GettyImages; p. 40 (B): Tuul and Bruno Morandi/Photolibrary/GettyImages; p. 41 (T): Boy_Anupong/Moment/GettyImages; p. 41 (B): John W Banagan/Lonely Planet Images/GettyImages; p. 46 (L): Allison Michael Orenstein/The Image Bank/GettyImages; p. 46 (R): Plume Creative/DigitalVision/GettyImages; p. 49: Jim Franco/Taxi/GettyImages; p. 52 (boots): StockPhotosArt/iStock/GettyImages Plus/GettyImages; p. 52 (cap): ljpat/E+/GettyImages; p. 52 (dress): pidjoe/E+/GettyImages; p. 52 (high heels): LOVE_LIFE/iStock/GettyImages Plus/GettyImages; p. 52 (jeans): gofotograf/iStock/GettyImages Plus/GettyImages; p. 52 (jewelry): DEA/L. DOUGLAS/De Agostini Editorial/GettyImages; p. 52 (necktie): WilshireImages/E+/GettyImages; p. 52 (shirt): Alex Cao/Photodisc/GettyImages; p. 52 (shorts): stocksnapper/iStock/GettyImages Plus/GettyImages; p. 52 (sneakers): Tevarak/iStock/GettyImages Plus/GettyImages;

p. 52 (suit): bonetta/iStock/GettyImages Plus/GettyImages; p. 52 (T-shirt): GaryAlvis/E+/GettyImages; p. 55 (T): Blake Little/Stone/GettyImages; p. 55 (C): Jenner Images/Moment Open/GettyImages; p. 55 (B): Kevin Kozicki/Image Source/GettyImages; p. 56: Barry Austin Photography/Iconica/GettyImages; p. 57 (photo 1): sutichak/iStock/GettyImages Plus/GettyImages; p. 57 (photo 2): Koichi Kamoshida/Photolibrary/GettyImages; p. 57 (photo 3): Westend61/GettyImages; p. 57 (photo 4): Paul Bradbury/OJO Images/GettyImages; p. 57 (photo 5): Jan Hetfleisch/GettyImages Europe/GettyImages; p. 57 (photo 6): Halfdark/GettyImages; p. 58 (T): Jupiterimages/Photos.com/GettyImages Plus/GettyImages; p. 58 (B): Nmaverick/iStock/GettyImages Plus/GettyImages; p. 59 (text messaging): skynesher/E+/GettyImages; p. 59 (rugby match): Stewart Cohen/Photolibrary/GettyImages; p. 59 (sushi): Steve Brown Photography/Photolibrary/GettyImages; p. 59 (houston): Gavin Hellier/Photographer's Choice/GettyImages; p. 60: Sam Edwards/Caiaimage/GettyImages; p. 61 (L): Martin Puddy/Stone/GettyImages; p. 61 (R): Karina Wang/Photographer's Choice/GettyImages; p. 62 (L): jimkruger/iStock/GettyImages Plus/GettyImages; p. 62 (C): AzmanL/iStock/GettyImages Plus/GettyImages; p. 62 (R): Jonas Gratzer/LightRocket/GettyImages; p. 63 (T): Alberto Manuel Urosa Toledano/Moment/GettyImages; p. 63 (B): DUCEPT Pascal/hemis.fr/GettyImages; p. 64 (BL): Sungjin Kim/Moment Open/GettyImages; p. 64 (TC): RODRIGO BUENDIA/AFP/GettyImages; p. 64 (BR): Andrea Pistolesi/Photolibrary/GettyImages; p. 65: JTB/UIG/GettyImages; p. 68: BSIP/UIG/GettyImages; p. 69: KidStock/Blend Images/GettyImages; p. 70: YinYang/E+/GettyImages; p. 71: Ariel Skelley/Blend Images/GettyImages; p. 73 (photo 1): Peter Dazeley/Photographer's Choice/GettyImages; p. 73 (photo 2): whitewish/E+/GettyImages; p. 73 (photo 3): Chuck Kahn/EyeEm/GettyImages; p. 73 (photo 4): lisafx/iStock/GettyImages Plus/GettyImages; p. 73 (photo 5): TUGIO MURATA/amanaimagesRF/GettyImages; p. 73 (photo 6): Creative Crop/DigitalVision/GettyImages; p. 74 (greasy): David Crunelle/EyeEm/GettyImages; p. 74 (bland): Howard Shooter/GettyImages; p. 74 (rich): Johner Images/GettyImages; p. 74 (salty): Creativ Studio Heinemann/GettyImages; p. 74 (healthy): Verdina Anna/Moment/GettyImages; p. 75 (Carlota): andresr/E+/GettyImages; p. 75 (Luka): NicolasMcComber/E+/GettyImages; p. 75 (Adam): David Harrigan/Canopy/GettyImages; p. 76 (broccoli): Kevin Summers/Photographer's Choice/GettyImages; p. 76 (sushi): Food Image Source/StockFood Creative/GettyImages; p. 76 (cream cone): dlerick/E+/GettyImages; p. 77: gchutka/E+/GettyImages; p. 79 (T): Richard Roscoe/Stocktrek Images/GettyImages; p. 79 (C): www.sierralara.com/Moment/GettyImages; p. 79 (B): Yevgen Timashov/Cultura/GettyImages; p. 80: Ulf Andersen/GettyImages Europe/GettyImages; p. 81 (Badwater Basin): David ToussaintMoment/GettyImages; p. 81 (Suez Canal): Jacques Marais/Gallo Images/GettyImages; p. 81 (Mount Waialeale): M Swiet Productions/Moment Open/GettyImages; p. 82: Christian Vorhofer/imageBROKER/GettyImages; p. 83 (Angel Falls): Jane Sweeney/AWL Images/GettyImages; p. 83 (Yangtze River): View Stock/GettyImages; p. 83 (Antarctica): Michael Nolan/robertharding/GettyImages; p. 83 (Rain forest): JohnnyLye/iStock/GettyImages Plus/GettyImages; p. 83 (Grand Canyon): Stephanie Hohmann/EyeEm/GettyImages; p. 84: GlobalP/iStock/GettyImages Plus/GettyImages; p. 86: Emilio Cobos/Euroleague Basketball/GettyImages; p. 87 (go to park): Feverpitched/iStock/GettyImages Plus/GettyImages; p. 87 (go to concerts): Yuri_Arcurs/DigitalVision/GettyImages; p. 87 (have parties): SolStock/E+/GettyImages; p. 87 (see plays): VisitBritain/Eric Nathan/Britain On View/GettyImages; p. 87 (watch horror movies): Crazytang/E+/GettyImages; p. 87 (go on picnics): Kentaroo Tryman/Maskot/GettyImages; p. 88 (Hannah): Dianne Avery Photography/GettyImages; p. 88 (Pablo): Jacqueline Veissid/Blend Images/GettyImages; p. 88 (Richard): Laura Doss/Image Source/GettyImages; p. 88 (Lien): iPandastudio/iStock/GettyImages Plus/GettyImages; p. 88 (Kalil): Juanmonino/iStock/GettyImages Plus/GettyImages; p. 88 (Rachel): Westend61/GettyImages; p. 88 (Eliana): billnoll/E+/GettyImages; p. 88 (Daichi): petekarici/iStock/GettyImages Plus/GettyImages; p. 90: ichaka/E+/GettyImages; p. 93 (L): Paul Bradbury/Caiaimage/GettyImages; p. 93 (TR): Hero Images/GettyImages; p. 93 (CR): Hero Images/DigitalVision/GettyImages; p. 94: Zero Creatives/Cultura/GettyImages; p. 95 (T): DragonImages/iStock/GettyImages Plus/GettyImages; p. 95 (C): agentry/iStock/GettyImages Plus/GettyImages; p. 95 (B): Digital Vision/Photodisc/GettyImages; p. 96: Deb Snelson/Moment/GettyImages.

1 Where are you from?

1 Write about yourself.

My first name is _____.

My last name is _____.

Please call me _____.

I'm from _____.

2 Put the words in order to make questions. Then answer the questions.

1. class   your   how   English   is

A: _How is your English class_ ?

B: _It's pretty interesting_ .

2. name   teacher's   your   what's

A: _____ ?

B: _____ .

3. from   your   teacher   where   is

A: _____ ?

B: _____ .

4. your   what   friends'   are   names

A: _____ ?

B: _____ .

5. classmates   what   your   are   like

A: _____ ?

B: _____ .

3 Choose the correct responses.

1. A: Hi, I'm Diane.

B: _Oh, hi. I'm Peter._
  - Oh, hi. I'm Peter.
  - What do people call you?

2. A: My name is Bill Matory.

B: _____
  - Nice to meet you, Bill.
  - Let's go and say hello.

3. A: Hello. I'm a new student here.

B: _____
  - Thanks.
  - Welcome.

4. A: I'm sorry. What's your name again?

B: _____
  - P-A-R-K.
  - Eun-ha Park.

5. A: How do you spell your first name?

B: _____
  - I'm Akira.
  - A-K-I-R-A.

6. A: What do people call you?

B: _____
  - It's Angela Young.
  - Everyone calls me Angie.

4 Look at the answers. What are the questions?

1. Agent: What _'s your name?_

  Silvia: My name's Silvia.

2. Agent: What _____

  Silvia: My last name's Garcia.

3. Agent: Who _____

  Silvia: That's my husband.

4. Agent: What _____

  Silvia: His name is Gustavo.

5. Agent: Where _____

  Silvia: We're from Venezuela.

6. Agent: Who _____

  Silvia: They're my children.

5 | Choose the correct words.

1. That's Antonio. _____He_____ is in my class. (He / His)

2. I'm from Barcelona, Spain. _____ is a beautiful city. (It / It's)

3. Excuse me. What's _____ last name again? (you / your)

4. They're my classmates. _____ names are Jill and Tae-min. (They / Their)

5. _____ name is Naoko. Please call me Nao. (I / My)

6. This is Ellen's husband. _____ name is Tim. (His / Her)

7. My parents are on vacation. _____ are in Australia. (We / They)

8. We have English at 10:00. _____ classroom number is 108-C. (Our / We)

6 | Complete this conversation with *am*, *are*, or *is*.

Amber: Who _____*are*_____ the men over there, Ethan?

Ethan: Oh, they _____ on my baseball team. Let me introduce you. Hi, Pablo, this _____ Amber Fox.

Pablo: Nice to meet you, Amber.

Amber: Nice to meet you, too. Where _____ you from?

Pablo: I _____ from Cuba.

Ethan: And this _____ Marco. He _____ from Brazil.

Lisa: Hi, Marco.

7 Hello and welcome!

A Read these four student biographies. Then complete the chart below.

>>> INTERNATIONAL LANGUAGE SCHOOL <<<

Every month, we meet new students at the school. This month, we want to introduce four new students to you. Please say "hello" to them!

Rafael is in English 101. He is from Puebla, Mexico. His first language is Spanish, and he also speaks a little French. He wants to be on the school volleyball team. He says he doesn't play very well, but he wants to learn!

Su-yin is in English 102. She is from Wuhan, China. She says she writes and reads English pretty well, but she needs a lot of practice speaking English. Her first language is Chinese. She wants to play volleyball on the school team.

Fatima is in English 103. She is from Tunis, Tunisia. She speaks Arabic and French. She is an engineering student. She wants to be an engineer. She says she doesn't play any sports. She wants to make a lot of new friends in her class.

Finally, meet **Arun**. He is in Fatima's class. He says he speaks English well, but his writing isn't very good! Arun is from Chennai, India, and his first language is Hindi. He is a soccer player, and he wants to be on the school soccer team.

Name	Where from	Languages	Sports
1. Rafael			
2.	Tunis, Tunisia		
3.		English and Chinese	
4.			soccer

B Write a short biography of a classmate.

_____

_____

_____

_____

_____

8 Choose the correct sentences to complete this conversation.

- ☐ You, too. Talk to you later.
- ☑ Hi, Stacey. I'm Omar. How are you?
- ☐ I really like biology.
- ☐ Yes, I am. I'm an exchange student from Egypt.
- ☐ Yes, he is. We're in Biology 300. Is he your friend?

Stacey: Hello, I'm Stacey.

Omar: _Hi, Stacey. I'm Omar. How are you?_

Stacey: Pretty good, thanks. Are you a student here?

Omar: _____

Stacey: Welcome. Do you like it here? What's your favorite subject?

Omar: _____

Stacey: Oh, really? Is Ben Jones in your class?

Omar: _____

Stacey: No, he's my brother! Actually, I have to go meet him now. Nice to meet you, Omar.

Omar: _____

9 Complete this conversation. Use contractions where possible.

Grammar note: Contractions	
Do not use contractions for short answers with *Yes*.	
Are you from Argentina?	Is he from Greece?
Yes, I am. (*not* Yes, I'm.)	Yes, he is. (*not* Yes, he's.)

Alex: Hello. ___I'm___ Alex Robles. And this is my sister Celia.

Paola: Hi. _____ Paola Vieira.

Celia: Are you from South America, Paola?

Paola: Yes, _____. _____ from Brazil. Where are you both from?

Alex: _____ from Puerto Rico.

Paola: Are you from San Juan?

Celia: No, _____. _____ from Ponce. By the way, are you in English 101?

Paola: No, _____. I'm in English 102.

10 Look at the answers. What are the questions?

1. A: _Who's Allison?_

B: Allison is my best friend.

2. A: _____

B: My favorite school subject is history.

3. A: _____

B: No, we're not from Germany. We're from Switzerland.

4. A: _____

B: Yes, it's an interesting class.

5. A: _____

B: Yes, Mary and Yuka are in my class.

6. A: _____

B: Ryan is funny and friendly.

7. A: _____

B: No, Ms. Rogers isn't my English teacher. She's my math teacher.

11 Read the expressions. Which ones say "hello" and which ones say "good-bye"?

	Hello	Good-bye
1. How are you?	☑	☐
2. See you tomorrow.	☐	☐
3. Good night.	☐	☐
4. Good morning.	☐	☐
5. Talk to you later.	☐	☐
6. How's it going?	☐	☐
7. Have a good day.	☐	☐
8. What's up?	☐	☐

12 Answer these questions about yourself. Use contractions where possible.

1. Are you on vacation? _____

2. Is your teacher from Canada? _____

3. Is your first name popular? _____

4. Is your English class in the morning? _____

5. Are you from Asia? _____

6. Are you a student at a university? _____

2 What do you do?

1 Match the correct words to make sentences.

1. A cashier _____d_____
2. A vendor _____
3. A babysitter _____
4. A doctor _____
5. A tutor _____
6. A pet sitter _____

a. helps sick people.
b. takes care of animals.
c. sells things.
d. takes money and gives change.
e. takes care of children.
f. helps students with their school work.

2 Write sentences using *He* or *She*.

1. I'm a mechanic. I fix cars. I work in a garage.

   He's a mechanic. He fixes cars.

   He works in a garage.

2. I'm a cook. I cook food. I work in a restaurant.

   She _____

   _____

3. I'm a math teacher. I teach math to students. I work in a school.

   She _____

   _____

4. I'm a taxi driver. I drive a car. I take people to places they want to go.

   He _____

   _____

3 Write *a* or *an* in the correct places.

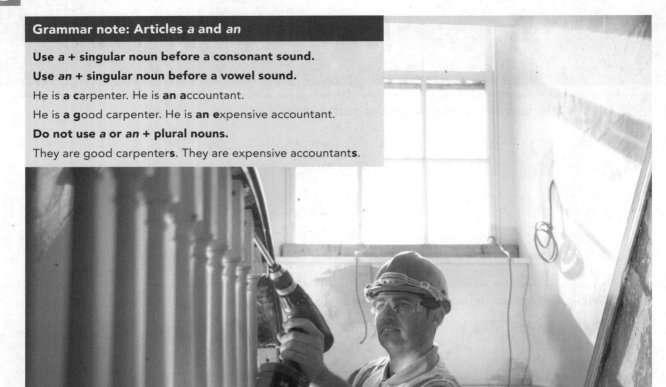

1. He's *a* ˄carpenter. He works for *a* ˄construction company. He builds schools and houses.

2. She's office manager. She works for large company. It's interesting job.

3. He works in restaurant. He's server. He's also part-time student. He takes business class in the evening.

4. She works for travel company. She arranges tours. She's travel agent.

5. He has difficult job. He's flight attendant. He works on airplane.

4 Choose someone in your family. Write about his or her job.

_____

_____

_____

_____

5 Complete this conversation with the correct words.

Tiffany: What _____*does*_____ your brother _____, exactly?
　　　　　　　　　　(do / does)　　　　　　　　　　　(do / does)

Kate: He _____ for the city. He's a firefighter.
　　　　　　　(work / works)

Tiffany: How _____ he _____ it?
　　　　　　　　　(do / does)　　　　(like / likes)

Kate: It's an interesting job. He _____ it very much.
　　　　　　　　　　　　　　　　　　(like / likes)

But he _____ long hours. And what _____ you _____?
　　　　　(work / works)　　　　　　　　　　(do / does)　　　　　(do / does)

Tiffany: I'm a student. I _____ geography.
　　　　　　　　　　　　　(study / studies)

Kate: Oh, really? Where _____ you _____ to school?
　　　　　　　　　　　　(do / does)　　　　(go / goes)

Tiffany: I _____ to Matthews University. My brother _____ there, too.
　　　　　　(go / goes)　　　　　　　　　　　　　　　　(go / goes)

Kate: Really? And what _____ he _____?
　　　　　　　　　　　　(do / does)　　(study / studies)

Tiffany: He _____ graphic design.
　　　　　　　(study / studies)

Kate: That sounds interesting.

6 Complete the questions in this conversation.

Tom: _*Where do you work?*_____

Ray: I work for Brady Corporation.

Tom: And what _____
there?

Ray: I'm an accountant.

Tom: An accountant? How

_____

Ray: I like numbers, so it's a great job.
And what _____

Tom: I'm a teacher.

Ray: Really? What _____

Tom: I teach accounting!

7 Interesting jobs

Read these two interviews. Answer the questions.

Today, Job Talk
interviews two people with interesting jobs.

Job Talk: Oliver, where do you work?

Oliver: Well, I guess I work in the sky.

Job Talk: In the sky? What do you do?

Oliver: I'm a flight attendant. I work on the international flight from Miami to Recife, Brazil.

Job Talk: That's really interesting. What do you like best about your job?

Oliver: I really like to travel and to meet people. So my job is perfect for me.

Job Talk: Do you speak Portuguese?

Oliver: I speak a little. I carry my dictionary everywhere I go!

Job Talk: What do you do, Lucy?

Lucy: I'm a security guard at Matthews University.

Job Talk: That sounds difficult. What is the hardest thing about your job?

Lucy: Well, people break the rules at the university, and I have to stop them.

Job Talk: Are people unfriendly to you?

Lucy: Sometimes, but most of the students are very nice.

Job Talk: And what do you like best about your job?

Lucy: Well, some days the university is quiet. I get to read a lot of books!

1. What does Oliver do? He _____

2. Where does he work? _____

3. How does Oliver learn Portuguese? _____

4. What does Lucy do? She _____

5. Where does she work? _____

6. What is the hardest part of her job? _____

8 Meet Patricio. Write questions about him using *What*, *Where*, *When*, and *How*.

1. _What does he do?_ _____

2. _____

3. _____

4. _____

Mercy Hospital

Patricio Cardozo
Registered Nurse,
Night Shift

9 How does Patricio spend his weekends? Complete this paragraph with the words from the box.

- ☐ around
- ☐ in
- ☐ at
- ☐ late
- ☐ before
- ☑ on
- ☐ early
- ☐ until

Everyone knows Patricio at the hospital. Patricio is a part-time nurse. He works at night on weekends. _____On_____ Saturdays and Sundays, Patricio sleeps most of the day and wakes up a little _____ nine _____ the evening, usually at 8:45 or 8:50. He has breakfast very late, _____ 9:30 or 10:00 P.M.! He watches television _____ eleven o'clock and then starts work _____ midnight. _____ in the morning, usually around 5:00 A.M., he leaves work, has a little snack, goes home, goes to bed, and sleeps _____. It's a perfect schedule for Patricio. He's a pre-med student on weekdays at a local college.

10 Choose the correct words to complete the sentences.

1. Avery is a tour guide. She _____takes_____ (answers / takes / writes) people on tours.

2. Stella _____ (does / goes / starts) to bed after midnight.

3. Bonnie _____ (answers / gets / starts) up early in the morning.

4. What _____ (does / goes / serves) your sister do?

5. Roland _____ (answers / serves / starts) work at 8:00 A.M.

6. My brother works in a bookstore. He _____ (answers / sells / works) books and magazines.

7. The Havana Garden restaurant _____ (serves / takes / writes) good Cuban food.

8. Dan _____ (serves / does / works) his school work on his new computer.

9. Nunu _____ (goes / sells / writes) about 30 emails a day.

10. David is a receptionist. He _____ (answers / starts / types) the phone and greets people.

11. Miguel _____ (does / takes / works) in a restaurant.

11 Choose the sentences in the box that have the same meaning as the sentences below.

- ☐ He goes to the university.
- ☐ She cares for people's pets.
- ☐ She stays up late.
- ☐ What does he do?
- ☑ She's a fitness instructor.
- ☐ He works part-time.

1. She teaches exercise classes.

She's a fitness instructor.

2. What's his job?

_____

3. She's a pet sitter.

_____

4. He's a student.

_____

5. She goes to bed at midnight.

_____

6. He works three hours every day.

_____

12 Fill in the missing words or phrases from these job advertisements.

1.
- ☐ at night
- ☐ part-time
- ☑ servers
- ☐ weekends

2.
- ☐ interesting
- ☐ Japanese
- ☐ tours
- ☐ student

3.
- ☐ at
- ☐ in
- ☐ manager
- ☐ weekends

Help Wanted

Larry's Diner needs
___servers___. Work during
the day or _____,
weekdays or _____,
full-time or _____.
Call 901–555–1977.

_____ job for a
language _____.
Take people on
_____. Evenings
only. Need good English and
_____ skills.
Email Brenda at Brenda44@cup.org.

We need a great office
_____! Work
Monday through Friday, no
_____. Start
work _____ 9:00
_____ the morning.

3 How much are these?

1 Choose the correct sentences to complete this conversation.

- [ ] Oh, James. Thank you very much.
- [ ] Which one?
- [✓] Which ones?
- [ ] Well, I like it, but it's expensive.
- [ ] Yes. But I don't really like yellow.

James: Look at those pants, Linda.

Linda: _Which ones?_

James: The yellow ones over there. They're nice.

Linda: _____

James: Hmm. Well, what about that sweater? It's perfect for you.

Linda: _____

James: This blue one.

Linda: _____

James: Hey, let me buy it for you. It's a present!

Linda: _____

2 Complete these conversations with *How much is/are . . . ?* and *this, that, these,* or *those.*

1. A: _How much is this_ blouse right here?

   B: It's $47.95.

2. A: _____ glasses over there?

   B: They're $87.

3. A: _____ sneakers right here?

   B: They're $79.99.

4. A: _____ cat over there?

   B: That's *my* cat, and he's not for sale!

3 Write the plurals of these words.

Spelling note: Plural nouns

Most words		Words ending in -*ss*, -*sh*, -*ch*, and -*x*	
cap	cap**s**	glass	glass**es**
shoe	shoe**s**	dish	dish**es**
		watch	watch**es**

Words ending in -*f* and -*fe*		Words ending in consonant + *y*	
shelf	shel**ves**	country	countr**ies**
knife	kni**ves**		

1. ring ____rings____

2. glove _____

3. party _____

4. boy _____

5. tie _____

6. box _____

7. scarf _____

8. blouse _____

9. T-shirt _____

10. hairbrush _____

11. computer _____

12. dress _____

4 What do you think of these prices? Write a response.

That's cheap.	That's not bad.	That's reasonable.	That's pretty expensive!

1. $250 for a wool sweater

   _That's pretty expensive!_____

2. $30 for a silk tie

   _____

3. $180 for a cotton dress

   _____

4. $40 for a gold necklace

   _____

5. $15 for three T-shirts

   _____

6. $80 for a leather belt

   _____

5 Choose the correct words to complete the conversations.

1. Shirley: I like ____*those*____ earrings over there.
(that / those)

    Clerk: Which _____?
(one / ones)

Shirley: The small gold _____.
(one / ones)

    Clerk: _____ $399.
(It's / They're)

Shirley: Oh, they're expensive!

2. George: Excuse me. How much
are _____ pants?
(that / those)

    Clerk: _____ only $65.
(It's / They're)

George: And how much is _____ shirt?
(this / these)

    Clerk: Which _____?
(one / ones)

They're all different.

George: This green _____.
(one / ones)

    Clerk: _____ $47.
(It's / They're)

3.   **Clerk:** Good afternoon.

Martina: Oh, hi. How much is
_____ watch?
(this / these)

    Clerk: _____ $195.
(It's / They're)

Martina: And how much is
that _____?
(one / ones)

    Clerk: _____ $99.
(It's / They're)

Martina: That's not bad. I'll take it!

6 **What do you make from these materials? Complete the chart using words from the box. (You will use words more than once.)**

belt	boots	bracelet	button	gloves	hairbrush
jacket	necklace	pants	ring	shirt	

Cotton	Gold	Leather	Plastic	Silk	Wool
gloves					

7 **Make comparisons using the words given. Add *than* if necessary.**

silver earrings

1. A: Hey, look at these silver earrings! They're nice.
And they're _____*cheaper than*_____ those gold earrings. (cheap)

B: But they're _____ the gold ones. (small)

A: Well, yeah. The gold ones are _____ the silver ones. (big) But $400 is a lot of money!

gold earrings

leather coat

2. A: This leather coat is _____ the wool one. (attractive)

B: Yes, but the wool one is _____. (warm)

wool coat

3. A: This orange shirt is an interesting color!

B: Yes, but the color is _____ the design. (pretty)

A: The design isn't bad.

B: I think the pattern on that gray shirt is _____ the pattern on this orange one. (good)

orange shirt

gray shirt

cotton dresses

4. A: These cotton dresses are nice.

B: Yes, but the silk ones are _____. (nice)

A: They're also _____. (expensive)

silk dresses

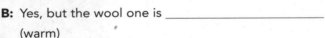

8 Complete the chart. Use the words from the box.

- ☑ boots
- ☐ bracelet
- ☐ dress
- ☐ earrings
- ☐ MP3 player
- ☐ necklace
- ☐ pants
- ☐ ring
- ☐ tablet
- ☐ television
- ☐ T-shirt
- ☐ smartphone

Clothing	Electronics	Jewelry
boots		

9 Answer these questions. Give your own information.

1	2	3	4	5
gold ring	tablet	hiking boots	wool gloves	black sunglasses
silver ring	laptop computer	sneakers	leather gloves	white sunglasses

1. Which ring do you prefer, the silver one or the gold one?

   I prefer the gold one.

2. Which one do you like more, the tablet or the laptop computer?

   _____

3. Which ones do you like more, the hiking boots or the sneakers?

   _____

4. Which ones do you prefer, the wool gloves or the leather gloves?

   _____

5. Which sunglasses do you like better, the black ones or the white ones?

   _____

10 Great gadgets!

A Read these ads. Match the pictures and descriptions.

1. _____   **2.** _____   **3.** _____   **4.** _____

a. Do you want to help the environment and do yard work at the same time? This machine knows when your lawn needs water. It waters your grass, and you don't have to do anything! Save time, save water, and save money! Only $124.99.

b. You can take this with you to the beach or on a picnic. No more uncomfortable towels or blankets! It fills with air in five minutes. Feel like you are sitting in your own living room in the great outdoors! Only $49.50.

c. What's a party without music? Indoors or outdoors, you can have a good time with this small item on a shelf or in a tree. Turn it down to set the mood, or turn it up to start the dancing! Only $299.99.

d. What's it like to swim like a fish? Now is your chance to find out! Put both feet in, get in the water, and feel what it's like to flap instead of kick. If you love to be in the water and dive deep, you need this! $36.

B Check (✓) True or False.

	True	False
1. The garden sensor waters your lawn when it needs more water.	☐	☐
2. The inflatable chair takes about five minutes to fill with air.	☐	☐
3. The Soundbook only works indoors.	☐	☐
4. You need two monofins, one for each foot.	☐	☐

C What's special about a gadget you have? Write a paragraph about it.

_____

_____

_____

_____

_____

_____

4 Do you play the guitar?

1 Check (✓) the boxes to complete the survey about music and TV.

A Do you like these types of music?	I love it!	It's OK.	I don't like it.
pop	☐	☐	☐
classical	☐	☐	☐
hip-hop	☐	☐	☐
rock	☐	☐	☐
jazz	☐	☐	☐

B Do you like these types of TV shows?	I love them!	They're OK.	I don't like them.
talk shows	☐	☐	☐
reality shows	☐	☐	☐
sitcoms	☐	☐	☐
soap operas	☐	☐	☐
game shows	☐	☐	☐

2 What's your opinion? Answer the questions with the expressions and pronouns in the box.

	Object pronouns
Yes, I do.	him
I love . . .	her
I like . . . a lot.	it
No, I don't.	them
I don't like . . . very much..	
I can't stand . . .	

Kendrick Lamar

1. Do you like horror movies?

   Yes, I do. I like them a lot.

2. Do you like Kendrick Lamar?

   _____

3. Do you like heavy metal music?

   _____

4. Do you like mystery books?

   _____

5. Do you like video games?

   _____

6. Do you like Adele?

   _____

Adele

3 Choose the correct job for each picture.

☐ an actor   ☐ an athlete   ☐ a pop group   ☐ a singer

1. Hope Solo is _____

2. Fall Out Boy are _____

3. Chris Hemsworth is

_____

_____

4. Luke Bryan is

_____

_____

4 Complete these conversations.

1. **Ken:** _____*Do*_____ you _____*like*_____ pop music, Janet?

Janet: Yes, I _____ it a lot. I'm a big fan of Beyoncé.

Ken: Oh, _____ she play the guitar?

Janet: No, she _____, but she's a great dancer.

2. **Alice:** _____ kind of music _____ your parents _____, Jack?

Jack: They _____ country music.

Alice: Who _____ they _____? Jason Aldean?

Jack: No, they _____ like him very much. They prefer Carrie Underwood.

3. **Harold:** Kelly, who's your favorite female singer? _____ you _____ Selena Gomez?

Kelly: No, I _____. I can't stand her. I like Etana.

Harold: I don't know her. What kind of music _____ she sing?

Kelly: She _____ reggae. She's really great!

5 Complete these questions and write answers.

1. <u>What kinds</u> of movies do you like?   I like _____

2. _____ is your favorite movie?   My favorite _____

3. _____ of movies do you dislike?   _____

4. _____ of TV shows do you like?   _____

5. _____ is your favorite actor or actress?   _____

6. _____ is your favorite song?   _____

7. _____ is your favorite rock band?   _____

8. _____ is your favorite video game?   _____

6 What do you think? Answer the questions.

1. Which are more interesting, action movies or historical dramas?

_____

2. Which movies are more exciting, westerns or crime thrillers?

_____

3. Which do you like more, musicals or animated movies?

_____

4. Which do you prefer, romantic comedies or science fiction movies?

_____

5. Which are scarier, horror movies or thrillers?

_____

7 Verbs and nouns

A Which nouns often go with these verbs? Complete the chart. Use each noun only once.

listen to	play	watch
music		

- [ ] a basketball game
- [ ] the piano
- [ ] the guitar
- [ ] videos
- [ ] the radio
- [ ] R&B
- [ ] the drums
- [x] music
- [ ] a movie

B Write a sentence using each verb in part A.

1. _____
2. _____
3. _____

8 Movie reviews

A Read the movie reviews. Write the type of movie for each review below the title.

comedy	historical drama	science fiction	crime thriller	horror
travel	documentary	romantic comedy	western	

● ● ● ⟨ / ⟩   ⌂

Movie Reviews   Search [   ] 🔍

Home   News   **Reviews**   Listings   Box Office   Sign in   Register

1 Ahead of Time

What are high school kids like in the future? This movie gives an answer. It's about a group of school kids in the year 2017. After class one day, they find a time machine behind the school. One of the teens sees a button marked "Year 2500" and presses it. They suddenly travel to the twenty-sixth century! They have many exciting adventures. But do they get back in time for school the next day? Watch and find out.

SCORE ★★★★☆

2 House of Laughs

This movie is about a group of six young people in London. They live in the same house in a suburb far from the city center. All of them come from different countries. They speak different languages and have different customs. What happens when they're all under one roof? Watch and laugh! The story is very funny, and the acting is very good. This movie is like a really good TV soap opera, but funnier.

SCORE ★★★★★

3 Coming Up for Air

The action never stops in this movie. Police officer Karen Montana wants to catch Mr. X, a notorious gold thief. Mr. X is stealing gold from an old shipwreck at the bottom of the ocean. The only way to catch him is under the water. But Montana's one weakness is that she can't swim and hates the water. Will she catch him? The plot isn't very good, but the surprise ending is worth waiting for. Watch for yourself.

SCORE ★★☆☆☆

B Write down the words in the review that helped you to decide what kind of movie it is.

1. Ahead of Time: _future,_____

2. House of Laughs: _____

3. Coming Up for Air: _____

9 Choose the correct responses.

1. A: What do you think of "The Voice"?

   B: <u>I'm not a real fan of the show.</u>

     • How about you?

     • I'm not a real fan of the show.

2. A: Do you like jazz music?

   B: _____

     • I can't stand it.

     • I can't stand them.

3. A: There's a soccer game tonight.

   B: _____

     • Thanks. I'd love to.

     • Great. Let's go.

4. A: Would you like to see a movie this weekend?

   B: _____

     • That sounds great!

     • I don't agree.

10 Yes or *no*?

A Fabiana is inviting friends to a movie. Do they accept the invitation or not? Check (✓) *Yes* or *No* for each response.

Accept?	Yes	No
1. I'd love to. What time does it start?	✓	☐
2. Thanks, but I don't really like animated movies.	☐	☐
3. That sounds great. Where is it?	☐	☐
4. I'd love to, but I have to work until midnight.	☐	☐
5. Thanks. I'd really like to. When do you want to meet?	☐	☐

B Respond to the invitations.

1. I have tickets to a classical concert on Saturday. Would you like to go?

_____

2. There's a soccer game tonight. Do you want to go with me?

_____

3. Meghan Trainor is performing tomorrow at the stadium. Would you like to see her?

_____

11 Choose the correct phrases to complete these conversations.

1. Eva: _Do you like_____ pop music, Anita?
(Do you like / Would you like)

Anita: Yes, I do. _____ it a lot.
(I like / I'd like)

Eva: There's an Ariana Grande concert on Friday.
_____ to go with me?
(Do you like / Would you like)

Anita: Yes, _____! Thanks.
(I love to / I'd love to)

2. Marco: There's a baseball game on TV tonight.
_____ to come over and watch it?
(Do you like / Would you like)

Tony: _____, but I have to study tonight.
(I like to / I'd like to)

Marco: Well, _____ basketball?
(do you like / would you like)

Tony: Yes, _____. I love it!
(I do / I would)

Marco: There's a game on TV tomorrow at 3:00.
_____ to watch that with me?
(Do you like / Would you like)

Tony: _____. Thanks!
(I like to / I'd love to)

12 Rewrite these sentences. Find another way to say each sentence using the words given.

1. Do you like rap?

_What do you think of rap?_____ (think of)

2. Chad doesn't like country music.

_____ (can't stand)

3. I think soap operas are great!

_____ (love)

4. Celia doesn't like new age music.

_____ (be a fan of)

5. Do you want to go to a soccer match?

_____ (would like)

5 What an interesting family!

1 Which words are for males? Which are for females? Complete the chart.

- ☑ aunt
- ☐ husband
- ☐ sister
- ☑ brother
- ☐ mother
- ☐ son
- ☐ daughter
- ☐ nephew
- ☐ uncle
- ☐ father
- ☐ niece
- ☐ wife

Males			Females		
brother			aunt		

2 Complete this conversation. Use the present continuous of the verbs given.

Jan: You look tired, Monica.
_____Are you studying_____ (study) late at night these days?

Monica: No, I'm not. My brother and sister _____ (stay) with me right now. They keep me up late every night.

Jan: Really, both of them? What _____ (do) this summer? _____ (take) classes, too?

Monica: No, they aren't. My brother is on vacation now, but he _____ (look) for a part-time job here.

Jan: What about your sister? _____ (work)?

Monica: Yes, she is. She has a part-time job at the university. What about you, Jan? Are you in school this summer?

Jan: Yes, I am. I _____ (study) two languages.

Monica: Oh, _____ (take) Korean and Spanish again?

Jan: Well, I'm taking Korean, but now I _____ (start) Portuguese classes.

Monica: Really? That's exciting!

3 **What is another way to say each sentence? Rewrite the sentences using the words in the box.**

| aunt | mother-in-law | ~~uncle~~ |
| granddaughter | son and daughter | wife |

1. Anita is Marco's niece.

  Marco is Anita's uncle.

2. John is married to Ann.

_____

3. My father's sister is a teacher.

_____

4. We have two children.

_____

5. My husband's mother is from Mexico.

_____

6. Willie and Mabel are Brooke's grandparents.

_____

4 **Choose the correct sentences to complete the conversation.**

☐ Yes, he is. He loves it there.
☑ No, I'm not. I'm living in Singapore now.
☐ Yes, we are. We really love Miami.
☐ Yes, I do. I like it a lot.
☐ No, they aren't. They're living in Atlanta now.

Kathy: Are you still living in Miami, Martin?

Martin: _No, I'm not. I'm living in Singapore now._

Kathy: Wow! Do you like it?

Martin: _____

Kathy: And is your brother still working in Seoul?

Martin: _____

Kathy: And how about your parents? Are they still living in Florida?

Martin: _____ How about you and your family, Kathy?
Are you still living here?

Kathy: _____

Singapore

5 Complete these sentences. Use the simple present or the present continuous of the verbs given.

1. This is my cousin, Martin.

He _____lives_____ (live) in Houston, but

he _____ (visit) Peru this summer.

He _____ (take) cooking classes there.

2. And these are my parents.

They _____ (work) in Paris this year.

They _____ (be) on vacation right now.

3. Here's a photo of my grandparents.

They _____ (not work) now.

They _____ (be) retired.

4. This is my sister-in-law, Amanda.

She _____ (want) to start her own company.

She _____ (study) business in Australia right now.

5. And this is my nephew, George.

He _____ (go) to high school.

He _____ (like) history, but

he _____ (not like) chemistry.

6 Choose a friend or a family member. Write about him or her using the simple present and present continuous.

_____

_____

_____

_____

7 Home or away?

A Answer these questions. Then read the passage.

1. Read the title below. What do you think a "boomerang kid" is?

_____

2. Are you going to live at home when you leave school? Why or why not?

_____

BOOMERANG KIDS

Today in the United States, many young adults are returning home to live after they graduate from college. They are being called "boomerang kids," like the Australian hunting stick that comes back after you throw it. Many college graduates can't find the jobs they want right away. Some also have college loans to pay back. They don't have enough money to rent expensive apartments, so they go back home to live with their parents. While they live at home, they are working at jobs with low pay and trying to save money for the future.

Meanwhile, the parents of boomerang kids are feeling the challenges of having their adult children back home. Most understand the problems their kids are having with money and accept that they're living with them again. But their relationships are different now. Some parents expect their kids to keep following their rules and to help around the house. Young adults, on the other hand, want to be independent and to make their own decisions. This creates tension between parents and kids. These boomerangs go out as kids, but they come back as adults.

B Check (✓) True or False. For statements that are false, write the correct information.

Young Adults	True	False
1. "Boomerang kids" are college graduates who don't want to live at home. _____	☐	☐
2. Many college graduates are having a difficult time finding a good job. _____	☐	☐
3. College graduates who live at home can't save money for the future. _____	☐	☐

Parents	True	False
4. Parents are seeing that it can be difficult to have their "boomerang kids" live at home again. _____	☐	☐
5. Parents want to do everything for their kids like they did when they were younger. _____	☐	☐
6. Parents and kids mostly agree about the rules and expectations of the house. _____	☐	☐

8 Arrange the quantifiers from the most to the least.

☑ all ☐ nearly all
☐ few ☑ no
☐ many ☐ some
☐ most

1. _____ all _____
2. _____
3. _____
4. _____
5. _____
6. _____
7. _____ no _____

9 Rewrite these sentences about the United States using the quantifiers given.

1. Ninety percent of children go to public schools. Ten percent of children go to private schools.

Most _children go to public schools._

Few _____

_____

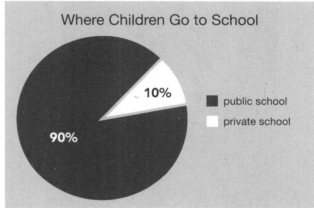

Where Children Go to School

10%
90%

■ public school
□ private school

2. Sixty-two percent of young people go to college after they finish high school. Thirty-four percent of young people look for work.

Many _____

_____

Some _____

_____

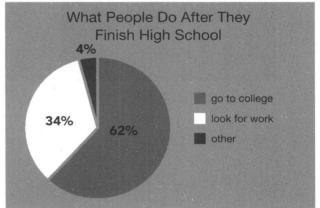

What People Do After They Finish High School

4%
34%
62%

■ go to college
□ look for work
■ other

3. Ninety-five percent of people over 65 like to talk to family and friends. Forty-three percent of people over 65 like to spend time on a hobby. Three percent of people over 65 like to play soccer.

Not many _____

_____

A lot of _____

_____

Nearly all _____

_____

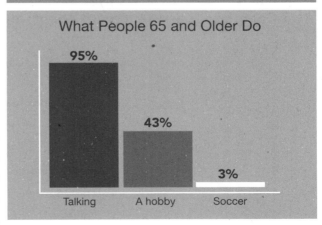

What People 65 and Older Do

95%
43%
3%
Talking   A hobby   Soccer

10 Choose the correct words or phrases to complete this paragraph.

In my country, some _____*couples*_____ (couples / cousins / relatives) get married fairly young. Not many marriages _____ (break up / get divorced / stay together), and nearly all _____ (divorced / married / single) people remarry. Elderly couples often _____ (divorce again / move away / live at home) and take care of their grandchildren.

11 Complete these sentences about your country. Use the words in the box.

all	a lot of	few	most	nearly all	no	some

1. _____ young people go to college.
2. _____ people study English.
3. _____ married couples have more than five children.
4. _____ elderly people have part-time jobs.
5. _____ students have full-time jobs.
6. _____ children go to school on Saturdays.

How often do you run?

1 **Complete the chart. Use words from the box.**

baseball	soccer	basketball	volleyball	football
walking	jogging	weight training	Pilates	yoga

Sports	Fitness activities
baseball	

2 **Arrange these words to make sentences or questions.**

1. often   mornings   play   on   we   tennis   Saturday

We often play tennis on Saturday mornings .

2. ever   Ryan   do   does   yoga

_____ ?

3. go   do   often   swimming   how   you

_____ ?

4. go   never   I   almost   jogging

_____ .

5. hardly   they   basketball   play   ever

_____ .

6. do   on   you   what   usually   Sundays   do

_____ ?

3 Use these questions to complete the conversations: *How often do you . . . ?*
Do you ever . . . ? What do you usually . . . ?

1. **A:** _Do you ever go bowling?_

   B: Yes, I often go bowling on weekends.

2. **A:** _____

   B: Well, I usually do martial arts or watch TV after work.

3. **A:** _____

   B: Yes, I sometimes play sports on weekends – usually soccer.

4. **A:** _____

   B: I don't exercise very often at all.

5. **A:** _____

   B: No, I never go to the gym on Saturdays.

6. **A:** _____

   B: I usually go jogging four times a week.

4 Keeping fit?

A Check (✓) how often you do each of the things in the chart.

	Every day	Once or twice a week	Sometimes	Not very often	Never
do martial arts	☐	☐	☐	☐	☐
play basketball	☐	☐	☐	☐	☐
exercise	☐	☐	☐	☐	☐
go jogging	☐	☐	☐	☐	☐
go bowling	☐	☐	☐	☐	☐
play soccer	☐	☐	☐	☐	☐
go swimming	☐	☐	☐	☐	☐
do weight training	☐	☐	☐	☐	☐

B Write about your fitness habits using the information in the chart.

_____

_____

_____

_____

_____

_____

_____

5 Complete this conversation with the correct prepositions. Write them in the correct places.

Kelly: What time do you go swimming ~~in~~ the morning? (around / in / on)

Neil: I always go swimming 7:00. (at / for / on)

How about you, Kelly?

Kelly: I usually go swimming noon. (around / in / with)

I swim about 30 minutes. (at / for / until)

Neil: And do you also play sports your free time? (at / in / until)

Kelly: No, I usually go out my classmates. (around / for / with)

What about you?

Neil: I go to the gym Mondays and Wednesdays. (at / on / until)

And sometimes I go jogging weekends. (for / in / on)

Kelly: Wow! You really like to stay in shape.

6 Complete the sentences. Use the words from the box.

do	ice hockey	soccer	treadmill	goes	jogging
swimming	watches	~~exercises~~	shape	training	

1. Katie never __*exercises*__.
   She's a real couch potato.

2. How often do you _____ martial arts?

3. I like to stay in _____. I play sports every day.

4. Jeff does weight _____ every evening. He lifts 50-pound weights.

5. Arturo goes _____ twice a week. He usually runs about three miles.

6. Miho often _____ TV in the evening.

7. Maria is on the _____ team at her high school. She's good at passing the ball.

8. Judy never goes _____ when the water is cold.

9. Kyle often _____ bike riding on weekends.

10. I run on the _____ at the gym three times a week.

11. In Canada, many people like to play _____ outside in the winter.

7 Sports around the world

A Read the descriptions of three unique sports that are played in different parts of the world. Which sport do you want to try? Why?

Capoeira

Capoeira is a sport that comes from Brazil. It is part martial art, part dance, and part game. The legs do most of the work in this sport. Capoeiristas kick, jump, and dance to the music of stringed instruments, drums, bells, and rattles. Although the two people are fighting and defending themselves, capoeira is really more about movement, speed, and knowing what your opponent is thinking.

Hurling

The game of hurling comes from Ireland. It is the fastest field sport in the world. Hurlers play on a field like soccer but use a stick and a small ball. The stick is used to carry or hit the ball, or players can kick it or slap it with their hands. They try to get the ball over a bar for one point or under the bar into a net for three points. Hurling is a very old sport and similar to modern rugby, soccer, field hockey, and football.

Bashi

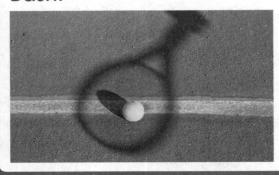

Bashi is a national sport in the Maldives, and only women play it. Between eight and eleven women play on a tennis court with tennis balls and one tennis racket. One player hits a ball with the racket on one side of the net, and players try to catch it on the other side. The woman who hits the ball faces away from the net and has to hit the ball backwards over her head! Women often get injured trying to catch the fast-moving balls with their bare hands.

B What sport do the activities describe? Check (✓) the answers.

	Capoeira	Hurling	Bashi
1. hit a ball backwards	☐	☐	☐
2. run very fast	☐	☐	☐
3. know what your opponent is thinking	☐	☐	☐
4. get a ball in a net	☐	☐	☐
5. move with music	☐	☐	☐
6. hit a ball over a net	☐	☐	☐

8 Choose the correct responses.

1. **A:** How often do you play golf, Monica?

   B: _Once a week._
   - I guess I'm OK.
   - Once a week.
   - About an hour.

2. **A:** How long do you spend on the golf course?

   B: _____
   - About four hours.
   - About average.
   - About three miles.

3. **A:** And how well do you play?

   B: _____
   - I'm not very well.
   - I almost never do.
   - I'm about average.

4. **A:** How good are you at other sports?

   B: _____
   - Not very good, actually.
   - I sometimes play twice a week.
   - Pretty well, I guess.

9 Look at the answers. Write questions using *how*.

1. **A:** _How long do you spend exercising?_____

   B: I don't spend any time at all. In fact, I don't exercise.

2. **A:** _____ at playing football?

   B: I'm pretty good at it. I'm on the school team.

3. **A:** _____ for a walk?

   B: Almost every day. I really enjoy it.

4. **A:** _____

   B: Baseball? Pretty well, I guess. Yeah, I like it a lot.

5. **A:** _____

   B: I spend about an hour jogging.

10 Rewrite these sentences. Find another way to say each sentence using the words given.

1. I don't go bike riding very often.

   I hardly ever go bike riding. (hardly ever)

2. Tamara exercises twice a month.

   _____ (not very often)

3. Patty tries to keep fit.

   _____ (stay in shape)

4. Ricardo often exercises at the gym.

   _____ (work out)

5. I go jogging every day after work.

   _____ (always)

6. How good are you at tennis?

   _____ (play)

11 What do you think about fitness and sports? Answer these questions.

1. Do you like to exercise for a short time or a long time?

   _____

   _____

2. Do you prefer exercising in the morning or in the evening?

   _____

   _____

3. Which do you like better, walking or jogging?

   _____

   _____

4. Which do you like better, team sports or individual sports?

   _____

   _____

5. How good are you at sports like basketball and tennis?

   _____

   _____

6. What is a sport or game you don't like?

   _____

   _____

7 We went dancing!

1 Past tense

A Write the simple past of these regular verbs.

1. watch ___watched___
2. play _____
3. invite _____

4. arrive _____
5. study _____
6. hurry _____

7. travel _____
8. wash _____
9. look _____

B Write the simple present form of these irregular simple past verbs.

1. ___eat___ ate
2. _____ did
3. _____ met
4. _____ saw

5. _____ slept
6. _____ spent
7. _____ drove
8. _____ went

C Use two of the verbs above and write sentences about the past.

Example: _We saw the Eiffel Tower in Paris last year._

1. _____
2. _____

2 Use the cues to answer these questions.

1. Where did you go this weekend?

   _I went to the zoo._____ (to the zoo)

2. Who did you meet at the party?

   _____ (a famous artist)

3. What did you buy?

   _____ (a new pair of jeans)

4. How did you and Mario like the movie?

   _____ (a lot)

5. Where did Faye and Bob spend their vacation?

   _____ (in the country)

6. What time did you and Allison get home?

   _____ (a little after 1:00)

3 **What do you like to do alone? With other people? Complete the chart with activities from the box. Then add one more activity to each list.**

	Activities I like to do alone	Activities I like to do with other people
cook dinner		
do homework		
exercise		
go shopping		
go to a sports event		
go to the movies		
have a picnic		
play video games		
take a vacation		
watch TV		

4 **Complete the questions in this conversation.**

A: How _did you spend the weekend_?

B: I spent the weekend with my sisters.

A: What _____?

B: Well, on Saturday, we went shopping.

A: That sounds like fun! What _____?

B: I bought a new pair of shoes and a new purse.

A: Where _____ on Sunday?

B: We went to an amusement park.

A: Oh, how _____?

B: We had a great time. In fact, we stayed there all day.

A: Really? What time _____?

B: We got home very late, around midnight.

5 Answer these questions with negative statements. Then add a positive statement using the information in the box.

- ☐ finish the project on Saturday
- ☐ go out with friends
- ☑ stay home all weekend
- ☐ take the bus
- ☐ watch it on TV
- ☐ work all day until six o'clock

1. A: Did you and John go to Anne's party on Saturday?

   B: _No, we didn't. We stayed home all weekend._

2. A: Beth left work at 2:00 yesterday afternoon. Did you go home early, too?

   B: _____

3. A: I watched TV all weekend. Did you spend the weekend at home, too?

   B: _____

4. A: I saw you and Amy at the library on Saturday. Did you work together on Sunday, too?

   B: _____

5. A: Giovanni drove me to work yesterday morning. Did you drive to work?

   B: _____

6. A: Sandy went to the baseball game last night. Did you and Martin go to the game?

   B: _____

6 Read about Pamela's week. Match the sentences that have a similar meaning.

A		B	
1. She was broke last week.	_f_	a. She had people over.	
2. She didn't work on Monday.	___	b. She did housework.	
3. She worked around the house.	___	c. She took the day off.	
4. She didn't wash the clothes.	___	d. She had a good time.	
5. She invited friends for dinner.	___	e. She didn't do the laundry.	
6. She had a lot of fun.	___	✓ f. She spent all her money.	

7 Did we take the same trip?

A Read the posts. Who went to Bangkok for the first time?

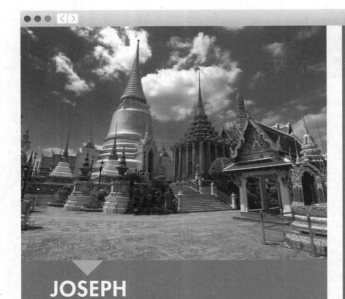

JOSEPH

We went to Thailand again for our summer vacation. We spent a week in Bangkok and did something every day. We went to the floating market very early one morning. We didn't buy anything there – we just looked. Another day, we went to Wat Phra Kaew, the famous Temple of the Emerald Buddha. Check out my pic!

Then we saw two more temples nearby. We also went on a river trip somewhere outside Bangkok. The best thing about the trip was the food. The next time we have friends over for dinner, I'm going to cook Thai food.

OLIVIA

Last summer, we spent our vacation in Thailand. We were very excited – it was our first trip there. We spent two days in Bangkok. Of course, we got a river taxi to the floating market. We bought some delicious fruit there. I'm posting a picture.

The next day we went to a very interesting temple called the Temple of the Emerald Buddha. We didn't have time to visit any other temples. However, we went to two historic cities – Ayutthaya and Sukhothai. Both have really interesting ruins. Everything was great. It's impossible to say what the best thing was about the trip.

B Who did these things on their trip? Check (✓) all correct answers.

	Joseph	Olivia
1. stayed for two days in Bangkok	☐	✓
2. visited the floating market	☐	☐
3. bought fruit	☐	☐
4. saw some historic ruins	☐	☐
5. traveled on the river	☐	☐
6. loved the food the most	☐	☐
7. enjoyed everything	☐	☐

8 Complete this conversation with *was*, *wasn't*, *were*, or *weren't*.

A: How _____was_____ your vacation in Thailand, Rich?

B: It _____ great. I really enjoyed it.

A: How long _____ you there?

B: We _____ there for two weeks.

A: _____ you in Bangkok the whole time?

B: No, we _____. We _____ in the mountains for a few days.

A: And how _____ the weather? _____ it good?

B: No, it _____ good at all! In fact, it _____ terrible. The city _____ very hot, and the mountains _____ cold and rainy!

9 Choose the correct questions to complete this conversation.

- [ ] And what was the best part?
- [ ] How long were you in Brazil?
- [✓] How was your vacation in South America?
- [ ] And how long were you in Argentina?
- [ ] How was the weather?

A: _How was your vacation in South America?_

B: It was a great trip. I really enjoyed Brazil and Argentina.

A: _____

B: I was in Brazil for ten days.

A: _____

B: For about eight days.

A: Wow, that's a long time! _____

B: It was hot and sunny the whole time.

A: _____

B: It was definitely the beaches in Brazil. Oh, and we learned the tango in Argentina!

Brazil

10 Complete the sentences with the correct words or phrases. Use the past tense when necessary.

1. We _____ a trip to Egypt last summer. (take / make / do)

2. My brothers _____ at home all weekend. (go dancing / play video games / take a bike ride)

3. I worked really hard in Germany last week. I was there _____. (in my car / on business / on vacation)

4. I'm sorry I was late. I had to _____ a phone call. (do / make / go)

5. I stayed home last night and _____ the laundry. (do / go / make)

11 My kind of vacation

A What do you like to do on vacation? Rank these activities from 1 (you like it the most) to 6 (you like it the least).

_____ go to the beach

_____ visit historical places

_____ go shopping

_____ visit museums

_____ spend time at home

_____ eat good food

B Answer these questions about vacations.

1. How often do you go on vacation?

_____

2. How much time do you spend on vacation?

_____

3. Who do you usually go with?

_____

4. Where do you like to go?

_____

5. What do you usually do on vacation?

_____

8 How's the neighborhood?

1 Places

A Match the words in columns A and B. Write the names of the places.

A	B		
☑ coffee	☐ campus	**1.**	_coffee shop_
☐ college	☑ shop	**2.**	
☐ gas	☐ hotspot	**3.**	
☐ grocery	☐ office	**4.**	
☐ hair	☐ mall	**5.**	
☐ movie	☐ salon	**6.**	
☐ post	☐ station	**7.**	
☐ shopping	☐ store	**8.**	
☐ Wi-Fi	☐ theater	**9.**	

B Write questions with _Is there a . . . ?_ or _Are there any . . . ?_ and the names of places from part A.

1. **A:** I need a haircut. <u>Is there a hair salon</u> near here?

   B: Yes, there's one on Grand Street.

2. **A:** I want to buy some new clothes. _____ near here?

   B: No, there isn't, but there's one in Center City.

3. **A:** I need to mail this package. _____ around here?

   B: Yes, there's one next to the bank.

4. **A:** I want to see a movie tonight. _____ around here?

   B: Yes, there's one in the shopping mall.

5. **A:** We need some gas. _____ on this street?

   B: No, there aren't, but there are a couple on Second Avenue.

6. **A:** We need to buy some cereal and some apples.

   _____ near here?

   B: Yes, there's one near the gym on Brown Street.

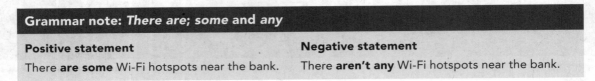

2 Look at these street maps of Springfield and Riverside. There are ten differences between them. Find the other eight.

Grammar note: *There are; some and any*

Positive statement	Negative statement
There **are some** Wi-Fi hotspots near the bank.	There **aren't any** Wi-Fi hotspots near the bank.

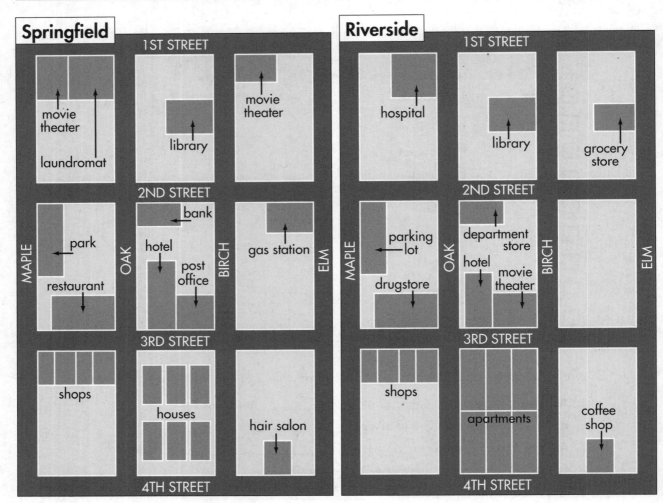

1. <u>There are some movie theaters on 1st Street in Springfield, but there aren't any in Riverside.</u>
2. <u>There's a park on the corner of 2nd Street and Maple in Springfield, but there isn't one in Riverside. There's a parking lot.</u>
3. _____
4. _____
5. _____
6. _____
7. _____
8. _____
9. _____
10. _____

3 Answer these questions. Use the map and the prepositions in the box.

☐ across from ☐ between ☐ in
☐ near ☑ next to ☐ on the corner of

1. Where's the nearest bank?

There's one next to the grocery store
on 1st Avenue.

2. Is there a post office near here?

Yes. There ·
_____

3. I'm looking for a drugstore.

_____

_____

4. Is there a laundromat in this neighborhood?

_____

_____

5. Is there a department store on River Street?

_____

_____

6. Are there any ATMs around here?

_____

_____

KING STREET

grocery store

hotel

ATM

bank · movie theater

PALM STREET

drugstore

gas station

library

post office

LINCOLN STREET

laundromat

department store

gym · hotel

gym →

RIVER STREET

1ST AVENUE · 2ND AVENUE · 3RD AVENUE

4 Answer these questions about your city or neighborhood. Use the expressions in the box and your own information.

Yes, there is. There's one on . . .   Yes, there are. There are some on . . .
No, there isn't.   No, there aren't.

1. Are there any good coffee shops around the school? _____

_____

2. Is there a drugstore near the school? _____

_____

3. Are there any grocery stores in your neighborhood? _____

_____

4. Is there a laundromat close to your home? _____

_____

5 The grass is always greener

A Read the interviews. Where would Charles like to live? Where would Arlene like to live?

MODERN LIVING

WE ASKED TWO PEOPLE ABOUT THE PLACES THEY LIVE.

Charles Bell

"My neighborhood is very convenient — it's near the shopping center and the bus station. It's also safe. But those are the only good things about living downtown. It's very noisy because the streets are always full of people! The traffic is terrible, and parking is a big problem! I can never park on my own street. I'd like to live in a small town."

Arlene Miller

"My family and I live in a nice small town. It has a great square where people meet for social events, and there's music on summer evenings. It's a safe place to raise children. But there is no privacy here. Everyone in town knows what you are doing all the time. And I don't meet as many interesting people as when I lived in the city. It can be too quiet here. I want more action! I think it's better downtown."

♡ LIKE   💬 COMMENT

B How do Charles and Arlene feel about their neighborhoods? Complete the chart.

	Advantages	Disadvantages
Downtown	convenient	
Small Town		no privacy

C Do you think it's better to live downtown or in a small town? Why?

_____

_____

_____

D How do you feel about the place you live? Write about it.

_____

_____

_____

6 Complete the chart. Use words from the box.

☑ bank   ☐ library   ☐ people   ☐ theater
☑ crime   ☐ noise   ☐ pollution   ☐ traffic
☐ hospital   ☐ parking   ☐ school   ☐ water

Count nouns		Noncount nouns	
bank		crime	

7 Write questions using *How much . . . ?* or *How many . . . ?* Then look at the picture and write answers to the questions. Use the expressions in the box.

☐ a few   ☐ a lot   ☐ many
☐ none   ☐ not any   ☑ only a little

1. trash   How much trash is there?   There's only a little.
2. buses
3. traffic
4. bicycles
5. police officers
6. crime

Choose the correct words or phrases to complete the conversation.

Andrea: Are there _____ any _____ (any / one / none) coffee shops around here, Carlos?

Carlos: Sure. There are _____ (any / one / a lot). There's a coffee shop _____ (across from / between / on) the Daily Market, but it's expensive.

Andrea: Well, are there _____ (any / none / one) others?

Carlos: Yeah, there are _____ (a few / a little / one). There's a nice _____ (any / one / some) near here. It's called Morning Joe.

Andrea: That's perfect! Where is it, exactly?

Carlos: It's on Third Avenue, _____ (between / on / on the corner of) the National Bank and the Chinese restaurant.

Andrea: So let's go!

Choose the correct words or phrases.

1. I'm going to the grocery store to get some _____.
(clothes / gas / food)

2. We're taking a long drive. We need to stop at the _____.
(laundromat / gas station / drugstore)

3. I live on the 8th floor of my _____.
(apartment building / neighborhood / theater)

4. Our apartment is in the center of the city. We live _____.
(downtown / in the neighborhood / in the suburbs)

9 What does she look like?

1 Write the opposites. Use the words in the box.

☑ light ☐ straight ☐ young ☐ short ☐ tall

1. dark / _____light_____   **3.** short / _____   **5.** elderly / _____

2. curly / _____   **4.** long / _____

2 Descriptions

A Match the words in columns A and B. Write the descriptions.

A	B	
☑ medium	☐ aged	**1.** medium height
☐ fairly	☐ brown	**2.**
☐ good	☑ height	**3.**
☐ middle	☐ long	**4.**
☐ dark	☐ looking	**5.**

B Answer the questions using the descriptions from part A.

1. A: How tall is he?

   B: _He's medium height._

2. A: What does he look like?

   B: _____

3. A: What color is his hair?

   B: _____

4. A: How long is his hair?

   B: _____

5. A: How old is he?

   B: _____

3 Complete this conversation with questions.

Marta: Let's find Arturo. I need to talk to him.

Alli: _What does he look like?_

Marta: He's very handsome, with curly brown hair.

Alli: And _____

Marta: It's medium length.

Alli: _____

Marta: He's fairly tall.

Alli: And _____

Marta: He's in his early twenties.

Alli: _____

Marta: Well, he usually wears jeans.

Alli: I think I see him over there. Is that him?

4 Describe yourself. How old are you? What do you look like? What are you wearing today?

_____

_____

_____

_____

_____

5 **Circle two things in each description that do not match the picture. Then correct the information.**

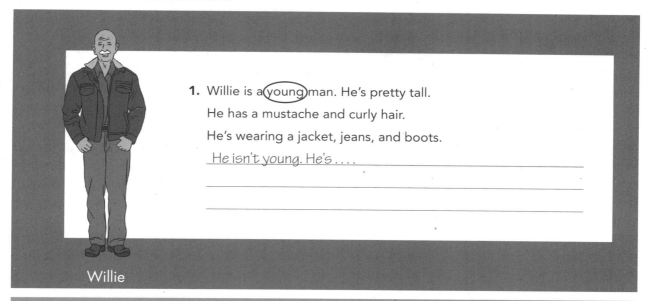

1. Willie is a (young) man. He's pretty tall.

   He has a mustache and curly hair.

   He's wearing a jacket, jeans, and boots.

   He isn't young. He's . . . .

   _____

   _____

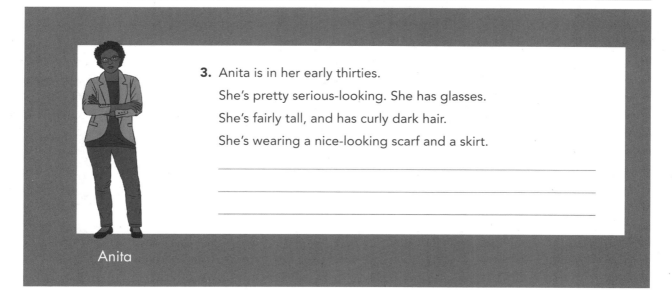

2. Sandy is about 25. She's very pretty.

   She's medium height. Her hair is long and blond.

   She's wearing a black sweater, a skirt, and sneakers.

   _____

   _____

   _____

   Sandy

3. Anita is in her early thirties.

   She's pretty serious-looking. She has glasses.

   She's fairly tall, and has curly dark hair.

   She's wearing a nice-looking scarf and a skirt.

   _____

   _____

   _____

   Anita

6 Which of these clothing items are more formal? Which are more casual? Complete the chart.

boots

cap

dress

high heels

jeans

necktie

shorts

sneakers

suit

jewelry

shirt

T-shirt

Formal	Casual
dress .	

7 Write a sentence about the people in the picture. Use the words in the box and participles.

- ☑ man
- ☐ one
- ☐ ones
- ☐ short man
- ☐ young woman

- ☐ carry a jacket
- ☐ wear sunglasses
- ☑ stand next to Angela
- ☐ talk to the man
- ☐ wear a suit and tie

1. _Brad is the man standing next to Angela._
2. _____
3. _____
4. _____
5. _____

Brad   Angela   Li Na   Matt   Tiffany   Rodrigo

8 Write sentences about the people in the picture. Use the words given.

1. <u>Charles and Natalie are the ones playing chess.</u> (ones / playing chess)
2. _____ (one / behind the couch)
3. _____ (ones / eating pizza)
4. _____ (woman / on the couch)
5. _____ (man / short black hair)

9 Rewrite the conversations. Find another way to say the sentences using the words in the box.

☑ near ☐ sitting ☐ wearing ☑ which ☐ who ☐ who

1. **A:** Who's Lucas?
   <u>Which one's Lucas?</u>
   B: He's the guy next to the window.
   <u>He's the guy near the window.</u>

2. **A:** Which ones are the servers?
   _____
   B: They're the ones in the red polo shirts.
   _____

3. **A:** Which one is Naomi?
   _____
   B: She's the one on the couch next to Lisa.
   _____

10 Which one is Jeff?

Complete Bill and Ruby's conversation at a party. Use the present continuous or the participle of the verbs in the box.

☐ cook   ☐ eat   ☑ look   ☐ play   ☐ sit   ☐ talk   ☐ use   ☐ wear

Ruby: I'm glad you brought me to this party, Bill. I'm _____looking_____ for someone here named Jeff.

Bill: Yeah, I don't know too many people here. But let's try to find him. Is he one of those guys _____ football? What about the guy with black hair and _____ the dark T-shirt?

Ruby: Hmm, no. That's not Jeff.

Bill: How about the one _____ the music system over there, in the white T-shirt.

Ruby: No, I know him. That's Ken.

Bill: Hmm. Oh, is that Jeff _____ at the table and _____ to the two women? It looks like they're already _____.

Ruby: No, not him, either. Gee, I wonder if Jeff even came to the party?

Bill: Well, he can't be the chef, right? The guy _____ vegetables at the grill?

Ruby: That's him! Hey, Jeff!

11 Choose the correct responses.

1. **A:** Who's Shawn?

   B: _The middle-aged man on the couch._
   - The middle-aged man on the couch.
   - That's right.

2. **A:** Where's Samantha?

   B: _____
   - She couldn't make it.
   - I'd like to meet her.

3. **A:** Is Avery the one wearing glasses?

   B: _____
   - That's right.
   - She's running late.

4. **A:** How tall is she?

   B: _____
   - Fairly long.
   - Pretty short.

10 Have you ever been there?

1 Match the verb forms in columns A and B.

A	B
1. make _g_	**a.** tried
2. ride _____	**b.** eaten
3. do _____	**c.** seen
4. eat _____	**d.** had
5. go _____	**e.** ridden
6. have _____	**f.** heard
7. be _____	✓ **g.** made
8. hear _____	**h.** done
9. see _____	**i.** gone
10. try _____	**j.** been

2 Complete the questions in these conversations. Use the present perfect of the verbs in Exercise 1.

1. A: _____Have you seen_____ Al's new dog?

   B: Yes, it's so cute!

2. A: How many times _____ to the gym this month?

   B: Actually, not at all. Let's go later today!

3. A: How many phone calls _____ today?

   B: I made two calls – both to you!

4. A: _____ your homework yet?

   B: Yes, I have. I did it after class.

5. A: _____ at the new Italian restaurant?

   B: Yes, we already have. It's very good but a little expensive.

6. A: How long _____ those boots?

   B: I bought them on Monday.

3 *Already* and *yet*

A Check (✓) the things you've already done. Put an ✗ next to the things you haven't done yet.

1. _____ graduated from high school
2. _____ gotten married
3. _____ ridden a horse
4. _____ been in an airplane
5. _____ learned to drive
6. _____ traveled abroad

B Write sentences about each activity in part A. Use *already* and *yet*.

> **Grammar note: *Already* and *yet***
>
> **Already** is used in positive statements with the present perfect.
> I've **already** graduated from high school.
> **Yet** is used in negative statements with the present perfect.
> I haven't gotten married **yet**.

1. _____
   _____
2. _____
   _____
3. _____
   _____
4. _____
   _____
5. _____
   _____
6. _____
   _____

4 Complete these sentences with *for* or *since*.

1. Jill has driven the same car _____*since*_____ 2004.
2. I have been a teacher _____ several years.
3. I haven't had this much fun _____ I was a kid!
4. I'm so sleepy. I've been awake _____ 4:00 this morning.
5. Kyoko was an exchange student in Peru _____ a whole semester.
6. Marcus has lived in Dubai _____ 2010.
7. How are you? I haven't seen you _____ high school.
8. Where have you been? I've been here _____ over an hour!
9. Mr. and Mrs. Lopez have been married _____ nearly 50 years.

5 Look at these pictures. How often have you done these things? Write sentences using the expressions in the box.

I've . . . many times.
I've . . . three or four times.
I've . . . several times.

I've . . . once or twice.
I haven't . . . lately.
I've never . . .

eat Thai food

go to a concert

1. _____

2. _____

go skiing

play an instrument

3. _____

4. _____

see an opera

play golf

5. _____

6. _____

A Read the two blog posts. Where did each blogger go? What activity did each one want to do?

NO WAY OUT!

Have you ever visited Mexico? If so, then you know it is famous for its Aztec ruins. Last summer my Spanish class visited Mexico City. We went on a tour of Aztec ruins that are found under the city's main square. We walked for two hours underground in the dark halls. It was like being in a cave. There are many interesting things to see. I wanted to get a better look at a statue, so I went around some ropes that are supposed to keep tourists out. Several minutes later, I came out on the other side, but my group disappeared! I couldn't hear any voices, and I didn't know which way to go. I was too embarrassed to shout, so I wandered around the halls trying to find my group. I started to get nervous. It seemed like I was alone for hours. I walked around in the darkness until I finally heard the professor calling my name. He was very worried, and I was relieved! For the rest of our trip in Mexico, he made sure I never left his sight. My friends still call me "Cave Woman."

NO WAY IN!

I have been to Europe many times but never to Greece until last summer. It was an unforgettable experience! I was staying at a small hotel in Athens. It was in a part of town where most tourists don't stay, but it was cheaper there, and I wanted to practice speaking Greek with people. One evening I went for a walk before dinner. Soon it started to get dark. I didn't want to get lost, and I remembered I had a small map of Athens in my wallet. My wallet! It wasn't in my pocket. I thought, "I've left it in the hotel room . . . and my hotel key is in my wallet!" It took me a long time to get back to the hotel, but I made it. The door was locked, of course. Sometimes I talk to myself when I'm upset. Well, I must have said out loud, "I've lost my wallet, I've locked myself out, and I've missed dinner!" Just then, the hotel manager appeared. I guess he heard me talking. He said something in Greek and pointed to his house. I followed him. He and his family were having a big Greek dinner. They wanted me to join them. The manager eventually let me into my room. But first, I ate one of the best meals I've ever had. And forgetting my wallet was the best mistake I've ever made!

B In which story or stories did the writer(s) do these things? Write *1*, *2*, or *1 and 2*.

___1___ went to ruins	_____ stayed at a hotel
_____ went to a foreign country	_____ went underground
_____ got lost	_____ made a mistake
_____ got help from someone	_____ went on the trip alone

C Write about an adventure you have had. What happened? What went wrong?

_____

_____

_____

_____

7 **Look at the answers. Write questions using *Have you ever . . . ?***

text messaging

rugby match

sushi

Houston

1. **A:** _Have you ever sent a text message during class?_

   B: No, I've never sent a text message during class.

2. **A:** _____

   B: Actually, I saw a rugby match last week on TV. It was awesome!

3. **A:** _____

   B: Yes, I love sushi.

4. **A:** _____

   B: No, I haven't. But my uncle lives in Houston.

5. **A:** _____

   B: Yes, I visited an amusement park last month.

6. **A:** _____

   B: No, I haven't. I don't think I would like camping.

7. **A:** _____

   B: Yes, I have. I once rode my aunt's motorcycle.

8 **Write your own answers to the questions (speaker A) in Exercise 7. Use expressions like the ones from the list.**

Yes, I have.	I . . . yesterday.	No, I haven't.	I've never . . .
	I . . . on Monday.		I . . . yet.
	I . . . last year.		
	I . . . in August.		

1. _____

2. _____

3. _____

4. _____

5. _____

6. _____

7. _____

9 Complete the conversation. Use the simple past or the present perfect of the words given.

A: _____Have_____ you ever _____lost_____ (lose) anything valuable?

B: Yes, I _____ (lose) my cell phone last month.

A: _____ you _____ (find) it yet?

B: No. Actually, I _____ already _____ (buy) a new one. Look!

A: Oh, that's nice. Where _____ you _____ (buy) it?

B: I _____ (get) it at the mall last weekend. What about you? _____ you ever _____ (lose) anything valuable?

A: Well, I _____ (leave) my leather jacket in a coffee shop a couple of months ago.

B: Oh, no! _____ you _____ (go) back and look for it?

A: Well, I _____ (call) them, but it was gone.

10 Choose the correct responses.

1. A: Has John visited his brother lately?

B: _____No, he hasn't._____
- How many times?
- No, he hasn't.

2. A: Are you having a good time?

B: _____
- Yes, in a long time.
- Yes, really good.

3. A: How long did Theresa stay at the party?

B: _____
- For two hours.
- Since midnight.

4. A: Have you had breakfast?

B: _____
- Yes, in a few minutes.
- Yes, I've already eaten.

5. A: How many times has Tony lost his keys?

B: _____
- Twice.
- Not yet.

6. A: Do you want to see that new movie?

B: _____
- I never have. What about you?
- Sure. I hear it's great.

7. A: Have you been here long?

B: _____
- No, not yet.
- No, just a few minutes.

8. A: Have you seen Sara today?

B: _____
- Yes, I saw her this morning.
- Yes, tomorrow.

11 It's a really nice city.

1 Choose the correct words to complete the sentences.

Singapore

Chicago

1. Prices are high in Singapore. Everything is very ___expensive___ there.
(cheap / expensive / noisy)

2. Chicago has amazing skyscrapers right next to a gorgeous lake. It's a really _____ city.
(beautiful / cheap / quiet)

3. My hometown is not an exciting place. The nightlife there is pretty _____.
(boring / nice / interesting)

4. Some parts of our city are fairly dangerous. It's not very _____ late at night.
(hot / interesting / safe)

5. The streets in this city are always full of people, cars, and buses. It's a very _____ city.
(spacious / crowded / relaxing)

2 Choose the correct questions to complete this conversation.

☐ What's the weather like?
☐ Is it big?
☐ Is the nightlife exciting?
☑ What's your hometown like?

A: _What's your hometown like?_ _____

B: My hometown? It's a pretty nice place, and the people are very friendly.

A: _____

B: No, it's fairly small, but it's not too small.

A: _____

B: The winter is wet and really cold. It's very nice in the summer, though.

A: _____

B: No! It's really boring. There are no good restaurants or nightclubs.

3 Choose the correct conjunctions and rewrite the sentences.

> **Grammar note:** *And, but, though,* and *however*
>
> **Use *and* for additional information.**
> It's an exciting city, **and** the weather is great.
> **Use *but, though,* and *however* for contrasting information.**
> It's very safe during the day, **but** it's pretty dangerous at night.
> The summers are hot. The evenings are fairly cold, **though**.
> It is a fairly large city. It's not too interesting, **however**.

Colorado

Dubai

Hong Kong

1. Colorado is beautiful in the summer. It's a great place to go hiking. (and / but)

   Colorado is beautiful in the summer, and it's a great place to go hiking.

   _____

2. Dubai is a very nice place. The summers are terribly hot. (and / though)

   _____

   _____

3. Hong Kong is an exciting city. It's a fun place to sightsee. (and / however)

   _____

   _____

4. My hometown has some great restaurants. It's not a good place for shopping. (and / but)

   _____

   _____

5. Our hometown is somewhat ugly. It has some beautiful old homes. (and / however)

   _____

   _____

4 Check (✓) if these sentences need *a* or *an*. Then write *a* or *an* in the correct places.

> **Grammar note: A and an**
>
> Use *a* or *an* with (adverb +) adjective + singular noun.
> It has **a fairly new park**. It's **an old city**.
> **Don't use *a* or *an* with (adverb +) adjective.**
> It's **fairly new**. It's **old**.

1. ✓ London has ⌃*a* very famous Ferris wheel.
2. ☐ Restaurants are very cheap in Ecuador.
3. ☐ Brisbane is clean city.
4. ☐ The buildings in Florence are really beautiful.
5. ☐ Apartments are very expensive in Hong Kong.
6. ☐ Sapporo is very cold city in the winter.
7. ☐ Beijing's museums are really excellent.
8. ☐ Mumbai is exciting place to visit.

5 Complete the description of Paris with *is* or *has*.

PARIS: City of Light

Paris _____ France's biggest city. It _____ a very lively city with an interesting history. It _____ a city of interesting buildings and churches, and it _____ many beautiful parks. It also _____ some of the best museums in the world. Paris _____ nice weather most of the year, but it _____ pretty cold in the winter. It _____ a popular city with foreign tourists and _____ millions of visitors a year. The city _____ famous for its fashion and _____ many excellent stores. Paris _____ convenient trains and buses that cross the city, so it _____ easy for tourists to get around.

It's a really nice city. **63**

A Scan the webpage. Where is each city?

SEOUL

Seoul was founded in 18 BCE. It is South Korea's capital and today has a population of 10.5 million people. Seoul is famous for producing popular music and films that are very well known in Asia, Latin America, and the Middle East. The city is surrounded by mountains and located on the Han River. It has an excellent transportation system that can take you to 115 museums, monuments, parks, and music festivals throughout the city. The best time to visit Seoul is in the fall and the spring. Winters can be quite cold and summers very hot.

QUITO

Quito sits 2,850 meters above sea level and is the highest capital city in the world. Its population is 2.6 million people. The city is located near the equator in the country of Ecuador (which means "equator" in Spanish). Quito's downtown center, one of the most beautiful in the Americas, has not changed much since the Spanish founded the city in 1534. On a day trip from Quito, you can go walking in the mountains and visit a volcano there. Because of the city's elevation and location on the equator, the weather there is pleasant all year.

RABAT

Rabat is located on the Atlantic Ocean. It was founded in 1146. Although Rabat is the capital of Morocco, its population is only about 580,000 people. The weather is cool at night with hot days in the summer and mild days in the winter. Mawazine, a famous world music festival, takes place in Rabat in the spring. You can visit the Kasbah, an old fortress, and enjoy the architecture, gardens, and the view of the ocean. Rabat's outdoor markets sell beautiful handmade goods. Explore the city and enjoy a delicious Moroccan meal!

B Read the webpage and complete the chart.

City	Date founded	Population	Attractions
Seoul			
Quito			
Rabat			

C Complete the sentences.

1. _____ and _____ have music festivals.
2. _____ is the capital city with the smallest population.
3. _____ is the oldest capital city.
4. _____ has the capital city with the highest altitude.

7 Complete the sentences. Use phrases from the box.

- ☐ shouldn't miss
- ☑ should see
- ☐ can get
- ☐ can take
- ☐ shouldn't stay
- ☐ shouldn't walk

1. You _____should see_____ the new zoo. It's very interesting.
2. You _____ near the airport. It's too noisy.
3. You _____ the museum. It has some new exhibits.
4. You _____ a bus tour of the city if you like.
5. You _____ alone at night. It's too dangerous.
6. You _____ a taxi if you're out late.

8 Complete the conversation with should or shouldn't and I or you.

A: I'm taking my vacation in Japan. What _____should I_____ do there?

B: _____ miss Kyoto, the old capital city. There are a lot of beautiful old buildings. For example, _____ see the Ryoanji Temple.

A: Sounds great. Hakone is very popular, too. _____ go there?

B: Yes, _____. It's very interesting, and the hot springs are fantastic.

A: _____ take a lot of money with me?

B: No, _____. You can use the ATMs in Japan.

A: So when _____ go there?

B: In the spring or the fall. You can see the cherry blossoms or the fall colors.

9 | Ask questions about a place you want to visit. Use *can*, *should*, or *shouldn't*.

1. the time to visit

What time of year should I visit?

2. things to see and do there

_____

3. things not to do

_____

4. special foods to try

_____

5. fun things to buy

_____

6. other interesting things to do

_____

10 | Rewrite the sentences. Think of another way to express each sentence using the words given.

1. It's a polluted city.

It isn't a clean city. _____ (not clean)

2. You really should visit the new aquarium.

_____ (not miss)

3. Apartments are not cheap in my country.

_____ (extremely expensive)

4. This neighborhood is not noisy at all.

_____ (very quiet)

5. When should we visit the city?

_____ (a good time)

12 It's important to get rest.

1 Any suggestions?

A Check (✓) the best advice for each health problem.

1. a backache

- ☑ use a heating pad
- ☐ get some exercise
- ☐ drink herbal tea

2. a bad cold

- ☐ see a dentist
- ☐ go to bed and rest
- ☐ go swimming

3. a burn

- ☐ take a multivitamin
- ☐ put it under cold water
- ☐ drink warm milk

4. a headache

- ☐ take some vitamin C
- ☐ take some pain medicine
- ☐ take a cough drop

5. an insect bite

- ☐ apply anti-itch cream
- ☐ use eyedrops
- ☐ drink lots of liquids

6. sore muscles

- ☐ drink lots of hot water
- ☐ take some cold medicine
- ☐ use some ointment

B Write a question about each problem in part A. Then write answers using the words from the box. Use the advice in part A or your own ideas.

> It's important . . .   It's sometimes helpful . . .   It's a good idea . . .

1. **A:** <u>What should you do for a backache?</u>
   B: <u>It's sometimes helpful to use a heating pad.</u>

2. **A:** _____
   B: _____

3. **A:** _____
   B: _____

4. **A:** _____
   B: _____

5. **A:** _____
   B: _____

6. **A:** _____
   B: _____

2 **Rewrite these sentences. Give advice using** *it's important . . . ,* *it's a good idea . . . ,* **or** *it's sometimes helpful . . . .*

Grammar note: Negative infinitives		
Problem	**Advice**	**Negative infinitive**
For the flu,	don't exercise a lot.	For the flu, it's a good idea **not to exercise** a lot.

1. For a toothache, don't eat cold foods.

   For a toothache, it's important not to eat cold foods.

2. For a sore throat, don't talk too much.

   _____

3. For a burn, don't put ice on it.

   _____

4. For insomnia, don't drink coffee at night.

   _____

5. For a fever, don't get out of bed.

   _____

3 **Check (✓) three health problems you have had. Write what you did for each one. Use the remedies below or your own remedies.**

Health problems

☐ a cough   ☐ a backache

☐ a headache   ☐ the hiccups

☐ insomnia   ☐ a sunburn

☐ a cold   ☐ stress

Some remedies

take some pain medicine

get some medicine from the drugstore

use some lotion

put some ointment on it

take some cough drops

see my doctor/dentist

go to bed

do nothing

Example: *Yesterday, I had a bad headache, so I took some pain medicine.*

1. _____

2. _____

3. _____

A Scan the article. Check (✓) the sentence that is the better summary of the article.

☐ People who laugh at least once a day live longer than people who don't.

☐ Laughter has important health benefits for your body.

LAUGH IT OFF

Have you laughed today? If so, you probably did a good thing for your health.

Psychologists now consider laughing to be an important practice for good health. Laughter is known to reduce stress, improve the body's ability to fight disease, and make life happier and more interesting. It adds to the pleasure we get from other people and the enjoyment other people get from us.

Dr. Madan Kataria, the founder of Laughter Yoga, discovered that laughter does not have to be real to be good for the body. In Laughter Yoga, people combine yoga breathing with laughter exercises in a group. This allows people to practice laughing without the presence of humor.

Dr. Kataria has found that the body responds well just to the physical act of laughing.

Dr. Annette Goodheart was one of the first doctors in the U.S. to promote laughter for health. In her book *Laughter Therapy: How to Laugh About Everything in Your Life That is Not Really Funny*, she writes, "Everyone usually knows what they think is funny or can laugh at. But I help people laugh about things that aren't funny and support them in re-balancing and resolving their pain."

People who say that laughter is the best medicine might be right. A laugh a day keeps the doctor away!

B Check (✓) True or False.

	True	False
1. Laughter can help the body fight disease.	☐	☐
2. The more you laugh, the more other people like you.	☐	☐
3. Laughter is healthier for you if it is real.	☐	☐
4. Psychologists believe it is healthy to laugh at all situations.	☐	☐
5. Dr. Goodheart helped patients focus only on funny things.	☐	☐

C Describe a time you laughed hard at something. How did you feel afterward?

_____

_____

_____

5 What do you suggest?

A Complete the word map with medicines from the list.

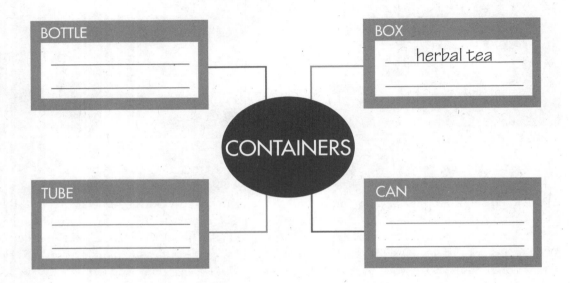

☐ anti-itch cream   ☑ herbal tea   ☐ pain medicine

☐ bandages   ☐ insect spray   ☐ shaving cream

☐ eyedrops   ☐ muscle ointment

BOTTLE
_____
_____

BOX
_herbal tea_____
_____

CONTAINERS

TUBE
_____
_____

CAN
_____
_____

B What should these people buy? Give advice. Use the containers and medicine from part A.

1. Danielle is having trouble sleeping.
   _She should buy a box of herbal tea._____

2. Simon has a bad headache.
   _____

3. Maria's shoulders are sore after her workout.
   _____

4. There may be mosquitoes where Brenda's camping.
   _____

5. Sam has a cut on his hand.
   _____

6. Graciela has dry, itchy skin on her feet.
   _____

7. Nathan cut his chin when he shaved with soap and water.
   _____

8. Sally's eyes are red and itchy.
   _____

6 Check (✓) the correct sentences to make conversations.

1. **Pharmacist:** ✓ Can I help you?

☐ Should I help you?

Customer: ☐ Yes. Can I have a bottle of pain medicine?

☐ Yes. I suggest a bottle of pain medicine.

Pharmacist: Here you are.

Customer: ☐ And what do you need for a sunburn?

☐ And what do you have for a sunburn?

Pharmacist: ☐ Do you suggest this lotion?

☐ I suggest this lotion.

Customer: Thanks.

2. **Pharmacist:** Hi. Can I help you?

Customer: ☐ Yes. Can I suggest something for sore muscles?

☐ Yes. Could I have something for sore muscles?

Pharmacist: ☐ Sure. Try this ointment.

☐ Sure. Could I try this ointment?

Customer: ☐ Thanks. And what should you get for the flu?

☐ Thanks. And what do you suggest for the flu?

Pharmacist: ☐ Can I have some of these tablets? They really work.

☐ Try some of these tablets. They really work.

Customer: ☐ OK, thanks. I'll take them. And you should get a box of tissues.

☐ OK, thanks. I'll take them. And could I have a box of tissues?

Pharmacist: Sure. Here you are.

7 Complete this conversation with the correct words.

A: Wow, you don't look very good! Do you feel OK?

B: No, I think I'm getting a cold. What should I do _____ it?
(for / to / with)

A: You should stay _____ home and go _____ bed.
(at / in / of)   (in / of / to)

B: You're probably right. I've got a really bad cough, too.

A: Try drinking some hot tea _____ honey. It really helps.
(for / of / with)

B: Anything else?

A: Yeah, I suggest you get a big box _____ tissues!
(at / in / of)

8 Give suggestions for these problems. Use words from the box.

> Try . . .   I suggest . . .   You should . . .

1. I can't stop sneezing.

   Try some allergy medicine.

2. I have a stomachache.

_____

3. I don't have any energy.

_____

4. I think I'm getting a cold.

_____

5. I'm stressed out!

_____

6. I have a very sore throat.

_____

1 **Show that you agree. Write sentences with the words given.**

1. A: I don't want fast food tonight.

    B: _I don't either._ (either)

2. A: I really like Mexican food.

    B: _____ (so)

3. A: I'm in the mood for Italian food.

    B: _____ (too)

4. A: I can't stand spicy food.

    B: _____ (neither)

5. A: I don't like greasy food very much.

    B: _____ (either)

6. A: I want to eat healthy food for lunch.

    B: _____ (too)

2 What do you think?

A Look at the pictures. Write sentences about the food. Use the expressions in the box and the given words.

> **Useful expressions**
>
> I love . . .   I'm crazy about . . .
> I can't stand . . .   I'm not crazy about . . .
> I don't like . . . very much. It's a little too . . .
> I like . . . a lot.

greasy

1. _It's a little too greasy._

bland

2. _____

rich

3. _____

salty

4. _____

healthy

5. _____

B What are three of your favorite kinds of food? Write what you like about them.

_____

_____

_____

_____

3 To your taste

A Skim the restaurant reviews. Match the reviewer with the number of stars.

1. Carlota   ★   Awful!

2. Adam   ★ ★ ★   Pretty good.

3. Luka   ★ ★ ★ ★ ★   Fantastic!!

YUM! Restaurant Reviews

Find a restaurant …

QUINOA CORNER
175 PLEASANT ST.

Carlota

Quinoa Corner is my latest discovery! This international food restaurant has everything: delicious steak, hamburgers, Mexican enchiladas, Mediterranean salads, and vegetarian and vegan dishes, too. When I was there last Saturday, I ordered a grilled salmon with baby asparagus and a baked potato. Delicious! And the atmosphere is wonderful. The servers are dressed as cowboys and cowgirls. Every hour they do a square dance and sing a song for the diners. I love this place!

Luka

Last Sunday I took my wife to Quinoa Corner. I had sushi with rice and a cucumber salad. My wife had lamb curry with spicy vegetables and garlic bread. For dessert we both had chocolate cake. The sushi was quite good, although the salad was not as fresh as I'd like. My wife said that her curry was delicious, but that the vegetables were a little too salty. And I thought the servers were kind of silly. Despite those problems, we still recommend this restaurant.

Adam

For dinner last Thursday, I visited Quinoa Corner for the first time. I ordered the quinoa burger and an almond milkshake. They served me a real hamburger! While I was trying to explain the mistake to my server, she stepped away and began to dance and sing with the other "cowboys"! It took another half hour before my quinoa burger got to the table. When it did, it was cold, bland, and greasy! I do not recommend this restaurant.

B Read the reviews and complete the chart.

	Carlota	Luka	Luka's wife	Adam
Ordered:				
Problems:	☐ yes ☐ no	☐ yes ☐ no	☐ yes ☐ no	☐ yes ☐ no
Recommends:	☐ yes ☐ no	☐ yes ☐ no	☐ yes ☐ no	☐ yes ☐ no

4 Check (✓) the item that does not belong in each group.

1. ☐ apples
   ☑ broccoli
   ☐ strawberries

2. ☐ sushi
   ☐ pasta
   ☐ bread

3. ☐ ice cream
   ☐ iced coffee
   ☐ iced tea

4. ☐ corn
   ☐ green beans
   ☐ pork

5. ☐ beef
   ☐ bread
   ☐ chicken

6. ☐ a cookie
   ☐ a turkey sandwich
   ☐ a hamburger

5 Use one or more words to complete this conversation between a server and a customer.

Server: May I take your order?

Customer: _____ Yes, I'll have _____ the salmon.

Server: What kind of dressing _____ on your salad – French, blue cheese, or vinaigrette?

Customer: _____ like French, please.

Server: And would you like _____ to drink?

Customer: Yes, _____ have iced coffee.

Server: With milk and sugar?

Customer: Yes, _____.

Server: Anything else?

Customer: No, _____. That'll _____ all.

6 Choose the correct responses.

1. A: What would you like?

B: _I'll have a beef burrito._

- I'll be your server today.
- Yes, I'd like to.
- I'll have a beef burrito.

2. A: Would you like soup or salad?

B: _____

- I guess I will, thanks.
- I'd like soup, please.
- Yes, please.

3. A: What would you like on your pizza?

B: _____

- I'll have pepperoni.
- I'd like a soda, please.
- Small, please.

4. A: Would you like anything to drink?

B: _____

- No, thanks.
- Yes, a hamburger, please.
- I'll have some noodles, please.

5. A: What flavor ice cream would you like?

B: _____

- Fresh, please.
- Vanilla, please.
- Ice cream, please.

6. A: Would you like anything else?

B: _____

- Yes, thank you very much.
- Not at all, thanks.
- That'll be all, thanks.

7 Choose the correct words.

1. Baked potatoes are less _____greasy_____ than french fries. (greasy / healthy / spicy)

2. In a restaurant, the server takes your _____. (table / order / service)

3. Many people like _____ on their salad. (dessert / dressing / soda)

4. Some people rarely cook with spices. They prefer food to be _____. (bland / hot / rich)

5. Strawberry is a popular ice cream _____. (drink / flavor / meal)

8 **Complete the conversation. Use the words and expressions in the box.**

☐ am   ☐ favorite kind of food   ☐ too
☐ can   ☐ like it a lot   ☐ I'll
☐ can't stand them ✓ neither   ☐ would
☐ do   ☐ so

Maria: I feel tired tonight. I really don't want to cook.

Courtney: _____Neither_____ do I. Let's order out. Do you like Chinese food?

Maria: It's delicious! I _____!

Courtney: I do, _____. It's my _____.
Let's call Beijing Express for home delivery.

Maria: Great idea! Their food is always good. I eat there a lot.

Courtney: _____ do I. Well, what _____ you like tonight?

Maria: I'm in the mood for some soup.

Courtney: So _____ I. And I think _____ have orange chicken
and fried rice.

Maria: OK, let's order. Oh, wait. They don't take credit cards, and I don't have any cash on me.

Courtney: Neither _____ I. Too bad! What should we do?

Maria: Well, let's look in the refrigerator. Hmm. Do you like boiled eggs?

Courtney: I _____!

Maria: Actually, neither _____ I.

14 It's the coldest city!

1 Geography

A Circle the correct word.

1. This is a mountain with a hole on top. Smoke and lava sometimes come out, and it can be dangerous.
   - **a.** waterfall
   - **(b.)** volcano
   - **c.** hill

2. This is a dry, sandy place. It doesn't rain much here, and there aren't many plants.
   - **a.** desert
   - **b.** sea
   - **c.** volcano

3. This is a low area of land between mountains or hills.
   - **a.** island
   - **b.** valley
   - **c.** beach

4. This is an area of water with land all around it.
   - **a.** hill
   - **b.** island
   - **c.** lake

5. This is a flow of water that happens when a river falls from a high place.
   - **a.** hill
   - **b.** canyon
   - **c.** waterfall

6. This is a large area of land that has lots of trees on it.
   - **a.** desert
   - **b.** forest
   - **c.** river

B Complete the names. Use words from the box.

☐ Canyon	☐ Falls	☐ Ocean	☑ Lake
☐ Desert	☐ Mount	☐ River	☐ Sea

1. _____Lake_____ Superior
2. Amazon _____
3. Grand _____
4. Atlantic _____
5. Mojave _____
6. Niagara _____
7. Mediterranean _____
8. _____ Everest

2 Write the comparative and superlative forms of the words given.

Spelling note: Comparatives and superlatives			
	Adjective	**Comparative**	**Superlative**
Add *-er* or *-est* to most words.	long	long**er**	the long**est**
Add *-r* or *-st* to words ending in *-e*.	large	large**r**	the large**st**
Drop the **y** and add *-ier* or *-iest*.	dry	dr**ier**	the dr**iest**
Double the final consonant and add *-er* or *-est*.	big	bi**gger**	the bi**ggest**

1. busy   _busier_   _the busiest_
2. cool   _____ _____
3. friendly   _____ _____
4. heavy   _____ _____
5. nice   _____ _____

6. noisy   _____ _____
7. old   _____ _____
8. safe   _____ _____
9. small   _____ _____
10. wet   _____ _____

3 Complete this conversation. Use the superlative form of the words given.

Keegan: So where did you go for your vacation, Kathy?

Kathy: Japan.

Keegan: How exciting! Did you have a good time?

Kathy: It was terrific! I think Japan is _the most exciting_ (exciting) country in Asia.

Keegan: Well, it certainly has some of _____ (interesting) cities in the world – Tokyo, Osaka, and Kyoto.

Kathy: Yeah. I had _____ (good) time in Kyoto. It's _____ (beautiful) city I've ever seen. Of course, it's also one of _____ (popular) tourist attractions. It was _____ (crowded) city I visited this summer.

Keegan: I've always wanted to visit Japan. What's it like in the winter?

Kathy: Actually, I think that's _____ (bad) time to visit because I don't like cold weather. However, I think the Sapporo Snow Festival is _____ (fascinating) festival in the world.

4 **Complete these sentences. Use the comparative or the superlative form of the words given.**

Badwater Basin

the Suez Canal

Mount Waialeale

1. Badwater Basin in California's Death Valley is _____ *the lowest* _____ (low) point in North America.

2. The Suez Canal joins the Mediterranean and Red Seas. It is 190 kilometers (118 miles) long. It is _____ *longer than* _____ (long) the Panama Canal.

3. Mount Waialeale in Hawaii gets 1,170 centimeters (460 inches) of rain a year. It is _____ (wet) place on Earth!

4. Canada and Russia are _____ (large) countries in the world.

5. Russia is _____ (large) Canada.

6. _____ (high) waterfall in the world is in Venezuela.

7. The Atacama Desert in Chile is _____ (dry) place in the world.

8. _____ (hot) capital city in the world is Muscat, Oman.

9. The continent of Antarctica is _____ (cold) any other place in the world.

10. The Himalayas are some of _____ (dangerous) mountains to climb.

11. Mont Blanc in the French Alps is _____ (high) the Matterhorn in the Swiss Alps.

12. The Pacific Ocean is _____ (deep) the Atlantic Ocean. At one place, the Pacific Ocean is 11,033 meters (36,198 feet) deep.

5 The coldest and the windiest!

A Scan the article about Antarctica. In what ways is it different from other places on Earth? Why do scientists work there?

ANTARCTICA is the most southern continent in the world. It's like nowhere else on Earth. It's much larger than Europe and nearly twice the size of Australia. It's an icy plateau with the South Pole at its center. Antarctica is the coldest and windiest place in the world, even colder and windier than the North Pole. Although 98 percent of Antarctica is covered in ice, it is considered a desert. Along the coast, annual precipitation is only 200 millimeters (eight inches) a year. Very few plants grow there, but there is some wildlife, including whales, seals, and penguins. In the summer, the sun shines for 24 hours a day, but in the winter, it's completely dark for about three months.

When Captain James Cook sailed around the continent in the 1770s, he found no one living there. Today, a few scientists work in Antarctica, but they only spend fairly short periods of time there. Many of these scientists live and work on the Antarctic Peninsula. This area is the closest part of Antarctica to South America, the continent's nearest neighbor. Many of these scientists are studying the effects of climate change there. Antarctica has warmed by about 2.5 degrees Celsius since 1950. Some ice is melting in certain parts of the continent. However, unlike the vast melting that is happening in the Arctic, the ice in Antarctica is actually growing in spite of global warming.

Scientists think that this cold and lonely place can teach us a lot about the earth and how to keep it safe.

B Read about Antarctica. Check (✓) True or False.

	True	False
1. Antarctica is bigger than Europe.	☐	☐
2. The North Pole is the coldest place in the world.	☐	☐
3. The coasts in Antarctica get a lot of snow.	☐	☐
4. In Antarctica, it never gets dark in the summer.	☐	☐
5. Captain Cook discovered a few people living in Antarctica.	☐	☐
6. The Antarctic Peninsula is the closest part of Antarctica to South America.	☐	☐
7. Ice in Antarctica is melting throughout the continent.	☐	☐

6 Geography quiz

Use the words in the box. Write questions about the pictures. Then circle the correct answers.

☐ How big   ☐ How deep   ☐ How long
☐ How cold   ☐ How far   ☑ How high

Angel Falls

1. <u>How high is Angel Falls?</u>
   a. It's 979 meters (3,212 feet) tall.
   (b.) It's 979 meters high.

2. _____
   a. It's 6,300 kilometers (3,917 miles) long.
   b. It's 6,300 kilometers high.

the Yangtze River

Antarctica

3. _____
   a. It gets up to –88.3 degrees Celsius (–126.9 degrees Fahrenheit).
   b. It gets down to –88.3 degrees Celsius.

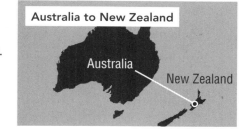

Australia to New Zealand

Australia   New Zealand

4. _____
   a. It's about 2,000 kilometers (1,200 miles).
   b. It's about 2,000 square kilometers.

the Amazon Rain Forest

5. _____
   a. It's 6 million square kilometers (2.5 million square miles).
   b. It's 6 million kilometers long.

6. _____
   a. It's about 1.6 kilometers (1 mile) big.
   b. It's about 1.6 kilometers deep.

the Grand Canyon

7 **Answer these questions about your country.**

1. How big is the largest city?

_____

2. What's the wettest month?

_____

3. What's the driest month?

_____

4. How hot does it get in the summer?

_____

5. How cold does it get in the winter?

_____

6. How high is the highest mountain?

_____

7. What's the most beautiful town to visit?

_____

8 **Match the words with their opposites.**

1. biggest ___f___   **a.** better
2. bad   _____   **b.** wettest
3. shorter _____   **c.** colder
4. worse   _____   **d.** drier
5. worst   _____   **e.** hottest
6. near   _____   **f.** smallest
7. lowest   _____   **g.** far
8. driest   _____   **h.** bigger
9. hot   _____   **i.** good
10. shortest _____   **j.** best
11. hotter _____   **k.** low
12. smaller _____   **l.** highest
13. coldest _____   **m.** longest
14. wetter _____   **n.** wet
15. dry   _____   **o.** taller
16. high   _____   **p.** cold

15 What are you doing later?

1 Match the words in columns A and B. Write the names of the events.

A	B	
☑ baseball	☐ appointment	**1.** baseball game
☐ birthday	☐ concert	**2.**
☐ car	☑ game	**3.**
☐ class	☐ match	**4.**
☐ medical	☐ party	**5.**
☐ rock	☐ race	**6.**
☐ tennis	☐ reunion	**7.**

2 Read Joe's calendar and write about his plans each day. Use the present continuous.

1. On Sunday afternoon, Joe is going to play tennis with Brock.

2. _____

3. _____

4. _____

5. _____

6. _____

7. _____

3 **Complete this conversation. Use *be going to* and the verbs given.**

Stacey: What _____ are _____ you _____ going to do _____ this weekend, Hannah? (do)

Hannah: I _____ to a jazz concert on Saturday. (go)

Stacey: That sounds interesting.

Hannah: Yeah. There's a free concert in the park. What about you, Stacey?

Stacey: Well, Ryan and I _____ a baseball game in the afternoon. (see)

Hannah: And what _____ you _____ in the evening? (do)

Stacey: Ryan _____ his mother in the hospital. (visit) But I _____ not _____ anything really. (do)

Hannah: Well, I _____ some friends over for a barbecue. (have) Would you like to come?

Stacey: Thanks, I'd love to!

4 **Choose the correct responses.**

1. **A:** There's a basketball game on TV tonight. Do you want to watch it?

   B: _I'm sorry. I'm working late tonight._

   • How about this evening?

   • I'm sorry. I'm working late tonight.

   • Yes, it does.

2. **A:** Would you like to have dinner at Bella's Bistro tonight?

   B: _____

   • No, I'm not doing anything.

   • Sorry, I'm going away next week.

   • Yes, that sounds great! But it's my turn to pay.

3. **A:** Do you want to go hiking tomorrow?

   B: _____

   • Yes, I'm going to.

   • Can we go to a late show?

   • Sure, I'd love to.

4. **A:** How about going to a movie on Saturday?

   B: _____

   • Oh, I'm sorry. I can't.

   • Nothing special.

   • No, I wouldn't.

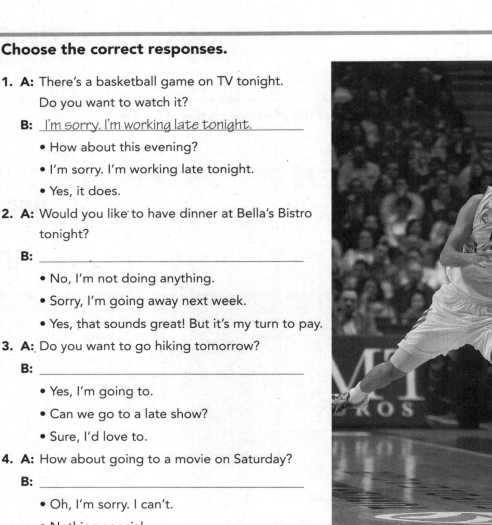

5 Write invitations to this week's events in Eagleton.

Exciting things to do this week in EAGLETON!

MONDAY	TUESDAY	WEDNESDAY	THURSDAY
Pop concert Ellie Goulding	**Summer Festival** Lots to do for everyone!	**Musical** Jersey Boys	**Museum** Modern art exhibition opening

1. *Are you doing anything on Monday evening? Do you want to see a pop concert?* OR
   I'm going to go to the Ellie Goulding concert on Monday. Would you like to come?

2. _____

3. _____

4. _____

6 Write about how often you do these leisure activities. Use the expressions in the box.

I . . . almost every weekend.
I never . . .
I often . . .
I sometimes . . . in the summer.
I . . . three or four times a year.

1. _____
2. _____
3. _____
4. _____
5. _____
6. _____

go to the park

go to concerts

have parties at home

see plays

watch horror movies

go on picnics

7 I need help!

A Read Hannah's social media post and the comments from her friends. Why does she need help?

| Wall | Find friends | Chat | | Profile | Sign out |

Hannah   1h ago
Guess what? I'm moving! Is anyone around Saturday morning and (maybe?) afternoon to help me move things to my new apartment? I only have a few heavy things, but I could use all the help I can get. I'll provide pizza for dinner! Tell your friends and let me know!

Pablo   58 minutes ago
Cool, where are you moving? I wish I could help you Saturday, but I'm going to the beach. Don't hate me. I'm available on Sunday . . . but that probably doesn't help you. Sorry!

Richard   55 minutes ago
Congratulations on the new place! I can help, but not until the afternoon. My study group is getting together to prepare for the chemistry exam on Monday (yikes!). See you after lunch?

Lien   50 minutes ago
Whoo-hoo, new apartment! Saturday morning I have to go to my little brother's baseball tournament. But I'll come over right after it's finished. What's the address?

Kalil   42 minutes ago
I'm so sorry, Hannah. I'm going to be working all weekend. I know, bummer. Can't wait to visit, though. Save me a slice of pizza! I like leftovers. ;-)

Rachel   30 minutes ago
I can't wait to see your new apartment! I'm going to visit my grandmother all day, so unfortunately I can't come until the evening – probably when the pizza arrives! Hope that's OK . . .

Eliana   24 minutes ago
Oh, bad timing! I have the city bicycle race on Saturday morning. But I can come when it's over. In fact, I'm going to keep riding past the finish line and straight to your place! See you in the afternoon.

Daichi   15 minutes ago
Pizza?! I'm in. But wait. I need to drive my sister to her dance class and then to her basketball game. Argh. Can she move in with you? Just kidding. I'll be there by 3:00.

B Match Hannah's friends with their reasons for not being able to help her or for showing up to help late.

1. _____ has a bicycle race.   **a.** Daichi
2. _____ has to study.   **b.** Eliana
3. _____ has to drive his sister around.   **c.** Kalil
4. _____ is going to the beach.   **d.** Pablo
5. _____ is going to work all weekend.   **e.** Rachel
6. _____ is going to a baseball tournament.   **f.** Richard
7. _____ is going to visit her grandmother.   **g.** Lien

8 **Read these messages. What did the caller say? Write the messages another way using *tell* or *ask*.**

> For: *Mr. Jones*
>
> Message: *The meeting is at 10:30. Arrive 10 minutes early.*

1. Please tell Mr. Jones that the meeting is at 10:30.
   Could you ask him to arrive 10 minutes early?

> For: *Ms. Rodriguez*
>
> Message: *We need the report by noon. Call Ms. Brady as soon as possible.*

2. _____

_____

> For: Mr. Welch
>
> Message: The new laptop is ready. Pick it up this afternoon.

3. _____

_____

9 **Look at the text messages. Write sentences asking someone to give these messages.**

Grammar note: Negative infinitives	
Request	**Message**
Don't call him today.	Please ask Jan **not to call** him today.
Don't go home yet.	Could you tell him **not to go** home yet?

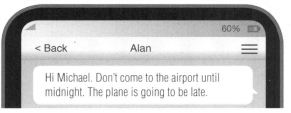

1. _____

_____

_____

2. _____

_____

_____

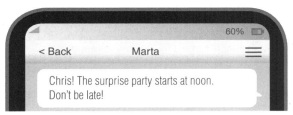

3. _____

_____

_____

10 Choose the correct words.

Receptionist: Hello. McKenzie Corporation.

Mr. Brown: _____ May I _____ speak to Mr. Scott Myers, please?
(May I / Would you)

Receptionist: I'm _____. He's not in. _____ a message?
(busy / sorry)   (Can I leave / Can I take)

Mr. Brown: Yes, please. This is Mr. Brown. _____ you _____
(Would / Please)   (tell him that / ask him to)

I have to reschedule our meeting? My phone number is 303-555-9001.

_____ you _____?
(Please / Could)   (ask him to call me / ask me to call him)

Receptionist: OK, Mr. Brown. I'll _____ the message.
(give him / tell him)

Mr. Brown: Thank you very much. Good-bye.

11 Match the questions with the correct responses.

☐ Let me see if she's in.	☑ That's OK. I'll call back.
☐ This is John. John Abrams.	☐ Sure, I'd love to come. Thanks.
☐ Oh, no. I don't eat meat.	☐ Yes. My number is 303-555-3241.

1. I'm sorry. She's busy at the moment.
That's OK. I'll call back.

2. Could I ask her to call you back?
_____

3. Who's calling, please?
_____

4. Would you like to come to a party?
_____

5. Could I speak to Tiffany, please?
_____

6. Why don't we eat at Sam's Steakhouse tonight?
_____

1 Choose the correct responses.

1. A: Hey, you really look different.

   B: _Well, I've grown a mustache._

     • I moved into a new house.

     • I'm more outgoing than before.

     • Well, I've grown a mustache.

2. A: I haven't seen you for ages.

   B: _____

     • I know. How have you been?

     • Well, I got a bank loan.

     • My new job is more stressful.

3. A: You know, I have three kids now.

   B: _____

     • No, I haven't graduated from college yet.

     • Wow, I can't believe it!

     • Say, you've really changed your hair.

4. A: How are you?

   B: _____

     • I hope to get my driver's license soon.

     • Well, actually, I turned 18.

     • I'm doing really well.

2 Complete the sentences. Use information in the box and the present perfect.

☐ fall in love   ☐ get two pay raises   ☐ start an online course

1. JoAnn _____ this year. Now she has enough money to buy a house.

2. Irvin _____. He's studying to become a graphic designer.

3. Gisela and Russ _____. They're going to get married in December.

3 Describe how these people have changed. Use the present or the past tense.

Before   Now

Before   Now

1. Mr. and Mrs. Kim _had a baby_____. **2.** Sara _____.

Before   Now

Before   Now

3. Ella _____. **4.** Ron _____.

4 Rewrite these sentences. Find another way to say each sentence using the words given.

1. I've grown out my hair.

  _My hair is longer now._____ (longer)

2. Raquel gained a lot of weight.

  _____ (heavier)

3. Ben goes to a new school now.

  _____ (change)

4. Helen and George got divorced last year.

  _____ (married)

5. Traci quit eating fast food.

  _____ (healthier)

6. We quit working out at the gym.

  _____ (not go)

5 | Life changes

A Read the passages on the left in part B. Complete these sentences.

   1. _____ had an interesting job two years ago.

   2. _____ had money problems two years ago.

   3. _____ was a student two years ago.

B Now read the passages on the right. Match the people's lives two years ago with their lives now.

Rafael

Diane and her husband

Krystina

Two years ago	Now
1. Rafael Two years ago, I was a student, and I thought life was really good. I got up late. I spent the day talking to friends, and then I studied all night. I wore jeans and sweatshirts and had long hair and a beard. I felt free. _____	**a.** Now my life has completely changed. I got married six months ago! My husband and I often have friends over for dinner. We're taking classes several nights a week. It's great! We're even talking about starting a family soon.
2. Diane I moved to a new town two years ago. My job was interesting, but I was single and I didn't have any friends. People at work were friendly but not very outgoing. We never did anything after work. _____	**b.** Now I work as a computer programmer for an international company. I've moved to Seoul and have started to learn Korean. Korean food is great, and I've gained a few pounds. I feel much happier and healthier.
3. Krystina My life seemed to come to an end two years ago. I lost my job. Then I lost weight and looked terrible. Money became a problem. I was very sad. I needed some good luck. _____	**c.** Now I actually look forward to getting up early in the morning and going to work. Of course, I dress up now, and my hair is shorter. But I don't really mind. At least my evenings are free!

C Underline at least two changes in each person's life.

6 Complete the sentences. Use the words in the box.

- ☐ broke   ☐ graduation   ☐ responsibilities
- ☐ career   ☑ loan   ☐ successful

1. Rhonda wants to pay off her student _____loan_____ before she buys a car.

2. I'd like to be _____ in my first job. Then I can get a better job and a raise.

3. I go to school, and I have a family and a part-time job. I have a lot of _____.

4. After _____, Amelia and Lee plan to look for jobs.

5. Max lost his job. Now he's _____, and he can't pay his rent.

6. What _____ are you most interested in pursuing?

7 Complete this conversation. Use the words given.

Mariko: What ____do you plan to do____ (plan, do) this summer, Brian?

Brian: I _____ (want, get) a summer job.
I _____ (like, save) money for a vacation.

Mariko: Really? Where _____ (like, go)?

Brian: I _____ (love, travel) to Latin America. What about you, Mariko?

Mariko: Well, I _____ (not go, get) a job right away. First, I _____ (want, go) to Spain and Portugal.

Brian: Sounds great, but how _____ (go, pay) for it?

Mariko: I _____ (hope, borrow) some money from my brother. I have a good excuse. I _____ (plan, take) courses in Spanish and Portuguese.

Brian: Oh, I'm tired of studying!

Mariko: I love to study. I also _____ (hope, take) people on tours to Latin America. Why don't you come on my first tour?

Brian: Count me in!

8 **Imagine you have these problems. Write three sentences about changing your situation. Use the words in the box.**

1. I just moved to a new town, and I don't know anyone. I never do anything after work. People at work don't really talk to me. I haven't had a date in about four months. And I never find anything fun to do on the weekends.

| I'm going to . . . | I want to . . . | I plan to . . . |

_____

_____

_____

_____

_____

2. I've become less careful about my health lately. I've stopped jogging because I'm bored with it. I've started eating more fast food because I'm too tired to cook after work. And I can't sleep at night.

| I'm going to . . . | I'd like to . . . | I'd love to . . . |

_____

_____

_____

_____

_____

3. My job is so boring. I spend two hours driving to and from work every day, and I don't make enough money! I can't find a new job, though, because of my poor computer skills.

| I hope to . . . | I want to . . . | I plan to . . . |

_____

_____

_____

_____

_____

9 Choose the correct words to complete each sentence. Use the correct form of the word and add any words if necessary.

1. Floyd hopes to _____ _move_ _____ to a small town.
   (move / live / change)

2. This job is _____ my last job.
   (outgoing / stressful / crowded)

3. After graduation, Kira plans _____ for an international company.
   (play / work / move)

4. Stephanie's salary is much _____ before. She had to take a pay cut.
   (low / short / high)

5. I hope to buy a house soon. I need _____ a bank loan.
   (open / start / get)

6. Neil and Kelly got _____ last summer. The wedding will be in April.
   (engage / marry)

10 Advise people how to make changes in their lives. Use expressions like the ones in the box.

| Why don't you . . .   You should . . .   You shouldn't . . . |

1. I've gained a lot of weight this year.

   _____

2. My hair is longer, but it doesn't look good.

   _____

3. I've gotten tired of wearing the same old clothes.

   _____

4. I want to start a successful business.

   _____

5. I'm often bored on weekends.

   _____

6. I don't really have any goals.

   _____

7. I've finished this textbook, but I still want to improve my English!

   _____